DIGGING FOR
HITLER

DIGGING FOR
HITLER

THE NAZI ARCHAEOLOGISTS SEARCH
FOR AN ARYAN PAST

Dr DAVID BARROWCLOUGH

FONTHILL

Fonthill Media Language Policy

Fonthill Media publishes in the international English language market. One language edition
is published worldwide. As there are minor differences in spelling and presentation, especially
with regard to American English and British English, a policy is necessary to define which form
of English to use. The Fonthill Policy is to use the form of English native to the author. David
Barrowclough was born and educated in England and now lives in Cambridge, United Kingdom;
British English has therefore been adopted in this publication.

Fonthill Media Limited
Fonthill Media LLC
www.fonthillmedia.com
office@fonthillmedia.com

First published in the United Kingdom and the United States of America 2016

British Library Cataloguing in Publication Data:
A catalogue record for this book is available from the British Library

ISBN 978-1-78155-500-2

Typeset in 10.5pt on 13pt Sabon
Printed and bound in Great Britain by CPI Group (UK) Ltd, Croydon, CR0 4YY

Preface

I first had the idea for this book when an undergraduate at Cambridge in the 1990s. I was frustrated that lecturers would often refer to the appropriation of archaeological science by the Nazis without being able to refer students to a confirmatory text. The Indiana Jones franchise, for all its value as entertainment, only served to enhance those frustrations with its confusing mix of historical fact and contemporary fiction. Thus was the seed sown for the production of this volume, which it is hoped goes some way to explaining how and why the Nazis looked to archaeology and anthropology during the Third Reich.

In writing this book, I have had support and assistance from a number of academics, institutions and friends. I would like to thank Dr Francisco Garcia Alonso, Prof Heinrich Härke, Pippa Payne, Dr Sarah Ralph, Prof Thomas Schneider, Prof Oebele Vries, and Prof Robert Williams for their contribution to the text, helpful conversations and access to images in their private archives and libraries. Access to original documents and secondary texts was given by the Academy of Natural Sciences, Philadelphia; Bundesachiv, Berlin; Federal Archives, Koblenz; *Institut für Zeitgeschichte*, Munich; Library of Congress, National Archives, Washington; Lancashire County Library Service; Oriental and India Office Collections, British Library; and the Public Record Office, Kew. Finally, I would like to thank my publisher and family for their support. Responsibility for any omissions or errors is my own.

Since the first stirrings of the idea for this book, things have moved forward somewhat, and the appearance of Heather Pringle's excellent *The Master Plan* (2006) and Christopher Hale's *Himmler's Crusade* (2006) are particularly welcome additions to the corpus. I recommend both, having drawn from them in writing this text. I have also found Léon Poliakov's *The Aryan Myth* (1974), Peter Levanda's *Unholy Alliance*

(2010), Nicholas Goodrick-Clarke's *Occult Roots of Nazism*, and Robert Bowen's *Universal Ice* (1993) very useful secondary texts when writing what follows. For anyone wishing to follow up the themes discussed in the following chapters, they make an ideal starting point. Many of the primary sources that underpin the text are now available online, and where possible I have indicated their location in the Endnotes.

Contents

1

Indiana Jones and Nazi Archaeology

If you want to be a good archaeologist, you gotta get out of the library.[1]

Introduction

Sometimes truth is stranger than fiction. That is certainly the case when it comes to the archaeological exploits of the Nazis during the 1930s and 1940s. In the famous *Indiana Jones* series of films, television shows, and comic stories, the eponymous hero takes on the forces of the Third Reich in a series of archaeologically themed adventures. Our hero was employed by the US secret services to take on the Nazis, who are searching the four corners of the world for archaeological treasures that they believe have supernatural properties. It may seem far-fetched, but these stories have more than a hint of truth in them. The Nazis really did send expeditions of archaeologists to South America, the Middle East, India and the Himalayas, as well as to occupied Europe. They truly believed that religious relics including the Holy Grail, the Ark of the Covenant, and the Spear of Destiny conferred superhuman powers upon their owner, and the Nazis invested considerable time and energy in locating them—even when they were busy fighting the Second World War. What is more—and here, truth really is stranger than fiction—they had their own theory for the creation of the world; it claimed that the Nazis were the survivors of an ancient Aryan race who originated in the icy northern latitudes, and whose ancestral home was the lost continent of Atlantis. All this they knew was true because the ancient Icelandic *Eddas*, rather than being mythological legend, were in fact the last traces of their ancient history. All this was controlled from within an ancient medieval castle, which was home to a secret sect of Nazi elite who, in addition to plotting world domination, were busy constructing a new pagan religion that would replace Christianity.

Indiana Jones

The chapters that follow reveal the true tales of Nazi archaeology that inspired the Indiana Jones stories, but first there will be a reminder of some of the adventures that were portrayed in the films. 'Indy', as he is often referred to, first appeared in the 1981 film *Raiders of the Lost Ark*, which was followed by *Indiana Jones and the Temple of Doom* in 1984 and *Indiana Jones and the Last Crusade* in 1989.[2] Between 1992 and 1996, he appeared on television in *The Young Indiana Jones Chronicles*, before returning to the big screen in *Indiana Jones and the Kingdom of the Crystal Skull* in 2008.[3] Alongside these were the video games *Indiana Jones and the Fate of Atlantis*, *Indiana Jones and the Infernal Machine*, *Indiana Jones and the Emperor's Tomb*, and *Indiana Jones and the Staff of Kings*.[4] The character has also featured in comic books and even theme parks. Since his first appearance in *Raiders of the Lost Ark*, he has become a worldwide star and remains one of cinema's most revered film characters. The American Film Institute ranked him as the second greatest film hero of all time, and *Raiders of the Lost Ark* was ranked second by *Empire* magazine in their list of the top 500 films of all time.[5]

Raiders of the lost Ark

In *Raiders of the Lost Ark*, Indiana Jones, Professor of Archaeology at Marshall College, finds himself pitted against the Nazis in a search for the Ark of the Covenant. To locate this elusive treasure, which the Germans believe will confer upon them supernatural powers, Indy is helped by Marion Ravenwood. The Nazis are led by Jones's arch rival, the French archaeologist and Nazi collaborator René Belloq, and the sinister Gestapo agent Arnold Toht. Most of the film's storyline is completely fictional; however, the ideas behind the story are all too real.

The adventure begins in 1936, when we find Indy searching for a priceless Chachapoyan fertility idol in South America. Using fragments of old maps, Jones makes his way through the jungle to a hidden temple. After navigating his way through a booby-trapped passageway, he finds the golden idol resting on a stone altar. He tries to remove it carefully, but his actions prove calamitous, initiating the famous action sequence in which a boulder chases Jones out of the temple and into the arms of Belloq and the deadly Hovitos, fictional descendants of the Chachapoyans.

In reality, there never was either an idol or Chachapoyan temple with a giant boulder, but there was a native population of Chachapoyans in the Andes of Peru. Spanish Chronicler Cieza de León records that they were known as the 'Warriors of the Clouds' until approximately 1450, when the Inca absorbed them into their culture.[6] All that survives today are archaeological ruins, some of which have similarities to the Chachapoyan temple found in *Raiders of the Lost Ark*. The fortress of Kuelap has walls 600 metres long and 19 metres high, within which are the remains of more than 400 buildings, along with the graves of many mummies. Radiocarbon dating indicates the site was constructed as early as the sixth century AD and was used throughout the pre-Columbian period. The entrance to Kuelap is long and very narrow, just as portrayed in the film; archaeologists believe it was designed this way so it could be easily defended.

Jones is next seen back at his college, where officers from Army Intelligence tell him darkly that Hitler is 'obsessed with the occult' and with finding religious and mythical artefacts that will increase his power. To this end, he has sent archaeologists from Germany to find the Ark of the Covenant. As far-fetched as it seems, the leading Nazi Heinrich Himmler did actively pursue religious relics from around the world, and there are some reports that suggest Adolf Hitler viewed himself as a messiah-like saviour of the German people. The artefacts the Nazis hunted included the Holy Grail, the Ark of the Covenant, the Bayeux Tapestry, and the regalia of the Holy Roman Empire, including the imperial sword of St Maurice, the Spear of Destiny (the Holy Lance), the Imperial Crown, and the Imperial Orb. Although the authenticity of these objects has been debated, the Nazis seemed to be unshakable in their belief that the objects existed and had mythical powers.

As they travelled across Europe, Africa, and western Asia, the Nazis looted thousands of priceless treasures from museums, churches, synagogues, homes, and private collections—further proof of the Nazi obsession with ancient objects. Many of these were taken by the Ahnenerbe Institute, which was created by Himmler, Herman Wirth, and Richard Walther Darré. The goal of the Ahnenerbe was to research the cultural history of the Aryans, the so-called 'master race' championed by Hitler. The Nazi expedition in *Raiders of the Lost Ark* would have been planned and led by the Ahnenerbe. The Institute sponsored expeditions around the world in an attempt to prove that the Nordic people had once ruled the world; these included expeditions to South America (see Chapter 3), Iceland (see Chapter 5), the Middle East (see Chapter 9), Tibet (see Chapter 4), and Ukraine and Poland (see Chapter 10). Following their expedition from India, through the Himalayas, and to Tibet, the Nazis claimed that

Germanic peoples had once conquered much of Asia and that Siddhartha Gautama, the Buddha, was himself of Aryan descent. Meanwhile, closer to home, the Nazis claimed that they had found Nordic runes in Italy that proved the Ancient Romans had Nordic heritage (see Chapter 6).

In *Raiders of the Lost Ark*, Indiana Jones is racing against the ruthless and brutal Nazis to find the Ark of the Covenant. Indy is first to locate the Ark, finding in the 'Well of Souls' only to have it snatched out of his hands by the Nazis, who, greedy for power, break it open—invoking the wrath of God in the process. According to the Book of Exodus, after Moses broke the original tablets containing the Ten Commandments, God commanded that they be placed in an ark.[7] The Book of Joshua tells us that the Ark was imbued with holy power and that it was this power that had famously destroyed the walls of Jericho.[8] There really is a Well of Souls; however, it is not in Egypt, as in the film, but instead lies beneath the Dome of the Rock in Jerusalem.[9]

Our best source of knowledge about the history of the Ark comes from the *Book of Kings*, according to which it was housed in Soloman's temple in Jerusalem. The Babylonians destroyed the temple in 586 BC, and from then on the location of the Ark has been uncertain.[10] The most widely held belief is that the invaders took the Ark as war booty, but there are other theories, including the idea that Pharaoh Shiskak captured it in *c.* 920 BC and took it back to Egypt.

It is the latter theory that underlies the script of *Raiders of the Lost Ark*, which places the Ark at Tanis. Tanis is a genuine archaeological site, first excavated in the nineteenth century by Flinders Petrie and Auguste Mariette. Needless to say, they did not uncover the Ark. The current whereabouts of the artefact are much debated; it is variously said to be in Ethiopia, Britain, Chartres Cathedral, and Egypt itself.[12] In the nineteenth century, the interest in all things Egyptian made it an appealing location for seekers of the Ark, especially since the deciphering of hieroglyphs made it possible to read ancient texts.[13]

Tanis lies in north-eastern Egypt, along the delta of the River Nile, in the ancient Land of Goshen.[14] The Hebrew story of Moses (Exodus 2:3–5), who was famously found among the bulrushes of the River Nile, is commonly located at Tanis, which was founded during the late Twentieth Dynasty (1187–1064 BC) and eventually became the capital of northern Egypt. The site hosts ruins of numerous ancient temples, at least two sacred lakes, and a royal necropolis containing the tombs of the Pharohs Psusennes I, Amenemope and Shoshenq II. Unusually, the tombs were found intact, containing all their jewellery, precious stones, gold, and funerary masks. However, no Ark was found, and there is little evidence to suggest it was ever at Tanis.

During the 1930s, Germany was one of many European countries excavating in Ancient Egypt. Their finds included a stunning bust of Nefertiti, which Adolf Hitler refused to return to Egypt.[15] Under the Third Reich, German Egyptology was realigned to fit with Nazi ideology, which met with unexpected admiration amongst the Muslim population following the lead of a young Egyptian named al Banna. It was al Banna who had formed the nationalist group the Muslim Brotherhood in the 1920s. He was an admirer of Adolf Hitler and the Nazis; ideologically, the Muslim Brotherhood shared the Nazi authoritarian hatred of Jews, addiction to violence, and desire to defeat the British, which was sufficient for the two movements to find common cause. In the 1930s, the Brotherhood's political and military alliance with Nazi Germany blossomed into formal state visits, *de facto* ambassadors, and overt and covert joint ventures, with the Muslim Brotherhood a virtual secret arm of the Nazi intelligence service. The Muslim Brotherhood adapted Nazi anti-Semitism for a local audience, providing Arab translations of *Mein Kampf*, which they translated as *My Jihad*. In 1933, the pro-Nazi sympathies of some Egyptians even extended to them founding the 'Young Egypt' party, which had its own Nazi-style storm troopers, torch-lit processions, and literal translations of Nazi slogans such as 'One folk, One party, One leader'. They also emulated Nazi anti-Semitism by calling to boycott Jewish businesses and physically attacking Jews.[16]

Indiana Jones and the Temple of Doom

The action in *Indiana Jones and the Temple of Doom* is set a year before *Raiders of the Lost Ark,* in 1935. Much like *Raiders of the Lost Ark*, the story of *Temple of Doom* is based on a certain amount of truth.

The opening of the film sees Indiana Jones in a nightclub, where he is poisoned over a disputed jade urn. The urn contained the remains of Nurhaci, the 'first emperor of the Manchu Dynasty'. He is a real historic figure (b. 1559) who was famed for his military conquests, which paved the way for the Qing Dynasty that ruled China until 1911.[17]

Although fictional, the film resembles the famous German expedition led by the explorer Ernst Schäfer in key respects. Schäfer had been in Shanghai when the German consul had approached him with an invitation to join the SS-Ahnenerbe, and he had subsequently travelled with his team of anthropologists through British-controlled India in order to reach Tibet (see Chapter 4). The aim of that expedition had been to record the religious and other customs of the locals and gather anthropological data on the population in order to establish their ultimate Aryan origin. In this respect, the expedition, like *Temple of Doom*, is more focused on anthropology than archaeology, although both relied on a certain amount of 'treasure hunting'.[18]

The Sankara Stone that Jones and his companions set off to retrieve was a creation of the filmmakers; however, the Sankara is an alternative name for the Hindu deity Shiva. Shiva, the Destroyer, is one of the three primary Hindu gods (the Trimurti) and is the bringer of new life, as out of destruction comes reincarnation. The actual Sankara Stone that Indy is searching for may not be real, but the use of similar stones called 'Lingam', or 'Shiva-Linga', is quite common in Hinduism. A lingam is a representation of Shiva usually linked with a 'yoni', which is a symbol of 'Shakti' (female creative energy)—suggesting that the two represent the inseparability of male and female.[19]

While staying in the Maharajah's palace, Jones, Willie, and Short Round discover a secret underground cavern where the Hindu goddess Kali is being worshipped by the Thuggee. The Hindu goddess—referred to as 'the black one' or 'black mother'—is considered sacred as the giver and destroyer of life.[20]

At the Maharajah's formal dinner, Indiana Jones makes small talk with the Maharajah, Prime Minister Chattar Lal, and other dinner guests, including representatives of the British. Schäfer and his party similarly met with high-ranking locals, probably in an attempt to woo them to the Nazi cause while also gathering intelligence on the strength of British forces in India ahead of a possible Nazi invasion. Indy and his friends are served 'snake surprise' and 'chilled monkey brains', while the conversation turns to discussion of the extinct Thuggees. The Thuggees are greatly fictionalised in *Temple of Doom* but, like in much of the story, there is truth behind Indy's adventure. The Thuggee were a religious sect who were renowned for joining travellers on they journey, sometimes accompanying them for hundreds of miles. During the trip, they would gain the travellers' confidence only to then murder them at an opportune moment. Thugs were known to quietly strangle their victims before looting their possessions, with one Thuggee, named Behram, claiming to have killed over 900 people. The Thuggee were active for several hundred years, during which time they are estimated to have killed between 50,000 and 2 million people, until the British finally ended their violence in the mid-1800s. Thuggee worship of Kali was also real, and although it has been argued that they actively killed travellers as sacrifices to Kali, it is more commonly believed that they were motivated by greed rather than religion in their banditry.[21]

Indiana Jones and the last Crusade

The third film, *Indiana Jones and the Last Crusade*, was set in 1938 and reintroduced the characters of Sallah and Marcus Brody from the first film. In this film, Indy is once again battling with Nazi mystics, this time in search of the Holy Grail, which takes him from beautiful canals of Venice to the deserts of Turkey. Perhaps more than any of the other films in the franchise, this story comes very close to recounting real-life events, as the Nazis really did send parties of archaeologists across Europe to search for the Holy Grail (see Chapter 12).

We first see Indy snatch the ancient 'Cross of Coronado' from some treasure-seeking bandits. There is no real Cross of Coronado, but the crucifix is of course Christianity's most recognisable symbol, representing the sacrifice Jesus made for all sinners by dying on the cross. There was, however, a real Spanish conquistador, Francisco Vásquez de Coronado, who travelled to the Americas in 1540. He was the first Spaniard to explore what are now the southwestern states of New Mexico, Arizona, Texas, Oklahoma, and Kansas. The driving force behind Coronado's explorations was the pursuit of treasure and wealth, but, as with most conquistadors, he brought with him a deeply rooted Christian faith that he planned to spread to the New World.[22]

While escaping his needy students at Marshall College, Indy is 'abducted' by enigmatic men who take him to their employer, Walter Donovan. At this meeting, Indy recounts the legend of the Holy Grail and the three brothers who dedicated their lives to finding and then guarding it. According to myth, the Grail was found by three knights during the First Crusade. The knights used the power of the cup to extend their lives; the bravest and most worthy of the three remained with it as the Guardian of the Grail while the other two returned to Europe, where they left two grail markers. Donovan reveals that he has found one of the markers and is very close to finding the second, but he requires Jones's help. Indy is reluctant to help until he finds out that his father has gone missing while searching for the Grail.

Behind the fictional account of the film lies an element of truth. In 1071, the Seljuk Turks conquered Jerusalem and appeared to be on the verge of invading the Byzantine Empire. Fearing defeat, the Emperor requested help from Pope Urban II and the leaders of Europe to defend against a Muslim invasion. Several hundred thousand Christians responded to the Pope's call to take up arms in what was considered a holy mission. The First Crusade saw the Christians regain Jerusalem only for the Muslims to retake it, setting the pattern for the next 200 years, during which time there were numerous Crusades, with nearly all ending in Christian defeat.[23]

In the film, Indy is pursued by the mysterious and deadly Guardians of the Grail, members of an imaginary organisation called the 'Brothers of the Cruciform Sword', which is based loosely based on the Knights Templar. The Templars were an elite group of warriors that pledged to defend Christian pilgrims as they travelled to the Holy Land. In their early days, the Knights Templar relied on donations to support their operations, but they became enormously rich after developing an early system of international banking. Before beginning their pilgrimage, travellers would deposit their money with the Knights and in return receive a letter of credit. Then, on arrival in Jerusalem, they would produce their letter of credit and receive the equivalent amount of money. Jealous and fearful of the power and wealth amassed by the Templars, in 1307 Pope Clement V ordered the arrest of all the Templar Knights, all but destroying the order within seven years.[24]

Conspiracy theories and myths have circulated concerning the survival of the sect as a secret underground organisation, some suggesting that they are custodians of the Ark of the Covenant, the Holy Grail, or both. One of the most persistent theories is that the Freemasons are the descendants of the Knights Templars. In reality, the Freemasons are a pretty poor substitute for the noble knights, consisting as they do of petty shopkeepers, postmen, and aspirant police constables; they are more concerned with their own advancement than guarding religious relics like the Holy Grail and the Ark of the Covenant.[25]

As Indy's meeting with Donovan continues, we learn that a team has been assembled to recover the Holy Grail, which is revealed to be the cup used at the Last Supper that also caught the blood of the crucified Jesus at his crucifixion. The earliest-known historical account of the Grail comes from *Perceval le Gallois*, a twelfth century romance written by Chrétien de Troyes.[26] In this story, the Grail is depicted as a bowl or dish, but in later versions it is usually described as a cup, chalice, and occasionally a platter. Subsequent authors combined Troyes' Grail with the legend of the Holy Chalice, the cup from which Jesus drank at the last supper. In legend, the Grail is linked to Joseph of Arimathea and Arthurian legend. There is also a tradition that Zeus, the Greek god, drank from a horn of cornucopia, a never-ending source of nourishment that parallels the never-ending love of Christ as represented by the Grail.[27]

Today, following Dan Brown's novel *The Da Vinci Code* and Michael Baigent, Richard Leigh, and Henry Lincoln's *Holy Blood, Holy Grail*, the traditional view of the Grail has been challenged.[28] In these books, the Grail is believed to be Mary Magdalene rather than either a cup or chalice. These 'theories' state that Mary Magdalene married Jesus and bore his children, and thus she was the Grail and recipient of his bloodline. This idea comes from the loose translation of *sangréal*. In Old French, '*san gréal*' means 'Holy Grail', while '*sang réal*' means 'royal blood'. Many contemporaries of the Grail legend use the latter translation to connect Christ's bloodline with Mary Magdalene and the Grail legend. This idea has met with much controversy, particularly from those of the Christian faith, because the thought of Jesus fathering children and maintaining his earthly presence casts doubt on his divinity. When evaluating these 'theories', the key is to remember that they are published as fiction.

There are many institutions across the world that believe they possess the true Grail; the most widely accepted of these is St Mary's Cathedral in Valencia, Spain. However, in reality we will never know which, if any, of the candidates is the 'real' Grail. We do know something of the temple that Indy finds in the 'Canyon of the Crescent Moon', where, in the film, the Grail is hidden:

> Let them bring me to your holy mountain in the place where you dwell. Across the desert and through the mountain to the Canyon of the Crescent Moon, to the Temple where the cup that holds the blood of Jesus Christ resides forever.[29]

The real temple is found in the ancient Nabataean city of Petra in Jordan and dates to 312 BC. Located within a mountainous region, access is controlled through a narrow mountain pass, making it an ideal fortress. The buildings themselves were carved out of the mountains; the most magnificent of these buildings, *Al Khazneh* ('The Treasury'), features as the Grail Temple in *The Last Crusade*.

Indiana Jones and the Kingdom of the Crystal Skull

Indiana Jones and the Kingdom of the Crystal Skull is set in 1957, nineteen years after *The Last Crusade*, and sets an older Indiana Jones against Soviet agents. The Soviets are bent on harnessing the power of a crystal skull associated with extra-terrestrials; the skull was discovered in South America by Harold Oxley, Jones's former colleague. Jones is aided in his adventure by his old flame, Marion Ravenwood, and her son, teenager Henry 'Mutt' Williams, who we later find out is Indy's son. We also discover that Jones had been a Colonel in the Office of Strategic Services, predecessor to the Central Intelligence Agency, during the Second World War, and that he had run covert operations with MI6 agent George McHale.

As ever, the story is fictional but draws heavily on real-life incidents. Clearly the Cold War setting of the film post-dates the defeat of the Third

Reich, but in reality many of the incidents and themes draw upon real Nazi occult ideology and their archaeological expeditions. The Nazis really did send archaeological expeditions to South America, and they wanted to possess the crystal skull so much that they sent secret agents on a mission to steal it from the vault of a museum in Brazil (see Chapter 3). It is also true that archaeologists have frequently worked for the secret intelligence services of many countries over the years; archaeological expeditions were able to provide the perfect cover for international travel. During the First World War, the British hero Lawrence of Arabia used his archaeological expeditions as cover for spying on and recruiting opposition to pro-German forces. During the Second World War, the Nazis Altheim and Trautmann used their archaeological expeditions through the Middle East to gather intelligence for the Third Reich (Chapter 9).[30]

The quest to locate the fictional city of Akator is the driving force behind the plot of *Kingdom of the Crystal Skull*. In the film, Indiana Jones also refers to Akator as the 'City of Gold' or '*El Dorado*'. The first known account of *El Dorado* is found in Juan Rodriguez Freyle's story *El Carnero* of 1638, which tells of a Muisca chief's initiation ceremony. The ceremony involved the chief covering himself with gold dust before diving into Lake Guatavita. This explains the meaning of *El Dorado*, 'gilded one', in reference to the story. The Muisca's association with gold, coupled with rumours of a 'city of gold', encouraged the Spanish conquistadors Francisco Orellana and Gonzalo Pizarro to search—unsuccessfully—for the place they called *El Dorado*.[31]

The *Kingdom of the Crystal Skull* also uses the Nazca Lines as a plot device; these are a series of geoglyphs constructed by Nazca Indians in approximately 400 BC at Nazca, Peru. Their complex designs, which include figures of humans, insects, and birds, have long intrigued people and led to extraordinary claims that they were constructed as tributes to alien beings, or possibly even the markings of landing sites for extra-terrestrial craft. Archaeologists dismiss such flights of fancy and consider that they were either astrological symbols or else designs made for the gods to look down upon. The lines are rather insignificant from the ground, and it is only from the air that it is possible to grasp their scale.[32]

One of the most memorable images from *Kingdom of the Crystal Skull* is the discovery of the crystal skull itself, which is found within the burial site of conquistador and explorer Francisco de Orellana. Crystal skulls first began appearing in the late nineteenth century, with their discoverers claiming that they had been found in either Latin or South America. The skilfully carved skulls are said to predate the arrival of Columbus in the New World, but there is no evidence in Mesoamerican mythology for their existence, and sceptics argue that the skulls were Victorian creations almost certainly made in Europe. In contrast, believers claim that the skulls have a strange, mystical power that overcomes them when they look into the eyes of the skull. Many of these people believe that the skulls were made by extra-terrestrial beings, citing their intricate carving and lack of machine marks. A study of the crystal skulls in the Smithsonian and British Museum published in the *Journal of Archaeological Science* in 2008 found that both had in fact been crafted using a highly abrasive substance that had left marks invisible to the human eye.[33]

Although crystal skulls are a bizarre, there is no evidence of any connection between them and Orellana. However, incredibly, it is true that governments were busy trying to develop methods of mind control. While the idea seems outlandish—if not simply impossible—the Soviets were interested in mind control and performed experiments in telepathy. The Nazis undertook psychological studies on human subjects during the Second World War, while the Central Intelligence Agency was involved in a covert research program known as MKUltra, which experimented with mind-altering drugs including LSD. None of these experiments seem to have amounted to anything, relegating mind control to the end of Blackpool Pier, where it belongs, nor is there any evidence for the supernatural powers ascribed to the crystal skulls.[34]

The Young Indiana Jones Chronicles, Video Games, and Comic Books

A television series named *The Young Indiana Jones Chronicles* ran between 1992 and 1996. It initially centred on the young-adult Indiana and his activities during the First World War as a solider in the Belgian Army; the series then followed his exploits as an intelligence officer and spy seconded to the French intelligence service. He also appeared in video games based around the films, including *Indiana Jones and the Fate of Atlantis*, which had an original storyline that built around the Nazi belief that Atlantis was their Aryan homeland (see Chapter 3). Comic books have extended the franchise even further and again build upon true stories taken from the Nazi preoccupation with the occult and supernatural. In *Indiana Jones and The Spear of Destiny*, a four-part mini-series published by Dark Horse Comics between April and July 1995, Jones is again battling to take possession of a holy relic imbued with supernatural powers, hoping to reach it before the Nazis. The action takes place in the United Kingdom and Ireland in 1945 and involves Irish authoritarian nationalist Blueshirts in league with the Nazis. Again this draws on real life, as there really were Nazi sympathisers and collaborators in Ireland—notably Lord 'Haw Haw' and the traitor James Jacques (see Chapter 8).

The Spear of Destiny, also known as the Holy Lance (*Heilige Lanze*) and the Lance/Spear of Longinus, is mentioned in the Gospel of John (19:31–37), which states that as Jesus hung from the cross, the Romans decided to break his legs—a practice known as *crurifragium*, which hastened death. However, they realised that he was already dead and that there was no reason to break his legs; to make sure, a Roman soldier—named in extra-Biblical tradition as 'Longinus'—stabbed him in the side. 'One of the soldiers pierced his side with a lance, and immediately there came out blood and water' (John 19:34).[35]

Although several churches throughout the world claim to possess the spear, it is the one housed in the Hofberg museum in Vienna that Hitler believed to be the true example. This spear had belonged to the Hapsbergs and had been carried into battle by, amongst others, Henry the Fowler and Frederick Barbarossa. It has been claimed that it held a special significance for Adolf Hitler, who is said to have confided to Dr Stein that he had seen a vision of his own future when he had first seen the spear.[36] Hitler was also heavily influenced the works of Richard Wagner, whose opera *Parsifal* identified the Holy Spear with two items that appear in Wolfram von Eschenbach's poem 'Parzival. This is the spear that injured the Fisher King and appears as a bloody instrument in the Grail Castle. The opera reveals how the spear was lost by the Grail knight and then rescued by Parsifal. It is assumed that the blood on the spear came from Jesus; however, Christ is never named in the opera. Wagner has the blood manifest itself in the Grail rather than on the spearhead.

Such was Hitler's fixation with the lance that on 12 March 1938, the day he annexed Austria, his first port of call on arriving in Vienna was the Hofmuseum, where he claimed the spear. It was immediately sent to Nuremberg, the spiritual capital of Nazi Germany, where it remained until the final days of the war. At 2.10 p.m. on 30 April 1945, the spear fell into the hands of the US Seventh Army under General Patton. Later that day, in fulfilment of the legend, Hitler killed himself.[37]

The Nazis and Archaeology

The Nazis used archaeology to strengthen their nationalist ideology.[38] Adolf Hitler and Heinrich Himmler particularly saw the potential of the German past to support an Aryan national prehistory. They employed archaeologists, anthropologists, linguists, and historians to research the German past.

Some of their strangest activities included the 1928 expedition of Edmund Kiss to Bolivia to study the ruined temples in the Andes Mountains.

He claimed their similarity to ancient European monuments indicated that they were designed by Nordic migrants millions of years earlier. This theory was linked to the Nazi belief that the Germans were descendants of the Aryan race that had originated on the lost continent of Atlantis. The search for Atlantis took Nazi explorers as far afield as Iceland and the Canary Islands.[39]

Ten years later, in 1938, the Nazis sent an expedition to Tibet with the intention of proving the superiority of the Aryan race. The study included measuring the skulls of 376 people and comparing native features to those associated with Aryans.[40] That same year, Franz Altheim and his research partner, Erika Trautmann, travelled to the Middle East to search for evidence to support their theory that there had been an ancient power struggle between Nordic and Semitic peoples within the Roman Empire.[41]

Yet another series of expeditions were organised in an attempt to locate the Holy Grail, which they believed would confer supernatural powers upon them.[42] They ultimately failed to find the Grail, but they were more successful when it came to the Bayeux Tapestry; when they captured it, they asserted that it was evidence of Germanic (Saxon) superiority.[43] The same beliefs in Aryanism and Germanic superiority underpinned a 1936 expedition to Scandinavia, which collected plaster casts of prehistoric rock art that the archaeologists concluded were 'proto-Germanic'.[44]

Background

Although the Nazi research organisations Amt Rosenberg and Ahnenerbe were responsible for developing the idea of a distinctly Germanic prehistory, it was not the Nazis who were first to suggest such a view of the world. These organisations built upon a small (but popular) existing body of literature that was nationalistic, anti-Semitic, and racist while also being idealistically pastoral, pagan, and anti-communist.[45]

One of the people whose theories they adopted was the prehistorian Gustaf Kossinna. Adapting his theories, the Amt Rosenberg and Ahnenerbe presented Germany as the place where civilisation began. They justified this claim by using the work of Kossina and Alfred Rossenberg, who had both used the theory of Social Diffusion to argue that Germany had a history equivalent to that of the Roman Empire. According to the theory of diffusion, influences, ideas, and models were passed on from advanced peoples to the less-advanced by contact. This theory supported the Nazi view of Germany as the origin of world civilisation.[46]

This nationalistic combination of culture and science was typical of what the Third Reich called the *Weltanschauungswissenschaften* or

'World View of Sciences'. This asserted that culture and science were as one and carried certain 'race-inherent values', one of which was the idea that German scientists—and their conclusions—were more reliable than the views of scientists of 'lesser-race'. Elsewhere, scientific approaches to history considered that sagas and legends were interesting cultural works, but unreliable sources of 'fact'. *Weltanschauungswissenschaften* theory suggested that the sagas, folk stories, and songs should be considered reliable sources of historic fact, as well as forming part of popular culture: 'the guiding principle in Germany must be to emphasise the high cultural level, and the cultural self-sufficiency, of the Germanic people'.[47]

Heinrich Himmler was Hitler's right-hand man and one of the most powerful of the Third Reich's leaders.[48] He was absorbed by a mythic Germanic past, which combined ideas from the occult, pseudoscience, and legend. His interests ranged across 'World Ice Theory', the lost continent of Atlantis, the Icelandic Sagas, Runes, prehistoric Venus figurines, ancient rock carvings, the Holy Grail, telepathy, homeopathy, astronomy, heraldry, and the Bhagavadgita. He particularly admired Karl Maria Wiligut, a celebrated clairvoyant who claimed to be the last in a long line of German sages, the Uiligotis of the Asa-Uana-Sippe, whose ancestry could be traced back to prehistoric times.[49] Wiligut's psychic powers were said to enable him to recall at will the experiences of his tribe over some 300,000 years. At that time, there were three suns in the sky and the earth was populated by giants, dwarves, and other mythical beings. Wiligut's 'memory' conjured up remarkable tales involving millennia of tribal conflicts, lost cities, and a final reconciliation instigated by his own ancestors, the Adler-Wiligoten. In 9600 BC, a struggle began between the Irminist religion and the Wotanists, which resulted in a long period of exile for the Irminists in Asia, where Wiligut believed they were persecuted by Jews and Freemasons. These truly unbelievable accounts were the product of a man whose grip on reality was at times very loose; indeed, Wiligut was admitted into a psychiatric hospital between 1924 and 1927, where he was diagnosed as having 'a history of megalomania and schizophrenia'.

Despite Wiligut's history of illness, Himmler was more than willing to accept his delusions as fact. Wiligut's 'ancestral memory' promised to open a door into German prehistory, and so it was that he was not only welcomed into the SS under the pseudonym 'Karl Maria Weisthor', but also appointed head of the Department for Pre- and Early History within Darré's Race and Settlement office. Relations between Himmler and Wiligut were warm. It was Wiligut who designed the death's-head ring (the *Totenkopfring*) worn by members of the SS. He also worked on developing Wewelsburg as the SS Order Castle and stage-managed the ceremonies and rituals that sustained the SS as an Order, bestowing on it an aura of fake tradition and elitism, racial purity, and territorial conquest (see Chapter 10). He founded his own anti-Semitic league and published a newspaper named *The Iron Broom,* which viciously excoriated his ancestral enemies.

After the First World War, Himmler, like other radical conservatives, turned to occultist groups like the Thule Society.[50] In the eyes of these occult, anti-Semitic groups, Jews were rootless predators who thrived only in the chaotic world of the modern city. Only the German peasants seemed free of the Jewish taint, and many saw them as blood banks of Nordic purity. The many strange occult sects were fuelled by disillusionment and uncertainty and led by inspirational, larger-than-life characters such as the occultists Madame Blavatsky and Guido von List.[51] They celebrated a mythic German past and revived pagan ceremonies, reintroducing into popular culture the swastika (later to be deployed by the Nazis) along with runic symbols and Aryan-styled regalia. This was tied into the concept of *Deutsche Reinheit,* or 'Pure German Man', which proposed that Germans were 'pure Aryans' who, having survived a natural catastrophe, had evolved a highly developed culture during a long migration to Germany. This theory also explained that Greeks were 'Germanic', claiming as supporting evidence certain 'Indo-Germanic' artefacts found in Greece (see Chapter 9). In support, they cited Kossina's *Kulturkreis* ('culture circles') theory, which stated that an ethnic region could be identified based on the artefacts excavated from archaeological sites. In *The German Ostmark,* Kossinna argued further that lands where 'Germanic' artefacts were found were ancient Germanic territory.[52] These 'Germanic' lands, which included Poland, had been 'wrongfully stolen' by 'barbarians' and should by right be a part of German Reich. This was music to the ears of the Nazis, who were happy to use Kossina's academic theory to justify their eastward expansion into Poland, Czechoslovakia, Ukraine, and Russia.

In short, the Nazis used archaeology to generate propaganda sympathetic to the Third Reich. The Amt Rosenberg openly stated as much in its published goal, which was 'the interpretation and dissemination of unclassified knowledge regarding the history and cultural achievements of [their] northern Germanic ancestors on German and foreign soil'. [54]

In order to draw the German people to the idea of Germany as the site of the origins of civilisation, a series of films were produced by Lothar Zotz. These included *Threatened by the Steam Plough, Germany's Bronze Age, The Flames of Prehistory,* and *On the Trail of the Eastern Germans.* These films used the appeal of myth, nostalgia, and German triumph to reinforce the idea that German history was something to be proud of.[55] The success of these films lay in the fact that these periods of history were little-known to the general public and so could be freely manipulated to include heavy doses of propaganda. Additionally, magazines such as *Die Kunde* (*The Message*) and *Germanen-Erbe* (*Germanic Heritage*), and new museums such as the open-air reconstructions of Neolithic and Bronze Age lake settlements at Unteruhldingen, became popular, fulfilling the newly created need of the population to learn about 'true' German prehistory through accounts of the latest excavations. Altogether, this worked to engender feelings of pride that were used to reinforce the nationalistic, fascist message that Adolf Hitler had carefully crafted.

Nazi Archaeological Institutions

The Nazis established two archaeological institutions in the 1930s, both tasked with documenting the superiority of the Germanic race and its historical right to the old Germanic areas. Both institutions organised international archaeological expeditions, although their primary focus was on North Germany and Scandinavia, since these areas were regarded as the old Germanic's core countries. Both institutions were led by men at the top of the Nazi hierarchy.

The first organisation was the Amt Rosenberg, which comprised a small group of professional archaeologists, at least in their background and training.[55] The organisation was led by Alfred Rosenberg, a former journalist who, for a time, worked as an editor of the NSDAP's main newspaper, the *Völkischer Beobachter.*[56] According to Rosenberg's Nazi-approved history *Der Mythus des 20 Jahrdunderts*, the world had been shaped by an eternal battle between the Nordic and Atlantean people and 'Semites' (Jews).[57] It was his belief that Germans (Atlanteans) were superior racially, something that later justified the Final Solution. The work of supporting this view with archaeological evidence fell to the Amt Rosenberg, aided by the 'Thule Society'.
Rosenberg became head of the Reich Ministry for the Occupied Eastern Territories in 1941, and after the war he was captured, sentenced to death, and executed at the Nuremburg trials in 1946.

The second institution was the *Ahnenerbe Forschungs-und Lehrgemeinschaft* (The Ancestral Heritage Research and Teaching Society), more usually referred to as the 'Ahnenerbe'.[58] Its motto was 'A people live happily in the present and the future so long as they are conscious of their past and the greatness of their ancestors'. The Ahnenerbe undertook historical and anthropological research focusing on the origins and distribution of the German ethnic group, which they preferred to describe as the Aryan race. Their job was to find the facts, the 'thousands of mosaic pieces', as Himmler described them, which they did by investigating the 'space, spirit, accomplishments, and heritage' of the Indo-Germanic peoples of the Nordic race and then disseminating their findings to the German people. Although working under the umbrella of 'science', much of what they did was pseudo-scientific, and their attempts to publicise their work often took the form of propaganda justifying Nazi ideology. The Ahnenerbe and Amt Rosenberg coexisted for a period, but in time, due in large part to the support of Himmler, the Ahnenerbe ousted the Amt Rosenberg and completely took over the work of recovering the archaeological traces of Germany's glorious past.

As with much Nazi history, there is ambiguity about the precise date on which the Ahnenerbe was founded. There is some evidence that it existed in a different form as early as 1928, when Wirth established the 'Ahnenerbe Society'—'an association for clan- and heraldry-research assistance, heredity science and race-cultivation'—in order to spread his theories. Another precursor of the Ahnenerbe was a research institute for 'spiritual prehistory' created by the German state of Mecklenburg in 1932, when it was governed by the NSDAP. The Ahnenerbe as we know it came into being in 1935, when the '*Deutsches Ahnenerbe Verein*' was formally established in Berlin as a private not-for-profit organisation. Its founders were Heinrich Himmler, Hermann Wirth (a Dutch historian obsessed with Atlantean mythology), and Richard Walter Darré, creator of the Nazi 'blood and soil' ideology and head of the Race and Settlement Office.[59] At this time, funding for the Ahnenerbe came primarily from Darré, through his position within the German Ministry of Agriculture. This association ended around 1936, leaving Himmler in total control.

SS-Reichsführer Heinrich Himmler was among Hitler's most trusted colleagues. According to Felix Kersten:

> His eyes were extraordinarily small, and the distance between them narrow, rodent like. If you spoke to him, those eyes would never leave your face; they would rove over your countenance, fix your eyes; and in them would be an expression of waiting, watching, stealth ... His ways were the orphidian [*sic.*] ways of the coward, weak, insincere and immeasurably cruel ... Himmler's mind was not a twentieth-century mind. His character was medieval, feudalistic, Machiavellian, evil.[60]

Himmler was an early adopter of Nazism, becoming leader of the SS in 1929 and head of the Gestapo (the secret police) by 1934. He had responsibility for the concentration camps and rose to Commander of the Home Army in 1944, following the unsuccesful attempt on Hitler's life. At the end of the war, he was captured by the British; he killed himself before he could stand trial.

Himmler was fascinated by 'Völkisch' beliefs and took control of the Ahnenerbe so that he could personally direct the 'development of Germanic heritage'. He deployed scientists to find evidence to underpin a 'Germanic' culture, incorporating the institute into the SS by 1940. All members of the Ahnenerbe were in any case members of the SS. Wolfram Sievers was *Reichsgeschäftsführer* (Reichs Manager) in 1935, and he was promoted to SS-Obersturmführer in 1937, rising to SS-Standartenführer by the end of the war.[61] Sievers was an autocratic leader who was joined by Professor Walter Wüst in 1937 as trustee and '*kurator*' (replacing Hermann Wirth).[62] The Ahnenerbe was well-funded, with a budget of more than 1 million German marks (*c.* $4 million). This money was used to fund expeditions and experiments in aid of Nazi ideology, its output being racist pseudoscience.

Besides financial support, membership of the Ahnenerbe was attractive because it placed scholars in the academic elite of Nazi Germany. Those that enlisted into the Ahnenerbe gained patronage, and sometimes the attention of the Reichsführer-SS himself. This academic status was confined to Nazi-controlled territory, as beyond the borders of the Third Reich the Ahnenerbe were considered, even at that time, as a sort of 'intellectual criminals'. A further attraction of the Ahnenerbe was that its work was considered 'war essential', allowing its members to escape military service.

The Ahnenerbe had fifty-one different research institutes that carried out more than 100 extensive research projects. The size of the institutes varied in size. Some could be quite large—particularly those responsible for the archaeological expeditions—but most made do with less than a dozen personnel. For example, the staff for experiments to make seawater drinkable consisted of a supervisor, three medical chemists, one female assistant, and three non-commissioned officers.

The first institute to be established specialised in the study of Norse runes. It was under the command of Hermann Wirth, placing linguistic study at the forefront of Ahnenerbe activity. Wirth was the author of an immense book called *The Rise of Mankind* (1928), which described thousands of runic symbols from different northern European cultures.[63] Inspired by the geological work of Alfred Wegener, the first person to suggest the theory of continental drift, Wirth proposed a theory of 'polar shift', which implied that the icy north had once been the original homeland of the northern Aryan peoples. Shifting poles and wandering continents had done for Wirth's 'Arctic Race', although they had survived in isolated settlements like Atlantis. Wirth cited the findings of Knud Rasmussen, a Dane who had led an expedition to Greenland in 1906–7 and had claimed to have found 'mysterious' blond and bearded Eskimos. Linguistics were also studied at Professor Wüst's institute, where the focus was on Sanskrit, his area of specialism, investigating the connection between language and the Aryan race. When Wirth left the Ahnenerbe in 1937, Wüst took over his role as well.

Central to the Ahnenerbe was the publication of materials as part of Himmler's initiative to 'revive' Germanic traditions. To do this, they established their own publishing house in the academic suburb of Berlin-Dahlem; there, they produced a monthly magazine (*Germanien*), two journals on genealogy (*Zeitschrift für Namenforschung* and *Das Sippenzeichen*), and countless monographs.

In 1938, the 'Institute for Germanic Archaeology' was formed; under its umbrella, excavations took place at Paderborn, Detmold, Haithabu, and Externsteine. To this day, Haithabu is recognised as an important archaeological site for the study of early medieval settlements. The site lies on the Danish border and is near both Detmold and Externsteine, which is a legendary site renowned as an ancient Aryan temple associated with Yggdrasil, the 'World-Ash' of Norse legend. The ancient Germanic heartland encompassed Paderborn, Wewelsberg, and Externsteine. It was there that the Saxons had valiantly fought the Romans first, and later the Franks under Charlemagne. This was an area firmly behind the Nazis and one of the first to elect an NSDAP government.

Archaeological expeditions continued even after the outbreak of hostilities. Scientists went to Bulgaria, Croatia, Poland, and Romania, where they worked in collaboration with local academics. Excavations were also undertaken in occupied Russia and northern Africa, and expeditions travelled as far afield as the Far East—particularly to Tibet—and also Kafiristan.

Tibet had a particular significance for the Ahnenerbe, which supported several research trips by their Institute for Inner Asian Research led by Ernst Schäfer. Interest in Tibet was in part due to the influence of the Swedish explorer Sven Hedin, whose memoirs *My Life As An Explorer* were popular worldwide.[64] His description of discovering the ancient Chinese city of Lou-lan in the Taklimakan Desert includes the artefacts he unearthed—a swastika-decorated rug nearly 2,000 years old and early examples of writing on paper sparked Nazi interest. He enthused: '... not a single one of our ancient Swedish runestones is older than the fragile wooden staffs and paper fragments that I found in Lou-lan'. Hedin was a friend and mentor of many in the Ahnenerbe, including Schäfer. Even after the institute was absorbed into the SS, he maintained contact, despite the horrors they were responsible for. Although never an official member of the Ahnenerbe (he was in his seventies during the war), Hedin corresponded with the organisation and was present when the Institute for Inner Asian Research was formally established in Munich in January 1943.

Schäfer's SS-Tibet mission began in April 1938 and ended in August 1939. The aim was to gather cultural information on the Tibetans that supported Nazi ideology. This included details of their religion, anthropological measurements, and politics. The latter was kept secret and aimed at laying the groundwork for a possible German invasion of India.

More obscure was the idea that Schäfer was looking for evidence of the Yeti, a 'missing link' between great apes and humans. They failed in this last regard, but did return with plant specimens and animals, along with the 108-volume sacred Tibetan text, the *Kangschur*. They also undertook secret geophysical research to try to prove the validity of the 'World Ice Theory'.[65]

Himmler considered the Icelandic *Eddas* to be a sacred text. Iceland was viewed as a mythical homeland, the last surviving connection to prehistoric Thule. Himmler believed that secret knowledge of prehistoric culture lay within the *Eddas*, and as such, he afforded them their own Ahnenerbe Insititute. In addition, fieldwork was planned, just as it had been for Tibet, to undertake anthropological measurements of the people.[66] In fact, a mission did travel to the island in 1938. The aim was to find a 'hof', a place of worship to the Norse gods Thor and Odin. The expedition ran out of money and failed to obtain the permits needed to excavate. It was a total disaster.

The Ahnenerbe also had an institute devoted to musicology. Expeditions were sent to collect folk music from such diverse places as Finland, the Faroe Islands, and South Tyrol; they believed that the presence of certain musical traditions was to be taken as evidence for Germanic ancestry, and used to justify German expansionism to the east.

Of all the Ahnenerbe institutions, the one devoted to '*Welteislehre*' (World Ice Theory) was perhaps the most curious. The theory had been developed by Hans Hörbiger, but the institute was led by Dr Hans Robert Scultetus.[67] The theory, first mooted by Blavatsky, was that in the distant past, there had been six moons orbiting the Earth. The gravitational effect of the moons had triggered a terrible ice age, out of which had emerged the Aryan race.[68] According to Himmler: 'Our Nordic ancestors grew strong amidst the ice and snow, and this is why a belief in a world of ice is the natural heritage of Nordic men'.

Even though Hörbiger had died in 1931, his theory went on to be adopted by some Theosophists. In South America, occultists relied on his ideas to 'prove' the existence of a link between ancient Andean civilisation and Atlantis and Thule. In turn, this led to the Ahnenerbe's expeditions to South America to investigate the supposed Aryan Atlantean link. The Ahnenerbe were most concerned with practical applications of the World Ice Theory focused on meteorology, vital to military operations. Scultetus sent Edmund Kiss, who was a popular author of novels about Atlantis, on an expedition to Abyssinia. Kiss's mission was to establish support for the World Ice Theory.

So-called 'research' was carried out on human subjects by the Institute for Scientific Research for Military Purposes, mostly on inmates of the Dachau concentration camp. Professor August Hurt collected over 100 human skeletons from live subjects as well as performing experiments on his victims.[69]

In charge of research on live subjects at Dachau was Dr Sigmund Rascher, an SS Hauptsturmführer and member of the Ahnenerbe. He infamously froze captives in the low-pressure chambers and vats of icy water before experimentally warming them in sleeping bags, with boiling water and even by having sex with prostitutes. Those who survived were shot. It was Rascher who developed the cyanide capsules carried by SS members, including Himmler, who swallowed one to avoid prosecution at the end of the war. In the end, Rascher received some rough justice himself when he was executed by the SS for plotting to pass off kidnapped children as his own.[70]

Other institutes within the Ahnenerbe included one for the study of the Celts, who assisted in the planning of the SS castle at Wewelsburg— another of Himmler's vanity projects.

Although the ideas of the Ahnenerbe quite often seem bizarre to us, they did serve to conceal secret intelligence-gathering activities and more overt '*kuturpolitische*' (cultural-political) missions in Norway, Denmark, and the Netherlands. These activities included distributing propaganda and recruiting volunteers for the Waffen-SS. The Ahnenerbe were also charged with 'collecting'—'stealing', in other words—works of art, historical artefacts, and valuable documents for the Third Reich.

As ever with the NSDAP, the Ahnenerbe were set against other Nazi organisations to compete for pre-eminence in the field of Germanic culture, a classic tactic of the Reich. In their case, the chief rivals were Alfred Rosenberg, who was constantly in conflict with Hermann Wirth, and Karl Maria Wiligut, known as 'Weisthor' and head of the Department for Pre- and Early History in the RuSHA (Race and Settlement Office) and a personal favourite of Himmler.

The Ahnenerbe had to work with Wiligut due to his close ties to Himmler, but they did so through gritted teeth. In private, they considered him to be 'the worst kind of fantasist'. Academics in the Ahnenerbe were acutely aware of the occult overtones of many Nazis and did all they could to distance themselves from them. Fortunately for them, Wiligut fell from grace in 1939.

In 1943, the Ahnenerbe was relocated to Waischenfeld, Franconia, to avoid Allied bombing raids. In the end, the Americans took the city in April

1945. Had the Third Reich emerged victorious in the war, it was planned that an SS university at Leyden, in the Netherlands, would be established; in reality, its high-profile members were tried for war crimes while the others slid back into academia, often under false names, after the war.

Historians have often viewed the Nazi obsession with the occult (and particularly Himmler's) as an exotic aside to an otherwise rather sombre story of brutal policing and ruthless genocide. The truth is that Himmler's enthusiasm for the rediscovery of lost civilisations, prehistoric archaeology, the Holy Grail, and especially the origins of the 'Indo-Germanic' races were intricately interwoven with the racial 'theories' that demanded the elimination of the 'unfit'.

The Archaeologists

Prior to the rise of the Third Reich, there was neither funding nor interest in Germanic archaeology. The Nazis stepped into this vacuum with their nationalistic representation of the past, a representation that the public were ill-equipped to challenge. After being starved of public funding in the past, German prehistorians welcomed the prestige and resources fed into their discipline by the Reich. From 1933 to 1935, the number of professorships in archaeology increased from one to nine under Nazi rule; meanwhile, generous funding allowed them to multiply the number of excavations and museum displays. However, there was a high price to pay for this newfound political support. In their enthusiasm, many German archaeologists became willing participants in the worst activities of the NSDAP in general, and the SS in particular. Answering to the requests of their political masters, they provided support for Nazi racist Aryan ideology, justified German expansion to the east, and, in some cases, participated in the holocaust.

It is impractical to list all the archaeologists, anthropologists, historians, and supporters that collaborated with the Nazis, following the lead of Alfred Rosenberg, but some of the more notorious were: Rolf Alber, Franz Altheim, Julius Andrée, Wilhelm Aspendorf, Bruno Beger, Assien Bohmers, Fritz Bose, Helmut Bousset, Werner Braune, Brugg (aka Rudolf von Elmayer-Vestenbrugg), Hermann Bunjes, Frans Bursch, Ludwig Ferdinand Clauss, Richard Walther Darré, Karl Diebitsch, Hans-Jürgen Eggers, Ola Forsell, Dogobert Frey, von Fritsch, Albert Funk, Bruno Galke, Edmund Geer, Werner Gerlach, Rudolf Gorsleben, Ernst-Robert von Grawitz, Yrjö von Grönhagen, Hans Günther, Heinrich Harrer, Reinhard Heydrich, August Hirt, Otto Huth, James Jacques, Hans Jacobsen, Herbert Jankuhn, Herbert Jeschke, Julius Jordan, Karl Kersten, Edmund Kiss, Wilhelm

Kottenrodt, Bruno Kress, Bernard Kummel, Paul Ladame, Langsdorff, Hans-Jürgen Lutzhöft, Gero von Merhart, Kajetan Mühlmann, von Motz, Gotthard Neumann, Otto Ohlendorf, Martinez Santa Olalla, Peter Paulsen, Otto Plassmann, Alfred Ploetz, Alfred Quellmalz, Werner Radig, Otto Rahn, Sigmund Rascher, Hans Reinerth, Herrman Reischle, Ludwig Roselius, Alfred Rosenberg, Alfred Rust, Ernst Schäfer, Arthur Scheler, Walter Schellenberg, Erwin Schirmer, Karl Schlabow, Hans Schleif, R. R. Schmidt, Gustav Schwantes, Bruno Schweizer, Dr Scultetus, Rudolf von Sebottendorff, Wolf von Seefeld, Hans Ulrich von Seneberg, Wolfram Sievers, Ernst Sprockhoff, Wilhelm Teudt, Erika Trautmann, Ursula Uhland, Ernst Wahle, Joachim Werner, Karl Wienert, Karl Maria Wiligut, Hermann Wirth, Dominik Wölfel, Richard Wolfram, Walter Wüst, Wilhelm Unverzagt, and Hans Zeiß. Most of these individuals escaped prosecution after the war, with many going on to hold important positions in German universities.

Before and during the Second World War, these men and women participated in German expeditions that ranged across the globe, from South America to Tibet. In Europe, archaeological expeditions were sent to Ukraine, Bulgaria, Croatia, Greece, Iceland, France, Cyprus, Finland, Poland, Czechoslovakia, Romania, Norway and Scandinavia, Spain, and the Canary Islands, as well as India, Tibet, and Kafiristan in Asia and Mexico, Brazil, and Bolivia in South America.

2
Ideology: Aryans, Anti-Semiticism and Racism

Among all the disputes and uncertainties of the ethnographers about the races of Europe, one fact stands out clearly—namely, that we can distinguish a race of northerly distribution and origin, characterised physically by fair colour of hair and skin and eyes, by tall stature and dolichocephaly (i.e. long shape of head), and mentally by great independence of character, individual initiative and tenacity of will.[1]

Introduction

The Nazis invested considerable resources into archaeology during the Third Reich, with the politically driven aim of establishing evidence to support their racist ideology.[2] The instructions given to archaeologists were to find evidence to support theories that the Nordic, 'Aryan', German people were racially superior to other races, and therefore justified in using military force to subjugate and even exterminate 'inferior' peoples. This policy was set out—without any embarrassment—by Hitler himself:

... [the Aryan] is the Prometheus of mankind, from whose shining brow the divine spark of genius has at all times flashed forth, always kindling anew that fire which, in the form of knowledge, illuminated the dark night ... As a conqueror, he subjugated inferior races and turned their physical powers into organised channels under his own leadership, forcing them to follow his will and purpose. By imposing on them a useful, though hard, manner of employing their powers he not only spared the lives of those whom he had conquered but probably made their lives easier than these had been in the former state of so-called 'freedom' ... While he ruthlessly maintained his position as their master, he not only remained master but he also maintained and advanced civilisation ... If we divide mankind into three categories—founders of culture, bearers of culture, and destroyers of culture—the Aryan alone can be considered as representing the first category ... Should he be forced to disappear, a profound darkness will descend on the earth; within a few thousand years human culture will vanish and the world will become a desert.[3]

Chillingly, Hitler was only articulating a view already shared by many German people, a view that had been in existence for at least two or three centuries across Europe. To understand how this came about, we need to consider two separate questions—why were Aryans considered superior, and why were Jews singled out for particularly harsh treatment?

Anti-Semiticism and the Origins of Racism

In the years 1940 to 1944, to be Aryan or Semitic was to either live or to die in Nazi-occupied Europe. What was the justification for persecuting Jews? To answer this, we need look no further than the writing of Adolf Hitler:

The Jew completely lacks the most essential prerequisite of a cultural people, namely the idealistic spirit ... He is and remains a parasite, a sponger who, like a pernicious bacillus, spreads over wider and wider areas according as some favourable area attracts him ... Wherever he establishes himself the people who grant him hospitality are bound to be bled to death sooner or later ... He poisons the blood of others but preserves his own blood unadulterated ... To mask his tactics and fool his victims, he talks of the equality of all men, no matter what their race or colour may be ... To all external appearances, [he] strives to ameliorate the conditions under which the workers live; but in reality his aim is to enslave and thereby annihilate the non-Jewish races ... The black-haired Jewish youth lies in wait for hours on end, satanically glaring at and spying on the unsuspicious girl whom he plans to seduce, adulterating her blood and removing her from the bosom of her own people. The Jew uses every possible means to undermine the racial foundations of a subjugated people ... The Jews were responsible for bringing negroes into the Rhineland, with the ultimate idea of bastardising the white race which they hate and thus lowering its cultural and political level so that the Jew might dominate.[4]

Hitler clearly had a vitriolic hatred of Jewish people that ultimately led to the industrialisation of murder perpetuated during the Holocaust.

Nazi archaeologists worked to justify the actions of the Third Reich, and in some cases they actively participated in the murder of innocent Jewish people. As we investigate this in greater detail, we will see that as with much of Nazi ideology, they took existing anti-Semitic beliefs and bent them to their own ends.[5]

The Bible taught that all men were descended from a common ancestor, Adam, via the patriarch Noah and his sons, whose descendants are listed in the Book of Genesis. The Fathers of the Christian Church took the Biblical genealogies and combined them with their own traditions; after Noah, the lines of descent passed through his three sons—Japheth, Shem, and Ham—to whom there was sometimes added a fourth son, Jenithon or Manithon. According to tradition, based on etymological clues contained in the Bible, the Europeans were the children of Japheth, Asians were the children of Shem, and Africans were the children of Ham. Ham's descendants were the subject of a mysterious curse that condemned them to serve their cousins as slaves ('And Canaan shall be his servant...' Genesis 19:27), which conveniently justified the enslavement of African people. A sixth century Arab text recounts how Jesus changed some Jewish children into goats, and has him saying to their mothers, 'The children of Israel have the same rank among the peoples as the Negroes'.[6] In one short sentence, anti-Semitism and racism are legitimised.

Through the next thousand or so years, Christians and Jews lived side-by-side in many European countries in varying degrees of harmony. These periods were interspersed by violent pogroms when Jews were singled out for persecution. After a period of relatively peaceful co-existence, the late nineteenth century (into which Hitler and the other leading Nazis were born) was marked by an increase in anti-Semitism. In Germany, the influential philosopher Nietzsche had distinguished between an Aryan and a Semitic essence in the *Birth of Tragedy* (1871).[7] Paul de Lagarde (1827–1891) repeatedly demanded 'the destruction of Judaism' throughout Europe, suggesting that Jews might be exiled to Madagascar.[8] Lagarde's extreme views were admired by many notable figures, including Thomas Carlyle, Thomas Mann, Paul Natorp, and Thomas Masaryk, as well as Adolf Hitler and Alfred Rosenberg. This demonstrates the intellectual climate of the time, which was increasingly concerned with the classification of people into a hierarchy of 'races'.

Herrenvolk: The Master Race

Between the nineteenth and mid-twentieth centuries, anthropologists divided people into races and sub-races. Europeans were assigned to the

Caucasian race, which was sub-divided into the Nordic, Alpine, Dinaric, East Baltic, and Mediterranean races. The inhabitants of the countries of Northern Europe belonged to the Nordic race and were described as having light-coloured hair and eyes, fair skin, and long and narrow skulls. They were thought to be tall, truthful, equitable, competitive, naïve, reserved, and individualistic. Hitler preferred the term 'Aryan'; in the Third Reich, this word became synonymous with the Nordic 'race', less any people with blond hair who also had Jewish grandparents.[9]

In the mid-nineteenth century, long before the emergence of Nazism, scientific racism developed the theory that the original speakers of the Indo-European languages were the Aryans. They also held that they were an innately superior branch of humanity, responsible for its greatest achievements. This idea was popular in the late nineteenth and early twentieth centuries in some central and northern European countries, as well as in North America. Nazism took this further and claimed that the Nordic, Aryan race constituted a master race or *Herrenvolk*.

The principal proponent of this theory was Arthur de Gobineau, who set out his ideas in his *Essay on the Inequality of the Human Races* (1855).[10] According to Gobineau, the Aryan race best represented the Germanic people. He relied upon snippets from Tacitus, the Roman historian, who argued that after the decline of the Roman Empire, it was the 'pure' German people who had regenerated Europe.[11]

In the late nineteenth century, Theodore Poesche, an anthropologist, located the origin of the Aryans in the 'Rokitno' 'or 'Pinsk' Marshes in southern Belarus, and north-western Ukraine. Karl Penka, on the other hand, posited that they originated in Scandinavia and were synonymous with blond-haired and blue-eyed people.[12, 13] Thomas Henry Huxley developed this idea, coining the term 'Xanthochroi' for the fair-skinned Europeans.[14] In *The Aryan Race* (1888), Charles Morris added the detail that Aryans could be distinguished from other races by their dolichocephaly (long skulls), an idea illustrated by Henry Keane in *Man, Past and Present* (1899), which shows a Dane exemplifying the 'Nordic type'.[15, 16] The notion familiar to Nazis, that the 'dolichocephalic-blond' peoples were born leaders destined to rule over others was first enunciated by the French anthropologist Vacher de Lapouge in *L'Aryan*.[17] It was an idea given philosophical credibility by Friedrich Nietzsche:

In Latin *malus* ... could indicate the vulgar man as the dark one, especially as the black-haired one, as the pre-Aryan dweller of the Italian soil which distinguished itself most clearly through his colour from the blonds who became their masters, namely the Aryan conquering race.[18]

By 1902, the German archaeologist Gustaf Kossinna (1858–1931) developed the *Siedlungsarchaeologische Methode*—a technique for finding ancient people by looking at the spatial distribution of artefacts. He led archaeological expeditions to try to prove his theories and also published books for a general readership, which served as Nazi propaganda. One of his most popular books, *Die deutsche Vorgeschichte—eine hervorragend nationale Wissenschaft* (*German Prehistory: A Pre-eminently National Discipline*), justified the invasion of neighbouring countries by the 'superior' Aryan race. The dedication reads: 'To the German people, as a building block in the reconstruction of the externally as well as internally disintegrated fatherland'.[19]

The first Aryans—who might be called 'Proto-Indo-Europeans'—were identified by Kossinna, with the north German Corded Ware culture. His views gathered acceptance over the next twenty years, with the location of the Indo-European Urheimat being in Schleswig-Holstein, from where it had dispersed across Europe. This theory was well-established by the early twentieth century, although far from universally accepted. Sociologists were soon using the concept of a 'blond race' to plot the routes taken by migrations of the supposedly more advanced, 'entreprenurial', and 'innovative' European populations. In 1939, Carleton Coon wrote:

> The Poles who came to the United States during the nineteenth century, and the early decades of the twentieth, did not represent a cross-section of the Polish population, but a taller, blonder, longer-headed group than the Poles as a whole.[20]

The high-brow *vs* low-brow distinction derived from such theories also became enshrined in language.

In the early twentieth century, British-German writer Houston Stewart Chamberlain (1855–1927) considered the Nordic race to be made up of Celtic and Germanic peoples in addition to some Slavs—an idea that subsequently influenced Adolf Hitler's Nazi ideology.[21] Chamberlain's most famous work was *The Foundations of the Nineteenth Century*. The 1,500-page-long book gave a vision of the world that seemed to support the superiority of the Aryan race. As Chamberlain understood it, modern science was exclusively the work of the 'Celto-Slavo-Teutons'—otherwise known as the 'Germans':

> The faultlessly mechanical interpretation of nature is unavoidable and the only true one. When I say 'the only true one', I mean that it can be the only true one for Teutons; other men may, in the future as in the past, think differently … so long as the Teuton predominates, he will force

this view of his even upon non-Teutons ... By this—and this alone—we have acquired a mass of perceptions and a command over nature never equalled by any other human race.[22]

According to Chamberlain, this unique knowledge of science was acquired thanks to an understanding of the laws of scientific necessity, enlightened by the religious instinct of the Aryans. This was dealt with in a chapter on 'Religion':

Take, for example, the conception of the Godhead: here Jehovah, there the old Aryan Trinity ... Thanks to the influence of Hellenic sentiment, the Christian Church ... had, in the moulding of its dogma, steered successfully past that most dangerous cliff, Semitic monotheism, and has preserved in her otherwise perilously Judaised [*sic*.] conception of the Godhead the sacred 'Three in Number' of the Aryans ... all human knowledge rests on three fundamental forms—time, space, causality ... In short, the threefoldness [*sic*.] as unity surrounds us on all sides as an original phenomenon of experience and is reflected in all individual cases...[23]

Chamberlain's work was undeniably anti-Semitic and was adopted later by the philosopher of the NSDAP, Alfred Rosenberg, whose own work, *Der Mythos des 20. Jahrhunderts* (*The Myth of the Twentieth Century*) shows Chamberlain's influence. Chamberlain's *The Foundations of the Nineteenth Century* became the new Bible of hundreds of thousands of Germans. The reason for its popularity is addressed by Kaiser Wilhelm II in a letter to Chamberlain:

I knew by instinct that we youngsters had need of another education in order to serve the new Reich. Our stifled youth needed a liberator like yourself, one who revealed to us the Indo-German origins, which no one knew about. And so it was only at the cost of a hard struggle that the original Germanic Aryanism (*das Urarische-Germanische*), which slumbered in the depths of my soul was able to assert itself. It showed itself in my open hostility to 'tradition' and it often tried to emerge in strange inarticulate ways since it was, to begin with, an obscure and unselfconscious presentiment. And now you come and with a wave of your magic wand create order where there was chaos and light where there was darkness. You explain what was obscure, you show the way of salvation to the Germans and to all the rest of mankind...[24]

Modern readers may be shocked to learn that the book was generally well-received when a translated version appeared in Britain in 1911.

Most British newspapers mentioned it; *The Spectator* praised it as a 'monument of erudition'; the *Birmingham Post* found it 'glowing with life, packed with fresh and vigorous thought'; and the *Glasgow Herald* declared that it would be difficult to 'over-estimate the stimulating qualities of the book'. The commentator in *The Times Literary Supplement* hailed it as 'one of the books that really mattered'. In *Fabian News*, Bernard Shaw called the book a 'historical masterpiece'. The concept of a 'masterly' Nordic race had become so familiar that in 1920, the British psychologist William McDougall wrote:

> Among all the disputes and uncertainties of the ethnographers about the races of Europe, one fact stands out clearly—namely, that we can distinguish a race of northerly distribution and origin, characterised physically by fair colour of hair and skin and eyes, by tall stature and dolichocephaly (i.e. long shape of head), and mentally by great independence of character, individual initiative and tenacity of will. Many names have been used to denote this type... It is also called the Nordic type.[25]

On the other side of the Atlantic, the American William Z. Ripley attempted to define scientifically a 'Teutonic race' in his book *The Races of Europe* (1899).[26] His approach was to identify three categories—Teutonic ('*Teutonisch*'), Alpine, and Mediterranean. The teutons were distinguished by their pale skin, fair hair, blue eyes, and tall, slender body; they occupied Scandinavia, the Baltic region, East Prussia, northern Poland, northern Russia, parts of central Europe, and Britain and Ireland. Madison Grant, in his book *The Passing of the Great Race* (1916), took up Ripley's classification. He described a 'Nordic' type:

> Long skulled, very tall, fair skinned, with blond or brown hair and light coloured eyes. The Nordics inhabit the countries around the North and Baltic Seas and include not only the great Scandinavian and Teutonic groups, but also other early peoples who first appear in southern Europe and in Asia as representatives of Aryan language and culture.[28]

According to Grant, the 'Alpine race' (shorter in stature and darker in colouring, with a rounder head) predominated in central and eastern Europe through to Turkey and the Eurasian steppes of central Asia and southern Russia. The 'Mediterranean race', with dark hair and eyes, aquiline nose, swarthy complexion, moderate-to-short stature, and moderate or long skull, was said to be prevalent in southern Europe, the Middle East, and north Africa.

Grant's theories were successfully used to justify United States immigration policies. The Immigration Act of 1924 reduced the number of immigrants from southern and eastern Europe and Russia and excluded Asian immigrants altogether, while favouring immigration from the British Isles, Germany, Denmark, Sweden, and Norway. According to Grant, the great advances of humanity were all down to the Nordic race. This was a view endorsed by Calvin Coolidge, who would go on to become the US President. Coolidge wrote: 'Biological laws tell us that certain divergent people will not mix or blend. The Nordic people propagate themselves successfully'.

Back in Germany, the eugenicists Erwin Baur, Eugen Fischer, and Fritz Lenz insisted on the innate superiority of the Nordic race in their 1921 work *Human Heredity*.[29] They believed that the so-called Nordic qualities had evolved in the harsh physical environment of the north, where any weaklings would have failed to survive. They went on to argue that 'the original Indo-Germanic civilisation' was carried by Nordic migrants down to India, and that the physiognomy of upper-caste Indians 'disclose a Nordic origin'. Hans F. K. Günther, (1891–1968), one of Fischer's students, wrote *The Short Ethnology of the German People* (1929) and *Rassenkunde des Deutschen Volks* (*Race-Lore of the German People*, 1922), both of which established him as a leading light in anthropology and a favourite of the Third Reich. [31, 32]

Julius Evola and Alfred Rosenberg wrote of a 'Nordic-Atlantean' master race in *The Myth of the Twentieth Century*. It was in the lost world of Atlantis, a landmass off the coast of Europe, that the Nordic race evolved. From there, Rosenberg argued, people spread throught northern Europe, making their was as far as Iran and India. It was there that they found Zoroastrianism and Hinduism, which he believed to be 'Aryan' in nature. However, when these Nordic people began to intermarry, they lost their 'energy' and became 'degenerate'. Hitler was a believer in these theories and its racial basis of civilisation, being influenced shortly before he wrote *Mein Kampf*.

With the rise of Hitler, Aryan theory became the norm within German culture. In some cases, the 'Nordic' concept became an almost abstract ideal rather than a mere racial category. For example, Hermann Gauch wrote in 1933 that the fact that 'birds can be taught to talk better than other animals is explained by the fact that their mouths are Nordic in structure'.[33] He further claimed that in humans, 'the shape of the Nordic gum allows a superior movement of the tongue, which is the reason why Nordic talking and singing are richer'. Grauch's views were extreme, even for many in the Ahnenerbe. Hans F. K. Günther's views were more mainstream, and much of the Nazis' racial ideology was based upon his work. Günther had joined the party in 1932 and soon won praise and even a medal—presented by Alfred Rosenberg. Others held in high regard included Madison Grant, who proudly displayed a letter from Hitler that praised him for his work—the Führer referred to it as 'The Bible'. As we know, the Nazis were quick to cite scholarly papers in support of the Final Solution. Such views were not new, and as early as 1869 Galton wrote:

> We are ceasing as a nation to breed intelligence as we did fifty to a hundred years ago. The mentally better stock in the nation is not reproducing itself at the same rate as it did of old; the less able and the less energetic are more fertile than the better stocks ... The only remedy, if one be possible at all, is to alter the relative fertility of the good and the bad stocks in the community.[34]

The SS were to feature centre-stage in a Nazi post-war Europe. They were Hitler and Himmler's model Nordic elite, and they would be charged with regenerating a racially pure continent. Addressing officers of the SS-Leibstandarte 'Adolf Hitler', Himmler stated:

> The ultimate aim for those eleven years during which I have been the Reichsführer SS has been invariably the same: to create an order of good blood which is able to serve Germany; which unfailingly and without sparing itself can be made use of because the greatest losses can do no harm to the vitality of this order, the vitality of these men, because they will always be replaced; to create an order which will spread the idea of Nordic blood so far that we will attract all Nordic blood in the world, take away the blood from our adversaries, absorb it so that never again, looking at it from the viewpoint of grand policy, Nordic blood, in great quantities and to an extent worth mentioning, will fight against us.[35]

According to Nordic scholars, Nero, Sulla, Cato, and other senior Roman leaders had all been blond or red-haired—a 'fact' that proved Nordic influence had been behind the success of the Roman Empire. Needless to say, this 'fact' is at best misleading and at worst a work of fiction.

Methodology: Linguistics and Craniology

> The linguistic specialists have one great advantage over us: they can do without us whereas we cannot do without them ... We are, therefore, the vassals of linguistics and grateful vassals; but we must not be, we cannot be, its slaves.[36]

Anthropologists, prehistorians, and archaeologists inherited a corpus of research from an earlier generation of philologists on the origins of 'the primitive peoples of Japheth's race'. The Belgian Honoré Chavée (1815–1877) thought he had scientifically demonstrated 'by the facts of the natural history of language, the essential differences in mental constitution and therefore in cerebral organisation' between Aryans and Semites.[37] The philologist A. F. Pott was prompted by his reading of Gobineau to write an essay on the 'Inequality of Human Races, Especially From the Point of View of Philological Science, Based on a Consideration of the Work of Count Gobineau which Bears the Same Title'.[38] However, it was the Genevan philologer Adolphe Pictet, in his *'Essai de paléontology linguistique'* (1859), that captured the racist, anti-Semitic feeling of the age:

> This was the race of the Aryans, who were endowed from the beginning with the very qualities which the Hebrews lacked, to become the civilisers of the world; and nowhere does the evidence for a providential plan emerge more clearly than in the parallel courses of these two contrasting streams, one of which was destined to absorb the other. The difference between the two races could not be more marked ... The religion of Christ, destined to be the torch of humanity, was adopted by the genius of Greece and propagated by the power of Rome, while Germanic energy gave it new strength, and the whole race of European Aryas, under its beneficent influence, and by means of endless conflict, raised itself little by little to the level of modern civilisation ... It is thus that the race of the Aryas, more favoured than any other, was to become the main instrument of God's plan for the destiny of mankind.[39]

The pioneer of cultural anthropology Edward B. Tylor (1832–1917) was suspicious of philology. He wrote:

> A man's language is no full and certain proof of his parentage... Much bad anthropology has been made by thus carelessly taking language and race as though they went always and exactly together.[40]

Paul Topinard (1830–1911) was similarly critical, pointing out that the French were not 'Aryans by blood, but a mixture of races superimposed on one another'. Nevertheless, in *l'Anthropologie,* he still found himself asserting that dark-skinned people struggled at 'counting beyond two, three or five' in contrast to 'the so-called Aryan races which have a great aptitude for mathematics'.[41]

German anthropologist Rudolf Virchow (1821–1902) stressed the usefulness of craniology and the study of other physical characteristics as an alternative to the study of language. He accused philologists of confusing races, nations, and languages: 'Language may nationalise and de-nationalise', he concluded, 'but it cannot be an indication of blood-relationships'. Virchow, a trained anatomist, approached the question scientifically.[42]

Nineteenth century craniology was developed by the Swedish scientist Andreas Retzius as a response to the 'phrenology' of Lavater and Gall, of which he was a critic.[43] Retzius developed the idea of a *cephalic index*, around which craniology was constructed. Extraordinary measuring instruments, which mostly sprang from Broca's ingenious mind, came into use in ever-increasing numbers. All manner of special characteristics— like the 'complexity of cranial dentures'—were put forward as proof of the superiority of European skulls over those of 'inferior races', and it was the common opinion that the most skilful craniologists could distinguish at a glance between a Roman, a Frankish, and a Saracenic skull. Within the space of ten years, European science was convinced that skulls would yield the information necessary to define human races, with their respective qualities, more accurately than languages. Retzius thought he had established that it was the dolichocephalic peoples such as the Scandinavians, the Germans, the English, and the French who were 'endowed with the highest faculties of the mind'. 'Brachycephaly' was an indication of a different origin, which he described as Turanian, as distinguished from Iranian or Aryan, and which was typical of 'retarded' peoples such as the Lapps, the Finns, or Finno-Slavs, and the Bretons.

To test the 'Finnish hypothesis', Virchow and his colleagues formed a commission 'to establish a statistical record of the shapes of skulls throughout Germany, following a method to be formulated by the commission'. They had wanted to measure the skulls of soldiers, but the Army refused to cooperate, and instead they fell back on a study of 'associated' characteristics—the hair, eye, and complexion colour of schoolchildren in Germany, Austria, Switzerland, and Belgium, using questionnaires sent to teachers. The investigation lasted ten years and involved approximately 15 million children. During this time, Virchow had travelled to Finland, where he had established that contrary to some views, the overwhelming majority of the population was blond. In 1885, he announced the results, which established that there was a predominance of blond hair and blue eyes in northern Germany, including the territory east of the Elbe, showing that the people there were of essentially Germanic stock. This was in contrast to the Germanic migrations to the west and south of Goths, Franks, and Burgundians, who were finally submerged by the native populations. Those in the east had resulted in a definitive Germanisation, 'the formation of a new, purely German, *Volkstum*'.

Although Virchow's work could be seen as laying the foundations for the justification of German expansionism, his own political views were to deplore the misuse of science for political ends. As time went by, his belief in craniology was shaken; he even cast some doubt that 'dolichocephaly', the totem of Germanomaniacs, was a malleable and mutable standard, and therefore suggested that it lacked all historic-anthropological value. However, he never abandoned craniology altogether.

While scientists were trying to unravel the future of the human race in the light of natural selection, a number of politicians were looking to Darwinism to support their political philosophy.[44] The 'survival of the fittest' translated into an excuse and justification for imperialist ambition. Using Darwinian language, Adolf Bastian wrote:

> The flood of Germans advancing towards the East had implacably rolled back the weaker race following the law of victory to the strongest, the law of the 'struggle for existence' ... Prussia is a country of warriors; so it was and so it will remain as long as it is necessary to protect the marches of the East, but above all those of the West, against the trouble-makers.[45]

This martial, nationalistic sentiment prefigured what was to follow.

The late nineteenth century was also a time of renewed interest in the occult, spiritualism, and theosophy. In Germany, it took a pagan and nationalistic turn. In approximately 1850, Richard Wagner identified Christ with Wotan, the supreme God.[46] His music introduced large audiences throughout Europe to Germanic legends. Wagner's world vision can be summarised briefly as follows. Long ago, in the golden age, men lived in a state of primitive innocence as vegetarians on the high plateaus of Asia. However, they were tainted by original sin when they killed the first animal. Ever since then, a thirst for blood had taken possession of the human race, so that murders and wars increased and were followed by conquests, exiles, and migrations. Christ, who was either Indian or Aryan, had tried to save whose significance he revealed to men at the Last Supper by changing bread into wine and flesh into bread. Finally, 'he gave up his life to expiate the blood shed by carnivorous men since the beginning of the world'. A Church, influenced by Jewry, had perverted the sense of this message, with the result that mankind had continued to degenerate, polluted by animal flesh and by the poison of Jewish blood. The Jew was 'the devil incarnate of human decadence' and western civilisation a 'Judaeo-barbaric jumble'. For this reason, an apocalyptic end could not be long delayed. Only one hope remained—a new purification, a new receiving of the holy blood according to the rites of the mystery of Parsifal, the Germanic redeemer.

Prof Leopold von Schröder of Vienna University summed up Wagner's contribution:

> After a separation of more than five thousand years, the Aryan tribes can meet together for the first time in a designated place to contemplate the ancient mysteries fulfilled in a new form. Thanks to Wagner, Bayreuth has become the centre of all the Aryan people, and this very fact guarantees an astonishing supremacy to Germany and the Germans ...[47]

Paul de Lagarde became the prophet, duly canonised by the Third Reich, of a new 'Germanic religion'. In his book *The Religion of the Future*, he wrote that their national faith (*deutscher Glaube*) should enable the Germans to find the path of true liberty:

> We want liberty, not liberalism; Germany, not Judaeo-Celtic theories about Germany; piety, not dogmatics ... we want our own nature to be acknowledged, educated and transfigured; we do not want to be driven by a Russian coachman holding French reins, or flogged by a Jewish whip.[48]

3

The Nazis in South America and the Search for the First Aryans of Atlantis

If we divide mankind into three categories—founders of culture, bearers of culture, and destroyers of culture—the Aryan alone can be considered as representing the first category ... Should he be forced to disappear, a profound darkness will descend on the earth; within a few thousand years human culture will vanish and the world will become a desert.[1]

Raiders of the Lost Ark opens with Indiana Jones exploring a lost Mayan Temple deep in the South American jungle. It is here that Indy encounters his arch-enemy, the Nazi collaborator Belloq, for the first time on screen. In truth, the Nazis were more interested in South America than you might think. They were searching for lost idols hidden in the ruined cities of the rainforest. The Nazis even sent a team of secret agents to steal a crystal skull for the Third Reich. Most bizarre of all, they thought South America held the key to finding the lost continent of Atlantis—proving that sometimes, truth really is stranger than fiction.

South America and Atlantis

In his book *Lucifer's Servants*, Otto Rahn, an SS-Obersturmführer, recalls an ancient Mexican legend that describes how settlers from the land of Thule had migrated to South America:

In the wake of Columbus ... the sails of Ferdinand Cortez crossed the seas. It was he who conquered the kingdom of the Aztecs and Mexico for the benefit of Spain. In an account that he sent to the imperial court one reads that the king of the Aztecs had bowed to the Emperor because he held [the Emperor] to be the same Lord of luminous beings and superior essence 'from which had issued his own ancestors.' Montezuma had also been about to permit Cortez to appropriate all the idols ... is until he, the king, imprisoned by the gold-hungry conquerors and mortally wounded by them, understood who they really were. He refused to allow them to treat his wounds and, energetically resisting the idea of converting to Christianity, wished for nothing more than death. And he did die, the victim of a frightful mistake. Cortez was the envoy of the Pope and the Catholic emperor and not at all of the 'White God' for whom [the king] and his people had been waiting so long. This White God was to have come from the ancient land of Tulla or Tullan (which, according to their beliefs, had once been 'a country of the sun' but 'where now ice reigned' and where 'the sun had disappeared'), that is to say: from *Thule*. Rather than the servants of Lucifer, those whom they had greeted ... were the representatives of that 'ilk' [i.e. the Catholic Church] which, shamelessly, dishonours the face of our mother the Earth with its filth and its horrors.[2]

Such legends fuelled the imagination of Herman Wirth, who believed that the Nordic race had evolved in an arctic homeland some 2 million years ago and then founded a civilisation on the lost continent of Atlantis in the North Atlantic.[3] Other writers, such as 'Brugg' (a pseudonym of Rudolf von Elmayer-Vestenbrugg), waxed lyrical about the fruitful island, calling it a 'wonderland'. He described its extensive agricultural development, which resulted in the production of two crops each year through a combination of favourable rainfall, the construction of a network of canals, and the associated devising of large-scale irrigation schemes. Brugg mentioned Mayan records in which Atlantis was called 'Poseidonis' and was said to have had 64 million inhabitants. The capital city was said to have been surrounded by mountains and to have covered 60,000 plots of land. Their owners, the lords of the island, were claimed to have disposed of a military strength of 200,000 riders, cart drivers, archers, catapulters, stone throwers, and spear wielders. Enormous palaces were pictured as gracing this royal city under a warm tropical sun, despite its postulated meridional location. This idea accorded with that of Alfred Rosenberg, who believed in Atlantis as a 'northern culture centre' whose children had travelled everywhere as sailors and soldiers.[4] Wirth speculated that perhaps strong Nordic women who possessed 'all seeing capabilities' had ruled this primeval empire as a matriarchy for thousands of years, until a great cataclysm drowned their lands, sending survivors fleeing to northern Europe and North America.[5] The evidence for this dispersal was to be seen in the pyramids and step-temples (the designs of which were believed to have originated on Atlantis) that are found scattered around the globe, along with symbols, art, and writing. All of these assertions were used to show that all culture had originated on Atlantis and was disseminated by 'lofty, educated artists and architects as well as incomparable warriors and colonists who ennobled mainlanders wherever they were'.

In order to prove these beliefs, Wirth, Brugg, and their contemporaries pored over Plato's accounts of Atlantis. They believed these accounts to be an accurate description of the fate of his imagined Nordic empire in the North Atlantic, and they set about trying to prove this theory.[6] The lost continent of Atlantis is known from the writings of the fifth century BC Greek philosopher Plato. Some have thought that the Atlantis of his dialogues *Timaeus* and *Critias* was a fictional creation, but the Nazis were convinced in the truth of his accounts. Plato's *Critias* claims that an island called Atlantis was swallowed by the sea some 9,200 years before his time. The dialogues locate Atlantis in the 'Atlantic Pelagos', taken to mean the 'Atlantic Sea', 'in front of' the Pillars of Hercules and facing a district called modern Gades or Gadira (Gadiron), a location usually understood to be modern Gibraltar. Plato claimed that the story of Atlantis had come to him via his grandfather, Dropides, in an account he heard from the early sixth century BC Greek traveller, Solon, who had in turn heard it from an Egyptian priest in the temple at Saïs in the Nile Delta. The Egyptian priests had an unbroken tradition of knowledge extending far back into prehistory, making it impossible to place the legend in time and more than likely that the legend had been distorted in its retelling.

Wirth combed through geological studies of the northern floor of the Atlantic Ocean, confidently concluding that the continent of Atlantis had occupied a region stretching all the way from Iceland to the Azores before tectonic activity had caused it to sink.[7] He insisted that a few scraps of the ancient continent remained above water, namely the Canary Islands and Cape Verde.[8]

Canary Islands

Travellers had long told tales of an ancient people with blond, golden hair and fair skin living on the Canary Islands, a small archipelago located off the coast of northwest Africa. These stories described how the ancestors of the native Guanche people had mummified their dead, who, when excavated, were found to have locks of blond hair. Studying these accounts from his office, Wirth concluded that the Canary Islands had formed the southern edge of a vast Aryan homeland, Atlantis, and had somehow escaped devastation intact.[9] In order to prove this theory, Wirth's colleague, Otto Huth, proposed an expedition to study the ancient islanders' racial origins, archaeological artefacts, and religious rites.

Huth was a protégé of Herman Wirth, from whom he acquired his passionate interest in the Canary Islands. He had a long face with pointed nose that supported heavy-rimmed glasses. He spoke seven languages, including Hebrew, and was a fervent Nazi. Huth worked in the Ahnenerbe offices in Dahlem as an expert in 'religious science', specialising in ancient Aryan spiritual beliefs.[10] He had read nearly everything ever written on the ancient inhabitants of the Canary Islands. It was a tribal society of prosperous farmers and herders who had shaved with stone knives, painted their bodies green, yellow, and red, dressed in dyed goatskins, and mummified the bodies of their leaders. Huth believed that the original islanders, who were separated from north-western Africa by 60 miles of ocean, were members of a pure, undiluted line of the Nordic race, and that they had preserved ancient Aryan religious practices well into the fifteenth century, when they were finally overcome by Spanish settlers.[11] The story of the Spanish invasion appalled Huth, who was no lover of Christianity. In one article, he observed:

> This conquering of the Canary Islands by the Christian Spaniards is a shocking tragedy and one of the most appalling examples of the poisonous effects of Jewish-Christianity on the soul of European people.[12]

Huth's sense of this tragedy was considerably compounded by his particular concept of the Canarians. He noted with delight that some early European chroniclers had observed islanders with golden hair, rosy cheeks, and white skin. He was also fascinated by the accounts of later travellers who found Canarian mummies with blond tresses. However, Huth was a very selective reader. He deliberately ignored the warning of a contemporary, the prominent American anthropologist Earnest Hooton, who had written a major book on the ancient Canarians. As Hooton pointed out, the chemical nature of the preservatives and time itself often had 'a bleaching effect' upon the mummies' hair.[13] Huth, however, saw only what he wanted to see. He wrote:

> Separated from the disturbances of European world history, the ancient Nordic civilisation blossomed undisturbed on the happy islands until it was destroyed.[14]

Huth was anxious to study the religious practices of the ancient Canarians, certain that they would shed valuable new light on the beliefs of the primordial Aryans. First, however, he had to clinch the racial origins of the Canarians.[15] For his expedition, he planned on taking a racial scientist to perform detailed measurements on both the living and the dead.[16] He also intended to take an archaeologist to sift through collections of Canarian pottery shards and stone tools in hopes of detecting similarities to those of ancient Nordic peoples. This, he firmly believed, would give 'numerous results'.[17]

Preparations for the expedition were well-advanced, as Huth wrote in a letter to Wüst:

> We have a head start in the source material, and now we have to obtain a head-start in the fieldwork, thereby securing the best Canary research for the Ahnenerbe.[18]

Unfortunately, he was to be disappointed, as the scheduled departure of the expedition in the autumn of 1939 was interrupted by the outbreak of the Second World War. The Spanish had continued to rule the Canary Islands, which, at the time, were governed by the regime of Francisco Franco. Although a fascist, Franco refused to publicly side with the Axis when the war started, meaning that Huth's expedition had to be cancelled.

Although the expedition was unable to proceed, this did not put a complete end to research by those sympathetic to Nazi ideology. Relations between Spanish and German archaeologists were formally established in 1939, when Julio Martínez Santa Olalla was appointed Commissioner-General for Archaeological Excavations at the Spanish Ministry of National Education and Fine Arts. In October 1940, Himmler made an official visit to Spain, where he met Olalla. A close personal relationship was quickly established, leading to a plan to develop a Falangist version of the Ahnenerbe.

The Austrian philologist Dominik Wölfel, for example, studied the ancient language of the Canaries, writing the *Monumenta Linguae Canariae*. He also claimed to have discovered Nordic runes in the ravine of Guayadeque on Gran Canaria. In true Nazi fashion, he tied this discovery to the Icelandic *Eyrbyggia Saga*, which recounts the voyage of a sailor from northern Iceland. Encountering a storm, the sailor's ship was blown onto the shores of the Canaries; he established himself on the island and had become the leader of the inhabitants by the year 1000. Several years later, a second sailor, named 'Guliev', found himself similarly blown off-course on a journey from Iceland to Dublin. Two weeks later, he reached 'a round island' with 'golden beaches', where he landed. To his shock, he found that the natives who greeted him were white-skinned and spoke a kind of Irish. More was to come; as their leader rode down to the beach, Guliev saw that he was a tall man with strong white hair. He greeted the sailor in Nordic and told Guliev that he was also from Iceland and that his name was Björn Asbrandsson. After several weeks, Guliev and his crew had repaired their boat and rested before they set off to return home. Asbrandsson gave them several gifts, including a gold bracelet and a sword, saying, 'If you have the good fortune to return to your land, give the sword to Kjartan, Master Frodo, Turid and bracelet to his mother'.

Such legends underlined the Nazi belief in the reality of Atlantis and of the dispersal from this lost continent of the Aryan people to places such as Bolivia. In 1928, Edmund Kiss (1886–1960) embarked on an expedition to Bolivia with 20,000 Reichsmarks he had won in a writing contest. Kiss was a German building contractor, novelist, and convinced Nazi. His aim in travelling to Bolivia was to study the ruined temples of the Andes in order to prove his thesis that their apparent similarity to ancient European monuments indicated they had both been designed by migrating Ayrans millions of years earlier, when they had left Atlantis. On his return to Germany, Kiss not only claimed that his findings supported his origin theory but also Hans Hörbiger's World Ice Theory.

Kiss was fascinated by Hörbiger and his World Ice Theory (*Welt-Eis-Lehre*), which was one of the most bizarre of Nazi beliefs. The theory was popularised by an Austrian engineer, Hans Hörbiger, who was, in his time, a favourite of both Eckart and Hitler. Hörbiger claimed that there had been four major intervals in geological time up to the present—Primary, Secondary, Tertiary, and Quaternary—each characterised by its own fauna—reptiles, saurians, large mammals, and the contemporary fauna respectively. Each of these periods had its own life-cycle, which began moonless, continued with the capture of a moon, and ended with the moon's disintegration, causing a catastrophe on earth that led to an ice age followed by a terrible flood.

Hörbiger's theory required that thousands of years ago, before the Tertiary-period flood, the tropical South American Andes, the Mexican Highlands, and other elevated landscapes must have been free of ice and occupied by 'asylums' of isolated groups of intelligent human beings. Primitive cultures developed in these locations, leaving ruins such as those found at Lake Titicaca and the temples of the Mexican plateau, which were destroyed by the flood referred to in the Book of Genesis and in Assyrian cuneiform writing.

This theory depended, incorrectly, on two beliefs—that the world was much older than geologists say, and that it was composed of spinning balls and particles of ice. Hörbiger likened the universe to a giant steam engine filled with hydrogen and water vapour. In the distant past, the universe had been very different, with a number of small stars that were hot and steamy and a number of others that were small and ice-covered. These two types of stars had collided, causing tremendous explosions that had ballasted debris into space. In time, this material had coalesced, forming the planets and moons of our solar system. According to this theory, the Earth had originally supported six moons. The serial destruction of the first five, he suggested, had led to vast, almost unimaginable environmental catastrophes on Earth. As each moon had spiralled downward into the atmosphere, it had revolved faster and faster, creating an immense gravitational pull. The force had then pulled the Earth's oceans toward the equator, forming an immense tide that resembled a giant spare tyre around the equator; beyond the edges of this towering wall of water, the earth froze beneath thick glacial ice.

The flora and fauna had survived only in certain mountain refuges—the Bolivian Andes, the Tibetan Himalayas, and the Ethiopian highlands. Each of the moons had in turn entered the earth's atmosphere, exploding in the process and freeing the oceans to flow back over the Earth. Hörbiger claimed that the last of these atmospheric explosions had taken place more than 11,000 years ago. The concept of a universe composed of little more than ice crystals corresponded neatly with the Nordic *völkisch* instincts of the Nazis. Nordic people were at home amongst the ice fields of the north and, as the natural ancestor of the human race, the people who should rightly rule the earth in a universe composed entirely of snow.

Calling on Nordic legends for further support, the Nazis pointed out that these stories refer to the land of ice at the top of the world, interpreted by the Third Reich as Atlantis, or Ultima Thule, where the Aryan race was said to have originated. The Nazis even pointed to the very whiteness of the ice and snow as evidence that Aryan racial characteristics were consistent with their special, elevated place in the universe. There is little that we would recognise as science in these theories, but they served the ideology of the Nazis well when called upon to justify their lack of humanity.

This theory was completely wrong. In the 1930s, it was condemned in the strongest terms by German astronomers and other serious scientists. The World Ice Theory, noted one prominent mathematician, combined:

> The tyranny of an Asiatic despot [and] the presumption of a mathematical illiterate who, with childish innocence, strides up to things about which he knows nothing and ventures to substitute a caricature for a scientific picture of the universe.[19]

However, Kiss and many other Nazis were deaf to such criticism. The Nazis regarded Hörbiger as a genius. Indeed, Kiss and four other prominent believers in the World Ice Theory signed an official declaration, known as the *Pyrmonter Protokoll*, in 1936, stating:

> Hans Hörbiger's World Ice Theory in its fundamental form is the intellectual gift of a genius that is important to all humanity in both practical and worldview terms. To Germans, it is a true Aryan gift of special importance.[20]

Hörbiger's talk of giant tides and vast sheets of glacial ice provided a neat explanation for the inability of the scientists to find any trace of an ancient Aryan civilisation in the far north. Hitler himself had become a supporter of the theory. One night, over dinner, he noted, 'I'm quite well inclined to accept the cosmic theories of Hörbiger.' [21]

What Hörbiger's supporters desperately needed to rebut their scientific critics was proof of the cataclysms that he had described. Kiss was acutely conscious of this, and in 1927 he began searching for evidence. Keen to pursue his thesis further, Kiss contacted Arthur Posnansky, a silver-haired Austrian expatriate who had been studying a Bolivian site called 'Tiwanaku'. Located south of Lake Titicaca in the Bolivian Andes, one of the places that the World Ice Theory described as a mountain refuge, Tiwanaku was spread over nearly 1,000 acres. The ancient city boasted massive stone ruins, huge carved figurines, inscribed tablets, and immense doorways carved with jaguars and strange mythological characters. Some blocks weighed more than 400 tons. Most impressive of all was the Gateway to the Sun in Tiwanaku, a magnificent, massive, carved megalithic structure, befitting what was once the capital of a powerful empire that stretched across the Andeas, south from Bolivia to Chile and northern Argentina. At its height, in the sixth century, Tiwanaku was home to 50,000 people who prided themselves in their mastery of civil engineering. Lakes and swampland were successfully drained and converted into fertile arable fields tended by skilful farmers, while others herded llamas and alpacas to supply the needs of the urban populace.

The city was so splendorous that European travellers who came to the city in the nineteenth century could not believe it had been built by the indigenous Aymara people who they saw cultivating fields and herding livestock in the area. Instead, they concluded that Tiwanaku must have been constructed by a powerful foreign civilisation that had once invaded South America. Thus the mid-nineteenth century writer Francis de Castelnau proposed that Tiwanaku was the work of wandering Egyptian pharaohs rather than the 'imbicilic race that inhabits the country today'. Castelnau was typical of many nineteenth century European writers in expressing views that today would be considered not only chauvinistic but also racist.

Most professional archaeologists of the day knew that an indigenous Andean people, forerunners of the Inca, had designed and built Tiwanaku. However, Posnansky strongly disagreed. He suggested that a mysterious group of immigrants from the far west designed the great capital and put Andeans to work building it. He also asserted that construction on at least one of Tiwanaku's great temples began 17,000 years ago—an erroneous contention based on his own calculations of certain astronomical alignments of the walls. Indeed, Posnansky concluded that some 27 degrees separated the current position of the sun from that when the temple was built.[22] Subsequent archaeological excavation and radiocarbon dating (an absolute method of dating that came into use after the Second World War) has shown that Tiwanaku is no more than 1,700 years old.[23] Lastly, Posnansky believed he had discovered an ancient calendar of some sort carved into the stone above a Tiwanaku portal.[24]

Kiss soaked up these ideas, convinced that the mysterious architects were none other than the Aryans. He was so fascinated that he journeyed to South America in 1928, subsidised by a 20,000 RM prize he had won in a writing contest. For months, Kiss studied Tiwanaku ruins, sketching their floor plans and their inscriptions. He was particularly struck by an ancient sculpture of a man's head unearthed from one of its ruins. He noted later that it was 'immediately clear that this man is not Indian nor does he have Mongolian characteristics, but rather pure Nordic ones'.[25] As he worked through the city, he noted what he thought were European elements in the stone monuments:

> ... the doors are framed as they were in the Baroque period ... the construction of the eastern facade shows a series of cross symbols underneath an entablature that is easily identified as Greek.[26]

Kiss dismissed suggestions that the ancient Andeans had designed the splendid temples:

> The works of art and the architectural style of the prehistoric city are certainly not of Indian origin, rather they are probably the creations of Nordic men who arrived in the Andean highlands as representatives of a special civilisation.[27]

Instead, Kiss busied himself with the question of when this migration had happened. He believed that he found the answer in the massive inscribed relief on the ruin known today as the Gateway to the Sun. Kiss convinced himself that the inscriptions marked out a calendar, and that he could decipher symbols for twelve months of the year, each possessing either twenty-four or twenty-five days. He also thought it certain that each of the days had thirty hours, and each hour twenty-two minutes.[28]

Kiss regarded the inscription as compelling proof of Hörbiger's theory. The Tiwanaku inscription, he concluded, was a calendar reflecting the prehistoric conditions on Earth when an earlier moon rapidly orbited the planet. He had no means of determining when this had happened, but this did not stop him from leaping to a wild conclusion:

One thing we do know, and it would be extremely hard to convince us otherwise, even if the age of Tiwanaku cannot even be guessed, it must be at least millions of years old.[29]

On his return to Germany, Kiss rapidly achieved popular support for his ideas. He was helped by the Nazi magazines *SA Mann* and *Die Hitler Jugend*, the official magazine of Hitler Youth, who presented Kiss's fantastical interpretations as if they were scientifically proven facts.[30] He also wrote two novels set in Atlantis and South America; his first was entitled *The Last Queen of Atlantis* (*Die letzte Königin von Atlantis*) and found him equating the mythical northern land of Thule to the origins of humanity. According to Kiss:

> The inhabitants of Northern Atlantis [Ayrans] were led by their leader Baldur Wieborg, a native of the mythical Thule who migrated all across the world.

He later described the return journey of the Nordic Thulians to their mythical homeland in *The Swans of Thule*. Through the press coverage given to his two novels and one reference book, he was able to claim Himmler amongst his supporters. Indeed, Himmler had a copy of his more scientific-sounding book entitled *The Sun Gate of Tiwanaku* bound in leather so that he could present it to Adolf Hitler as a Christmas gift.[31] He illustrated the latter with his own architectural drawings of massive, Nazi-style monumental temples and tall, slim inhabitants dressed in a strange futuristic fashion.

Kiss longed to return to Bolivia with a large interdisciplinary team of scientists to search for fossil evidence of ancient flooding, and to conduct extensive excavations at both Tiwanaku and nearby Siminake. He hoped to unearth compelling new evidence of the ancient master race in the Americas and requested backing from the Ahnenerbe. After contacting Posnansky, the foremost authority on the site, Kiss approached Wüst for help planning an expedition and then Himmler. Both were wildly enthusiastic. 'One can now quite certainly expect results which might have a revolutionary importance for the history of mankind,' enthused Wüst.[32]

Kiss was exactly the kind of man with whom Himmler enjoyed socialising. At fifty-three, he was a commanding presence, standing at 6 foot 3 inches.[33] He possessed a broad, sturdy face, ears that splayed out from his head, wire-rimmed spectacles that curled around them, and a determined stamp to his mouth.[34] He spoke bluntly, kept his word faithfully, conducted his affairs with a gentleman's sense of honour, and was, judging from the testimonies of his friends and co-workers after the war, kindness personified toward his subordinates.[35] He also possessed a distinguished military record; in the First World War he had won two Iron Crosses, with one of them being first class.[36]

Kiss spent more than a year drawing up detailed plans for the expedition, relaying his needs to Sievers. The team would consist of twenty scientists who would excavate for a year and also explore Lake Titicaca, in addition to taking aerial photographs of ancient Incan roads that they believed had Nordic roots. Having carefully cultivated Heinrich Himmler's support through his writing and lectures, Kiss was able to secure funding for his expedition from Himmler's SS-Ahnenerbe.

He would have been ready sooner, but Himmler dispatched Kiss on a brief research trip to Libya to scour the Mediterranean coast for fossil evidence of the World Ice Theory. Himmler had earlier taken a flight over Libya and, while soaring over mountains there, noticed what he believed to be the tell-tale white layers of fossil shorelines. He insisted that Kiss put aside his South American plans, take a leave of absence from his government post, and prepare immediately to depart for Libya. Kiss strongly suspected that the trip to Libya, an Italian possession at the time, would be futile. The North African coast was strewn with fossil records of rising and falling sea levels, but Kiss knew that these geological formations had nothing to do with the purported cataclysms of the World Ice Theory. Still, he agreed to take a look; he did not want to antagonise his powerful patron. He also agreed to include Sardinia on his itinerary when someone in the Ahnenerbe pointed out an apparent similarity between stone towers there and the architecture at Tiwanaku.

Kiss set off by train for Rome in February 1939, with a cameraman and an assistant in tow. A short stint in a library there convinced him that a trip to Sardinia would be unnecessary. A few days later, he arrived in the Libyan capital of Tripoli. The Libyan governor, an ardent aviator and a friend of Charles Lindbergh, placed a plane, a pilot, and a truck at his disposal, and over the next two weeks, Kiss and his associates explored the Libyan countryside. The weather was not terribly conducive to aerial scouting; thick grey clouds heavy with rain hung over the coastal mountains, refusing to budge for most days, but Kiss kept busy. He drew neat, draughtsman-like maps of the mountains, carefully noting the coastal terraces and the notches of deep canyons and occasionally jotting down the word '*Zeugen*' where he thought he had found 'pieces of evidence'. He walked across plains and through canyons dotted with occasional palm trees, sketching profiles of the low mountains, and mulled over the origins of the Nalut Canyon not far from the Algerian border. The more he looked at it and at a number of similar gorges in the Libyan mountains, the more intrigued he became. 'Strong water currents on the scale imagined by the World Ice Theory most likely formed them through erosion', he later wrote. 'There is no other explanation'.[37]

By late August 1939, Kiss was back at his desk, finalising his plans. The expedition called for a team of twenty, consisting of archaeologists, geologists, zoologists, botanists, meteorologists, pilots, and underwater experts, all of whom would work for a year in Bolivia.[38] In addition to the archaeological excavations, Kiss planned to explore the deep waters of Lake Titicaca by underwater camera. He also proposed flying across the Andes so that film crews could shoot footage of the famous Inca roads, which Kiss believed were the work of Nordic lords.[39] Last but certainly not least, he also intended to conduct extensive geological fieldwork from Colombia to Peru to find evidence of ancient celestial cataclysms.

Sievers estimated that the salaries of the team members alone would cost 100,000 RM, or some $520,000 today (taking inflation into account).[40] Himmler did not flinch at the cost, and by late August 1939, Sievers was deeply immersed in the final arrangements for the trip, booking the team's passage to South America, locating a pilot experienced enough to undertake aerial photography in the high Andes, and organising payment of all the team members' salaries. It was a mammoth task greatly complicated by the plodding bureaucracy of the Nazi state and the pressing nature of Sievers's other duties. By late August 1939, the expedition was on the verge of embarking for South America, but then fate intervened in the form of Germany's invasion of Poland. The invasion, and the war that it triggered, caused the expedition to be postponed indefinitely. The cancellation of the Bolivian expedition left Kiss rudderless. He joined the SS, where his mundane duties were to serve as Guard Staff to high-profile Nazi buildings for the rest of the war. After this, he found himself facig a court at Nuremburg, where his involvement with the Nazi regime was excused on the basis that he had been nothing more than an arhaeologist. His best years were now behind him, and although he wrote another two books in the 1950s—one of which, *Some Comments on Critias*, was another attempt to locate Atlantis—he lived the remainder of his life in obscurity.

Brazil

The outbreak of war may have ended Kiss's hopes of returning to Bolivia, but it was not to put an end to Nazi expeditions to South America. In one of the most secret episodes of the war, members of the Ahnenerbe were sent to Brazil in 1943, tasked with 'procuring' (stealing, in other words) an enigmatic crystal skull found among the Mayan ruins of Lubaatun and stored in the vaults of one of the country's most secure museums. In a story that sounds like it has come straight from the Indiana Jones films, the mission went seriously awry when the Ahnenerbe agents were arrested after trying to infiltrate and rob the Brazilian museum storing the artefact.[41]

The story begins some years before in 1927, with an expedition to the Yucatan peninsula in modern-day Belize led by the famous English archaeologist Albert Mitchell-Hedges. It was decided to burn down thirty-three hectares of jungle forest that covered the ancient buildings of the Mayan ruin of Lubaantun. With the tree cover removed, the adventurers were amazed to see the stone ruins of a lost city, complete with a pyramid and an amphitheatre with a capacity for several thousand people. Most striking of all was Mitchell-Hedges' discovery of crystal skulls. These skulls—arguably one of the twentieth century's most enigmatic archaeological finds—eventually found their way to a museum in Brazil.

In Germany, Karl Maria Wiligut read of the events with great interest. Wiligut was a mercurial character who fully believed in the reality of a lost Atlantean continent that had been the birthplace of the Aryan race. He interpreted the crystal skulls as the work of Atlantean craftsmen, with the objects designed for use by priests in their pagan ceremonies. As a black magician, Wiligut also imbued the skulls with magical powers that, if harnessed by him, would give the Nazis an advantage in the ongoing conflict. Strange as many of Wiligut's ideas may seem, he exerted considerable influence on high-ranking Nazi officials, and it was he that gave the order to steal the crystal skull.

When the Brazilians interrogated the captive Ahnenerbe agents in 1943, the admitted being tasked with a mission to steal what they called 'the crystal skulls of the Goddess of Death'. This particular phraseology is pregnant with the occult influence of Wiligut; after all, it was he who had designed the SS Death Head motif most familiar to us from the ring worn by every member of the SS.

Tibet and the Search for the Aryan Homeland

At dinner [Himmler] talked to me on various scientific questions and told me about an expedition to Tibet.[1]

In *Raiders of the Lost Ark*, after returning from South America, Indiana Jones is sent on a mission to thwart the Nazi attempt to discover the lost Ark of the Covenant. His first journey takes him to the Himalayas, where he meets his lost love, Marion, whose father, Abner Ravenwood, has the headpiece to the Staff of Ra. Indy finds himself in Asia once again in the next film, *Indiana Jones and the Temple of Doom*, which begins in China and then takes him to India. As ever, behind the fictional films lies a story of Nazi intrigue, secret missions, and the search for holy relics.

In the 1930s, Tibet was little-known and much mythologised. Himmler, perhaps inspired by a legend that Aryans led by Thor fled a cataclysm to settle in the Himalayan kingdom of Tibet, decided that he could increase the Ahnenerbe's visibility by sending an expedition to the secretive nation. This would allow archaeologists to investigate the theories of Hörbiger— that the Tibetan Himalayas, like the Bolivian Andes, had been an Aryan refuge; and Günther, who proposed that Aryans had conquered much of Asia (including parts of China and Japan) in approximately 2000 BC, and that Buddha himself was an Aryan.[2] This latter idea was one that Walther Wüst developed, stating in a public speech that Adolf Hitler's ideology corresponded with that of Buddha since the two shared a common heritage. The expedition was led by Dr Ernst Schäfer of the Ahnenerbe, Germany's most experienced Tibetan explorer, who was a real-life Nazi Indiana Jones—part SS officer, scholar, explorer, and scientist. This official SS-Tibet Expedition began in April 1938 and lasted until August 1939.[3]

Schäfer was born in Cologne (Köln) on 14 March 1910. He was an able student and seems to have had an interest in Tibet from an early age.

He first travelled there in 1930 as a member of the Philadelphian Academy of Sciences expedition, when he was just twenty years old. The following year he returned, this time as a member of the American Brooke Dolan expedition, which travelled to Siberia and China as well as Tibet. Schäfer therefore had genuine expertise in Tibetan studies, and he had established his academic credentials through several publications in both German and English. In German he wrote *Berge, Buddhas und Bären* (*Mountains, Buddhas and Bears*); *Unbekanntes Tibet* (*Unknown Tibet*); and *Dach der Erde* (*Roof of the World*). In English, he had written 'Four New Birds from Tibet' in *Proceedings of the Academy of Natural Sciences, Philadelphia. 1937.*[4] Schäfer's interest in the anthropology of Asiatic people can be traced back to his early expeditions. His notes show that he observed and recorded the religious and cultural practices of the Tibetans. Included amongst his records are accounts of the various lamaistic festivals that he observed, as well as observations and comments on the Tibetan attitudes to marriage, rape, menstruation, childbirth, and homosexuality.[5]

In January 1936, the twenty-five-year-old Schäfer was in Shanghai, China. He was already a seasoned explorer who had achieved a name for himself through the publication of an account of his exploits. Having completed his last trip, he was considering whether his future lay in America or Germany when he met the German consul General Walther Greibel. Schäfer later said:

> [Greibel] was very friendly. I said, 'I'm going to America.'
> He said, 'That is impossible. You have to go back to Germany. I'll smooth the way for you. I'll write to Germany and recommend you.'

Greibel was so impressed with Schäfer and so alarmed that he might not return to Germany that he immediately sent a letter back home. The letter was brought to the attention of Heinrich Himmler, who was intrigued by this young SS officer's accomplishments.[6] Meanwhile, Schäfer had travelled to the US to complete his contract with the Academy at Philadelphia, where he began to be bombarded by telegrams from Berlin. The first congratulated him on his success; a second, from Himmler's office, told him that he had been awarded an honorary promotion to 'SS Untersturmführer *honoris causa*'. Schäfer was flattered and replied:

> I am so proud and happy I am not able to express it. I hope I will be able to show my gratitude through my actions. All my expectations were in each and every respect exceeded though the greatest honour for me is to have been promoted...[7]

Schäfer immediately sailed back to Germany on the SS *Bremen,* arriving in Hamburg. He was met by his father, who warned him, 'Be as clever as a snake. It is extremely dangerous.' [8]

Schäfer met Himmler and the two discussed plans for a German expedition to Tibet. Himmler was enthusiastic, as Schäfer himself recounted:

> Having been a member of the Black Guard since a long time, I was only too glad that the highest SS leader, himself a very keen amateur scientist, was interested in my work of exploration. There was no need of convincing the Reichsführer SS, as he himself had the same ideas; he simply promised to give me all the help necessary.[9]

Himmler's interest in the expedition may have owed much to the possibilities it offered to confer prestige upon the SS and the Ahnenerbe. Himmler was also fascinated by Asia and believed, like Hans Günther, that there might be Aryan refugees somewhere in the Himalayas. He was keen to have a propaganda triumph that would seal the reputation of the SS and Ahnenerbe. Himmler had his own rivals for political power, and he also resented the cultural status of Alfred Rosenberg, the man who had translated the *Protocols of Zion*, the phoney document that implied there was a Jewish conspiracy to seize global power.[10] He called himself a 'Fighter against Jerusalem'. He produced books such as *Immorality in the Talmud* and *The Myth of the 20th Century*. Like Himmler, he was obsessed with Aryan origins, the fate of Atlantis, as well as a clutch of pseudoscientific meta-theories about history. He was also chief editor of the *Völkischer Beobachter*, the Nazi newspaper. By 1936, Reichsleiter Rosenberg had his own rival organisation to the Ahnenerbe, known as the 'Amt Rosenberg', and was a bitter rival of Himmler. A celebrated expedition would give Himmler a powerful advantage. As well as being an accomplished explorer, Schäfer also enjoyed popular success as a writer. His first book, *Berge, Buddhas und Baren* (*Mountains, Buddhas and Bears*) had been a success in 1933, following his first expedition to Tibet.[11] Now he started work on a two-volume account of his second expedition—*Dach der Erde* (*Roof of the World*) and *Unbekanntes Tibet* (*Unknown Tibet*).[12] This would give Himmler just the sort of propaganda boost that he needed.

As Schäfer's plan took shape, Himmler began to pressure him to recruit team members from within the Ahnenerbe. Himmler wanted staff on board that would investigate his pet theories in the Himalayas. Looking for the Aryan homeland was one of them, and investigating Hörbiger's *Welteislehre* (World Ice Theory), another. At their first meeting, Himmler told Schäfer about the theory and of how the supernatural ancestors of the Aryans had once been sheathed in ice before being released from their frozen bondage by divine thunderbolts. He also told Schäfer about the work of Kiss in Bolivia, whose experience in 'proving' the World Ice Theory made him ideally qualified to take part in the expedition to the icy Himalayas and undertake further investigation of the *Welteislehre*.[13]

Schäfer had no idea who Kiss was and began to investigate. What he discovered dismayed him. Although the ruined Bolivian city of Tiwanaku is less than 2,000 years old, Kiss had proposed (on the basis of flimsy astronomical calculations) that it was a South American refuge for the people of Atlantis, which was abandoned 15,000 years ago after calamitous volcanic eruptions and floods. According to Kiss, Tiwanaku provided evidence for a lost Master Race and the violent upheavals predicted by Hörbiger's theory. High in the Andes, Kiss claimed to have discovered a monumental 'Nordic Head', which was more evidence of an Atlantean flight from an inundated world into the Andes. Kiss's head has never been seen by anyone else.

Schäfer considered Kiss a fantasist and not a scientist. He was fearful that his work would be ridiculed if Kiss were to be involved. However, he could not tell Himmler this directly; Hörbiger's *Welteislehre* provided an Aryan alternative to the 'dreadful and mistaken ... Jewish theories' of science, and had therefore won over the usually sceptical Hitler. In *Table Talk*, Hitler said he planned to build an observatory in Linz dedicated to 'the three great cosmological conceptions of history: those of Ptolemy, Copernicus and Horbiger'. To criticise Kiss openly was tantamount to criticising Hörbiger and the judgement of both Hitler and Himmler. As his father had advised, he had to proceed cautiously.[14]

Schäfer therefore had no alternative but to agree to meet with Kiss, but as soon as he did, he realised that there was a way out of the dilemma. He contacted Himmler and told him that it would be impossible to work with a man who was so much older than he. His experience in the wilds of Asia had made it clear that the key to success was youth. Nor, he said, did he want his authority questioned by an older man. His move was clever, and Himmler agreed he could proceed without Kiss.

This move shows Schäfer's determination to keep his expedition 'scientific', by keeping a distance from what he quietly considered the cranks of the Ahnenerbe. He decided next to try to decouple his work from the Ahnenerbe altogether. To do this Schäfer ensured that the detailed plans for the expedition, which he had to present to Wolfram Sievers, head of the Ahnenerbe, were on such a scale that they could not be afforded by the organisation, thus leading them to reject him rather than him rejecting them. In this he was again successful; Sievers rejected the project proposal, stating that 'The task of the expedition ... had diverged too far from the targets of the Reichsfuhrer SS ...' and that in any event the Ahnenerbe seemed to have no available funds, and nowhere near the 60,000 RM that Schäfer needed. Himmler was unhappy, but he could do nothing; Schäfer had successfully detached himself from the Ahnenerbe without losing Himmler's support.[15]

Schäfer had achieved what he wanted, although he now had to raise the money to fund the expedition himself. This would have been an overwhelming task for most people, but Schäfer seems to have raised the money without too much difficulty. Himmler had been happy to lend his name to the project as official patron, but Schäfer's business connections seem to have been more important. This suggests that the father and son had collaborated in extracting the project from the grip of the Ahnenerbe from the beginning.

Schäfer did not have it all his way, however. A real possibility is that Schäfer had been engaged in espionage on behalf of the Nazis, gathering intelligence on the British military presence in India. His various expeditions had taken place against the backdrop of the 'phony war' that predated the German invasion of Poland in September 1939. Although there is no direct record of this, it may be more than coincidence that within two months of his return to Germany, the Nazis were preparing to organise a Tibetan-North Indian strike force to remove the British from India. Schäfer's rapid rise through the SS ranks suggest that he was more than willing to accommodate the needs of his masters. He had joined the Nazi SS in the summer of 1933 (Party membership number 4690995), rapidly rising through the ranks. In 1936, he was Untersturmführer; then he was rapidly promoted to Obersturmführer in 1937; Hauptsturmführer in 1938; and Sturmbannführer in 1942. He was also awarded the much-coveted SS *Totenkopfring* (Death's Head Ring), which had been designed by *völkisch* occultist Karl Wiligut complete with runic inscriptions.

Schäfer also had to compromise in the area of science. The quest for a Nordic empire in central Asia was not, on the face of it, Schäfer's own obsession. He was a zoologist by training, and his personal aim was to use the expedition to further his research in zoology and botany, as well as in geology and ethnology, whereas Himmler's priority was to support the occult racial, anthropological and archaeological theories of the Third Reich through the study of the Ayran race and the associated World Ice Theory. There was, however, some convergence. Schäfer (along with other scientists in America and elsewhere) was convinced that all species of mammals must have evolved somewhere in between the Americas and Europe—in other words, central Asia. An influential American scientist at New York's powerful Museum of Natural History wrote:

The fact that the same kind of animals appear simultaneously in Europe and the Rocky Mountains region has long been considered strong evidence for the hypothesis that the dispersal centre is halfway between. In this dispersal centre, during the close of the Age of the Reptiles and the beginning of the Age of the Mammals, there evolved the most remote ancestors of all the higher kinds of mammalian life which exist today...

Anthropologists were quick to adopt the idea of an Asian origin for mammals. The central location made it the obvious epicentre for successive waves of dispersal west into Europe, east into China, and south into India. This hypothesis found popular support among scientists in the United States and Germany, prejudiced against the idea that the 'Dark Continent' could in any way be the 'cradle of mankind' that Darwin had suggested.

This idea of a central Asian dispersal centre was embraced by Schäfer. Although it is unlikely that either he or his American colleagues would have admitted to reading Madame Blavatsky and her followers, both *The Secret Doctrine* and the science of human origins sprang from a common source. For both, the key was the Tibetan plateau. Since Schäfer insisted that his new expedition was scientific, it followed that he would look for an anthropologist who would endorse the idea of a central Asian origin. There was one outstanding German anthropologist and SS officer with a unique interest in central Asia, and that was Bruno Beger.[16]

Dr Bruno Beger was a willing member of both the expedition and the SS. He was an anthropologist who later infamously went on to work at Auschwitz. He worked there under Professor Hirt on behalf of the Ahnenerbe, tasked with the collection of 115 human skeletons for inclusion in the Nazi Anthropological Museum. Gruesome as that may sound, what marked out Beger for all time was that he selected the 'skeletons' while their Jewish, Polish, and Asiatic owners were still alive and held captive at Auschwitz. The 'specimens' were transported to the Natzweiler concentration camp, where they were murdered in such a way as to avoid damaging the skeleton. The bodies of these poor souls were then shipped out for scientifically managed decomposition. Beger seemed to excel at this nasty trade, and while he was collecting over 100 'Jewish Commisar' skulls for the Berlin Institute, he still found time to supply his old friend Schäfer with a collection of Asian skulls.[17]

At the time of the Tibet Expedition, Beger was head of the RuSHA's Race Division (*Abteilungsleiter für Rassenkunde*), and in order to leave this post he joined Himmler's personal staff as a *Referentstelle* (consultant). For the moment, he confined himself to non-lethal examinations and the collection of measurements, photographs, and plaster casts. The text of *Geheimnis Tibet* shows that Schäfer and Beger shared the same ideas about race; when Schäfer discussed the Nepalis, he described them as 'part Indo-Aryan, part Mongoloid', 'intellectually very superior', and 'biologically robust'.[18] Beger's approach was very much that of the nineteenth century anthropologist. As European nations had conquered the world, anthropologists saw that the new colonies offered a unique scientific opportunity as laboratories of human types and different races. Indigenous peoples were measured, photographed, and collected using callipers and cameras to measure and record. While other colonists sent back material bounty, the scientists returned to their museums bearing cases packed with trophy animals and sometimes trophy people.

No nation, least of all Germany, had a monopoly on such scientific brutality. American anthropologists like Samuel Morton acquired skulls of Native Americans in their thousands, and usually by the most unscrupulous means, while British anthropologists preyed on Australian aborigines both living and dead.[19] Francis Galton, the British inventor of eugenics, was a pioneer of anthropometry.[20] He had a passion for numbers and statistical comparisons. In the 1850s, Galton joined a scientific expedition to south-west Africa, where he met an extraordinary woman—a striking African he called the 'Hottentot Venus'. He made her stand against a tree and, as he put it, lacking the standard equipment, used a sextant to make a precise measurement of her proportions. He wrote:

> I took a series of observations upon her figure in every direction, up and down, crossways, diagonally and so forth. I worked out the results by trigonometry and logarithms.

Nevertheless, Galton's cruelty in this instance was exceptional, and apart from the 'Hottentot Venus', there is no evidence at all that he exploited anyone or stole their bodies.

The mania for measuring withered out in England, but in Germany it was a different matter. Felix von Luschan (1854–1924), curator at the Ethology Museum in Berlin, built up sections devoted to Africa and Oceania, collecting human skeletal material, which assumed the superiority of the German.[21] In Germany, a tradition developed of referring to people as *Naturvölker* and *Kulturvölker*—people of nature and people of culture. Europeans were people with culture and history, while Africans and Pacific Islanders had no culture or history and were part of 'nature'. An entirely new science was required to develop this thesis as history was not appropriate to study these people. Anthropology emerged as this new science, devoted to studying the colonised. These people without history were considered pristine—humans in the raw—and thus offered anthropologists a unique chance to study authentic human nature.

Anthropologists looked for ways to rid their new science of subjectivity. They viewed history as an impossibly soft science contaminated by interpretation. Anthropologists had to adopt a position of 'pure objective observation', sharply distinguished from history. German anthropologists would seek out only the 'physical properties of humans'. Like Galton, they would measure the bodies and above all the skulls of *Naturvolker*. Anthropologists turned to the camera, the calliper, and the face-mask; they photographed, measured, and sculpted. This led to discomforting encounters between scientists and their subjects—being measured was not comfortable, and the arrival of anthropologists brandishing callipers came to be feared.

In the 1870s, the German explorer and amateur student anthropologist Hermann von Schlagintweit added a new technique to the anthropologist's armoury.[22] This was the face-mask, which was made from gypsum plaster and cast on the spot from the subject. Anthropologists like von Luschan seized on the new technique, and it became a vital part of an anthropologist's education. The process involved having one's face covered in slowly hardening clay, with only tiny vents and lengths of straw up one's nostrils to breathe through. The process lasted forty minutes. The gypsum plaster could irritate and even burn the skin; the dead were easier to work with. Rudolf Virchow, one of the most high-profile German anthropologists, cultivated German colonial administrators in East Africa to send back alcohol-filled zinc containers containing freshly severed heads acquired from native burials.

After the First World War, German anthropologists became increasingly preoccupied with their own Indo-German or Aryan race. Madame Blavatsky and the German occult thinkers she inspired led anthropologists to begin to investigate the origins of the Aryan race. The Germans turned to central Asia, the land of Blavatsky's Great White Brotherhood, rather than study Africans. It was into this intellectual climate that Beger was acclimatised as a student of Hans 'Rassen' Günther at Jena University. It was Günther who turned Beger, who was by all accounts a hard working student, into an anthropologist. He read Günther's, *The Racial Elements of European History*, in which he tells his readers that physical anthropology concerns itself with the 'calculable details of bodily structure'.[23] From a study of bodily structures, Günther concludes that there are five European races, but most Europeans, including Germans, are a mixture of blood lines, and it is the physical anthropologist who has the task of calculating the proportion of each race embodied in an individual. This can be determined only by intricately measuring bodies and skulls, recording hair types and eye colour, and then meticulously crunching the numbers. Günther believed that the evidence was worrying; German stock was increasingly mixed, and only the pure in blood could sustain a high civilisation.

A great deal of Günther's evidence is subjective. He depends, like most racists, on appearance, and the book contains page after page of mug shots that stand for the different racial types or mixtures of types. Many are anonymous, but others show history's great and good. There is Macchiavelli ('predominantly Dinaric'), alongside Leonardo (who was 'Nordic'); Tennyson was Nordic too, as were Byron and the Duke of Wellington, but Dickens is merely 'predominantly Nordic' since the crinkly texture of his hair betrays the presence of a different strain. Generic American professors (from Yale) and most statesmen are Nordic; marble statues, portraits and antique busts show that Greeks, Romans, and Germans too were of the Nordic type. Günther has a rogue's gallery as well—Socialist leader Ferdinand Lasalle is representative of a 'Jew from Germany' and is 'Predominantly Hither Asiatic with Nordic strain? Texture of hair Negro?' Camille Saint-Saëns is simply a 'Jew from France'.[24]

Günther's conclusion is simple and dangerous. The message of science is that the Nordic or Aryan race embodies all that is great and good. Aryans alone are endowed with a sense of competitive achievement and leadership, and highly developed senses of reality, prudence, duty, calm judgement, angelic creativity, and 'roguish humour'. What a piece of work is a Nordic man! However, if the weaker elements betray their inheritance by contaminating its purity, these attributes begin to wither—'an age of unlimited racial mixture has left the men of the present day physically and mentally rudderless'.

Günther then turns to the villains in the drama of race history. One racial type above all posed the most insidious threat to Nordic culture:

> The Jews give an example of the physical and mental hereditary endowment, for their inherited characteristics are the source of that strangeness which they themselves feel within the racially different European peoples and which these people feel with regard to the Jews...[25]

According to Günther, Jews exhibit particular gestures and traits which, thankfully, make them easy to identify. They are, for example, preoccupied by materialism and have a tendency towards obesity and 'lustfully sensual lips'. In his chapter 'Jewish Nation', Günther recommends that a 'worthy and evident solution of the Jewish question lies in that separation of the Jews from the Gentiles ... which Zionism seeks to bring about'. Thus the scientist became a propagandist.

From the beginning of the nineteenth century, many had come to believe that the Aryan races had expanded from a central Asian homeland, perhaps in Tibet. Günther turned the idea on its head. According to him, north-west Europe was the original home of the Nordic people, and Günther laboriously followed their trail eastwards to Persia, through the Caucasus and into India. In an echo of the Atlantis myth, Günther's Nords brought with them the art of building and sophisticated social systems. In some regions of the world, they left behind dolmens and stone circles; in India, they created the Hindu *Veda*. But as they spread across Asia, the weaker kind of Aryan began to lust after lesser races and poison their inheritance. The great Nordic empire collapsed and its people retreated back to their ancestral heartland in the north.

Günther found evidence for this in the *Veda*, which lament the mingling of races. Its proscriptions, he suspected, led to the emergence of the Hindu *varna* system of hierarchical castes that both Günther and Himmler admired. On the other hand, he blamed Buddhism for encouraging mixed marriage. The teachings of the Buddha 'wholly and irretrievably broke down the racial discipline and forethought of this wonderfully gifted people'. This is all strikingly similar to Ernst Schäfer's lament for the tough old Tibet corrupted by Lamaism. According to Günther, the original Aryans had no priests, and it was the emergence of a priestly caste that signalled the 'weakening' of their blood. Indian peoples, Günther believed, now contained barely a trace of their original Nordic blood, but he believed that some residual evidence might be found in remote areas of the North-West frontier. This is the key that unlocks Beger's intentions in Tibet.

Beger read Günther's *Die Nordische Rasse bei den Indogermanene Aliens* (1933).[26] The book is full of maps with arrows pointing south and then east from the Nordic heartland in northern Europe. They push through ancient Persia and deep into central Asia and the icy peaks of Tibet. When Beger read the book, he became fascinated by a possibility; Beger studied photographs of Tibetan nobles and noted their slim, perhaps even Nordic appearance. He described them as 'tall, with long head, thin face, drawn back cheek bones, springing out straight or slightly bent nose with high nose ridge, straight hair and imperious, self-confident behaviour'. Beger, and his professor became interested in the possibility that the last Aryans might be discovered on the roof of the world, in Tibet. Beger said that his intention would be:

To study the current racial-anthropological situation through measurements, trait research, photography and moulds [face masks] and especially to collect material about the proportions, origins, significance, and development of the Nordic race in this region.[27]

He also proposed to search for human fossils and for skeletal remains that could prove a former Nordic presence on the Tibetan plateau. Bruno Beger would turn Schäfer's expedition into a quest for the master race.

The expedition team also included Schäfer's right-hand man and technical expert, Edmund Geer, the entomologist and photographer Ernst Krause, who was also the official expedition cameraman, and the geophysicist Karl Wienert.[28] All were members of the SS, a condition of Himmler's patronage. Germany led the world in geomagnetic research in the 1930s, and Wienert's presence added real lustre to the expedition. Wienert's teacher Wilhelm Filchner had completed a number of gruelling geomagnetic and topographical surveys across the high interior of Asia, the first in 1903 and the most recent between 1935 and 1937. He had returned with spectacular new data, the pride of German science. Filchner had established a chain of magnetic stations across the northern borders of Tibet in the Kunlun Range; Wienert's task was to do the same in the Himalayas, to the south.

In the nineteenth century, unmapped regions of the world were simply shown as white spaces. The explorer's mission was to fill in those provocative lacunae, 'to trace lines upon the unknown corners of the earth'. For geophysicists, Sikkim and southern Tibet were magnetic white spaces. The problems were, of course, intertwined. For the last 700 years, explorers and navigators have been able to exploit one astonishing property of the Earth. Inside its core is a mass of liquid iron that slowly rotates below the crust. Its slow movement works like a dynamo, turning the Earth into an immense magnet with a magnetic field and a north and South Pole.[29] The invention of the compass some seven centuries ago made it possible for navigators and explorers to fix their direction of travel in relation to the north magnetic pole, the direction in which the tiny needles of their compasses always pointed. These magnetic poles lie close to the geographic North and South Poles, but hold a compass in the palm of your hand in Berlin and its needle will point 4 degrees away from north to west; in San Francisco, 20 degrees to the east. This is the declination. If your compass was constructed so that its needle could hang freely in space, it would not only be in error horizontally but vertically too; this is called the inclination. Scientists like Filchner and Wienert measured these discrepancies to create a three-dimensional image of magnetic variation. It was also realised that magnetic readings varied over time, so Wienert had to record both exactly where he was and the precise time when he made the measurements. In the field, quite complicated and cumbersome apparatus is needed to record as precisely as possible declination and inclination as well as the exact location and time of each reading.

Almost everything scientists like Filchner and Wienert were measuring was connected with that liquid iron dynamo slowly rotating deep down in the Earth's core. So, standing in the Himalayas, not far from the highest place on the planet, Wienert was actually measuring something that was being generated near the planet's centre. However, when Wienert was taking his measurements in 1938, scientists knew virtually nothing about the core; Wienert probably did not understand where or how the magnetic field was generated in the first place. In effect, then, he was making measurements in the dark, blindfolded, hoping that a few extra statistics would somehow throw light on this great mystery of the Earth.

Nevertheless, his measurements would be of more immediate practical use for future travellers or mapmakers in Tibet who might need to rely on a compass, including a possible Nazi invasion force. As an explorer moved across a landscape, filling in the blanks on his maps, he had to be aware that his compass needle was fickle, and the geomagnetic data gathered by men like Filchner and Wienert allowed him to make appropriate adjustments. German scientists were very good at geomagnetic measurement; the unit of magnetic force, the *Gauss*, was named after one of the most outstanding of all scientists, Carl Friedrich Gauss.[30] There is nothing intrinsically sinister or 'Nazi' about measuring earth magnetism. It is conceivable that Himmler believed Wienert's work could make some contribution to the *Welteislehre* (the World Ice Theory); after all, Wienert was in the very region where the Aryan ancestral race, wrapped in icy shrouds, was alleged to have descended to Earth. Beger remembered that Himmler's 'theories' about human origins were often discussed around the camp fire.

The very particular (and indeed peculiar) world view of the NSDAP (which Wienert had done so much to underpin) had its origins in the thinking of the late nineteenth century anthropologists such as Günther and Ludwig Ferdinand Clauss. It was, however, geographers who gave birth to the link between people and space; this ended after 1943 with the destructive *Lebensraum* policy and the *Drang nach Osten* (the drive to the east).

The German *Herrenvolk* demanded space to live, in the East or in Africa, which it deserved as a sacred right; geographers were called on to define not merely Germany as a state within political borders, but also as a *Volksboden* and a *Kulturboden*, an ethnic and cultural territory, which stretched minds to thoughts of colonisation and conquest. Geographers surveyed places and regions, anthropologists measured and calibrated living people, but both could come to the same conclusions about races and landscapes—that they belonged together, fed each other. A pure-blooded *Volk* was naturally wedded to a landscape; mixed races were estranged. Jews and gypsies were victimised by these ideas because they were viewed as races without a homeland. In fact, most geographers welcomed the new regime in 1933; very few were driven into exile. One claimed that 'German geography today is proud to make its results and its work ... available to the leadership of the state'. After 1939, German geographers worked hand in hand with German conquerors, mapping new conquests as 'Germandom' expanded in the wake of the tanks and stukas of the Reich.

Departing in April 1938, Schäfer led his expedition to Tibet, arriving the following January. Beger began his anthropological work in Gangtok ('High Hill') in Nepal. Gangtok was a large village straddling a densely forested ridge, the sides of which fell steeply to the river. At one end of the ridge was the royal palace and the private temple of the Chogyal, whom the British always referred to as the Maharaja. The British residency faced the palace on higher ground, behind pink dahlia trees and green ferns.[31]

Beger wanted to experiment making a head cast or mask, a difficult and time-consuming process that demanded the considerable patience and endurance of the subject. Beger used Passang, a Sherpa, who he realised was unwell following a bad head injury the previous week. Despite this, Beger, helped by Geer, pressed ahead. It was a reckless decision. The rushes of their film, *Geheimnis Tibet*, held in the Library of Congress in Washington DC, show the making of an anthropological mask in detail. The raw gypsum has to be mixed with water and disinfectant, and then globs are plastered over the subject's face. Two straws are inserted into the nostrils, although they do little to relieve the feelings of intense claustrophobia. When the mask is finished, the subject has to sit completely still, resembling nothing so much as a mummy from a horror film. Every now and then, in Krause's film, he turns without expression to the camera. When the mask is at last removed it forms a negative, a reversed image of the subject's face, so the final stage is to mix a synthetic rubber solution that is poured into the mask. When it has set it is peeled away, revealing a precise simulacrum of the subject's face, a portrait in latex.

On that day in Gangtok, nothing went to plan. Beger prepared the plaster and smeared it meticulously over Passang's face, but he failed to insert the straws and merely wiped away the clay from the nostrils. Passang soon began to experience difficulties with his breathing. As Beger covered his eyes he saw he was very frightened, but he decided to continue. With most of Passang's face completely covered, they all settled down to wait. Beger held a stopwatch and smoked a cigarette. Then he realised with horror that Passang's head had begun to jerk grotesquely, and the fragile globular mask had begun to break apart. With horror, Beger saw that Passang was having an epileptic seizure. Gurgling and foaming through the clay, he fell to the ground, his body arcing upwards and then slumping violently down. He was sucking the wet clay into his mouth and nostrils and turning blue. Beger began to scrape away the mask from his face, plunging his fingers into Passang's throat. It was a scene of repulsive horror, but Passang was saved. Beger reported that Passang described the feeling to his companions:

> ...he was taken over by thoughts of torture ... Everything started to rotate around him when the clay flowed into his nostrils ... The mountain god Kangchendzonga had appeared before him, seized him and shaken him violently.

Beger's inexplicable (to him) activities, which he had tolerated full of fear and suspicion, had transported him into a world of demons.[32]

Passang and the other porters found a picture of a grotesque demon god and showed it to Schäfer. It was a warning to unbelievers. Schäfer was outraged and turned on Beger. By this time, Geer had set off to find the local doctor and Schäfer was fearful of the repercussions. If the British discovered what had happened, the Germans could be expelled. There had been a confused discussion about whether getting a local doctor was in fact a good idea, but Kaiser and Geer failed to find him anyway. Schäfer gave Passang one of his best white shirts, which seemed to pacify him; he then told his men that they would be sacked without pay if anything was said to outsiders. No more face-masks would be made in Gangtok.

Leaving Gangtok, they headed to Chungtang, then Lachen, following the road that would allow them to cross the Himalayas into Tibet. As they travelled, Beger did all he could to impress the Sikkimese with his skills as a 'medicine man'. He hoped that by helping the locals, his reputation would spread, which would allow him to take his anthropological measurements and masks more easily—he would simply use his patients. He began by treating the caravan's porters, but soon others heard and he had a queue of people most days as they passed through the small hamlets. He had a supply of basic drugs, which impressed the locals. Many of his patients were the higher Bhutia class, who were less inclined to rely on traditional medicines than the Lepchas. Beger offered treatments for malaria, diarrhoea, eye infections, sores and skin problems, and even broken limbs.

The measurement of the Tibetan people proved no easy matter. High on the Himalayan plateau, *en route* between the Kangra La Pass and Khampa Dzong, Beger can be seen in the grainy black-and-white film, calipers in hand, with his human subject. The pretty girl seems uncomfortable, giggling nervously and gently pushing Beger away. Not to be deterred, he insistently brushers her aside, bent on measuring her arms; he then moves onto her hips, at which point she strikes him across the face in rage. These moments were edited out of the finished film, but the outtakes are in the Library of Congress in the US. They demonstrate that violence underpinned the practice of physical anthropology. Measuring bodies and making masks was not much different from possessing them or turning them into lifeless cadavers.

The expedition was allowed to enter Tibet on the condition that they were not to undertake scientific work. They decided to ignore this, of course, and so Beger and Wienert had to work in secret. They silently crept out of their accommodation and retrieved Wienert's geomagnetic equipment. Officially they were tourists, not working scientists. Very few of their companions could be completely trusted, but the Christmas celebrations provided good cover. With only the moon to guide them, they stumbled along a path they knew led to a side valley, their boots crunching through ice and snow. They crossed a stream and ended up on a narrow ridge with a good view of the night sky and a brilliant vista of stars.

The magnetometer used to take astronomical measurements was tricky to use at the best of times, but at high altitude and after a few drinks, it was more difficult than ever. It was bitterly cold, and their fingers were stiff and clumsy. They tipsily set up Wienert's equipment and somehow, in spite of the Tibetan beer, the cold, and the dark, took readings. Yatung is there in Wienert's data at 9,780 feet, latitude 27° 29′, longitude 88° 54′. He was always meticulous, however challenging the circumstances. As they travelled closer to Lhasa, his work would become much more difficult, and a great deal was at stake:

If these activities had been discovered by the Tibetan authorities this would have meant the end of the expedition. The Tibetan as an individual is rather harmless and extremely helpful, but in congregations, especially when involved in religious service, he becomes easily excited and dangerous.

Despite this, between Yatung and Lhasa he found ways to set up fourteen geomagnetic stations, most often working in the very early hours of the morning. During the day, Wienert often let the rest of the caravan pass by, and as soon as he was out of sight he would seize another opportunity to set up his tripod and magnetometer. Whenever he was discovered, one of the Sherpas would strike a pose as if Wienert were taking a photograph.

As they crossed the Tibetan plateau on their way to Lhasa, Beger noted many swastika designs on the sides of houses, and even what he called 'Rune-like' figures, which implies that he had listened to Weisthor or the other SS mystics more than he cared to recall later. Schäfer travelled with swastika flags and SS banners whenever he was not observed by the British, as his film shows very clearly. In Tibet, the swastika is called a *yungdrung* and is represented with its arms both clockwise and counter-clockwise. In its oldest form it is an image of the wind turning aside the rays of the sun; later, it came to represent good fortune. The Chinese call it *lei-wun* ('rolling thunder'), and Indians call it the *swasti*. You see them everywhere today. Swastikas adorn temples, houses, and even lorries. In Tibetan temples, they are often made from Chinese money and pasted on walls. For the German occult mystics, the swastika stood for Eastern wisdom. The Nazis had turned it into a sign of brutal aggression, but Schäfer shamelessly used his swastikas and thunderbolts to imply a cultural link with the Tibetans.

Kruase re-staged the arrival in Lhasa for his cameras, making the expedition party look like conquering heroes. The team then began to explore the city at the beginning of 1939. They encountered bustling streets lined with excrement, pigs, and rubbish, crowded by shops, beggars, and the like.

Beger needed better data to prove a connection between Tibetans and his own race, but so far his data was inconclusive. He hoped the streets of Lhasa would contain clues to the origins of the Aryan race. There were Tartars, Chinese, Muscovites, Armenians, Kashmiris, Hindustanis, and Nepalis. Beger could see nomads from Kham, Ngolok, and the Chungtang. Aristocrats strutted past in gold-embroidered robes, their long hair tied in a double topknot. In their wake came their wives in big head-dresses, tottering carefully in their heavy silk dresses layered with silver jewellery.

They left Lhasa on 20 March 1939. As they travelled across Tibet, Beger sought fresh subjects for his anthropometric work. He measured, photographed, and cast face-masks at every opportunity. Karl Wienert, for his part, was now free to resume his work. He set up fifteen magnetic stations between Lhasa and Shigatse.

The packs the expedition carried back were laden with animal skins, hundreds of reels of film, magnetometers and theodolites, radios, and the 108 volumes of the Tibetan Buddhist 'Bible', the *Kangyur*. They had collected an enormous number of plants and butterflies. Krause had shot 18,000 metres of 16-mm black-and-white film and coloured film and had taken 40,000 photographs. There is speculation that Schäfer had personally sought to prove that the Yeti was a species of bear, and though he did not find a specimen, he did send more than fifty animals back to Germany for further study, as well as 5,000 different grains. Beger had collected 2,000 ethnographic artefacts documenting Tibetan and regional culture and recorded the measurements of 376 people—mainly Tibetans, but also from other ethnic groups. He had also taken 2,000 photographs, made casts from the heads, faces, hands, and ears of seventeen people, and taken the fingerprints and handprints of another 350.

As the men walked out of Tibet, Schäfer became increasingly concerned that the expedition would find itself interred by the British, given the war in Europe. In Berlin, Himmler had no desire to see his precious Tibet Expedition interned, and so he organised their return. Arriving in Calcutta, the Germans boarded a British Indian Airways Sunderland flying boat, which flew them from the Bay of Bengal to Baghdad, where they found a Junkers U90 waiting to fly them on to Vienna. From there, a U52 took them to Munich, where they were met by Himmler himself. They all then flew to Berlin for a celebration and reception where Schäfer was presented with a Totenkopfring by Himmler. He would not publish his findings until 1950, under the title *Festival of the White Gauze Scarves: A Research Expedition through Tibet to Lhasa, the Holy City of the God Realm*.[33] Some of his more sensational findings found their way into the German press straight away, where the public avidly lapped them up. For example, the Nazi *Völkischer Beobachter* of 29 July 1939 relates:

Dr Ernst Schäfer, SS-Hauptsturmführer, has now completed the first German SS-Tibet Expedition with extraordinarily great success and will soon return to Germany with his guides. The participants of the expedition visited, as the first Germans, the capital of Tibet, Lhasa, the seat of the Dalai Lama, as well as Tibet's second-largest city, Shigatse, the capital of the Panchen Lama, and visited the huge monastery of Taschtimmps first visited in 1907 by Sven Hedin. By comparison, Sven Hedin's Trans-Himalaya's discoveries required several trips to accomplish. The harvest of the expedition regarding botanical and zoological collections is uncommonly rich and rare and of great value.[34]

An Article from *Der Neue Tag* dated 21 July 1939 is even more informative:

Sacred Tibetan Scripture Acquired by the Dr Schäfer-Expedition on Nine Animal Loads Across the High Country

(SPECIAL) FRANKFURT—20 JULY. The Tibet Expedition of Dr Ernst Schäfer, which during its expedition through Tibet stayed a long time in Lhasa and in the capital of the Panchen Lama, Shigatse, is presently on its return trip to Germany. Since the monsoons began unusually early, the return march of the expedition was hastened in order to secure the shipment of the precious collections. The expedition has singularly valuable scientific research results to inventory. In addition to outstanding accomplishments in the areas of geophysical and earth-magnetic research they succeeded in obtaining an extra rich ethnological collection including, along with cult objects, many articles and tools of daily life.

With the help of the regent of Lhasa it was Dr Schäfer who also succeeded in obtaining the *Kangschur*, the extensive, 108-volume sacred script of the Tibetans, which required nine animal loads to transport. Also especially extensive are the zoological and botanical collections that the expedition has already shipped, in part, to Germany the remainder of which they will bring themselves. The zoological collection includes the total bird-fauna of the research area. Dr Schäfer was also able, for the first time, to bag a Schapi, a hitherto unknown wild goat. About 50 live animals are on the way to Germany, while numerous other live animals are still with the expedition. An extensive herbarium of all existing plants is also on its way. Furthermore, valuable geographical and earth-historical accomplishments were made. Difficulties encountered due to political tensions with the English authorities were eliminated due to personal contact between Dr Schäfer and members of the British authorities in Shangtse, so that the unimpeded return of the expedition out of Tibet with its valuable collections was guaranteed.[35]

Following the celebrations, the members of the expedition were quickly assigned to duties fighting in the war. Himmler had something different in mind for Schäfer—a secret military plot. It was another piece of evidence to suggest that Schäfer had been a spy all along. The plan was for Schäfer to return to Tibet in order to incite rebellion against the Raj. Lord Curzon would have immediately understood the Soviet Union's interest in such a plan; it was, after all, his fear of Russian ambition that made him send Younghusband and his 'escort' to Lhasa in 1903. Germany too had an historic interest in playing the 'Great Game', and Schäfer's plot would be one of the last hands to be played.

It might seem obvious that on the eve of war, a German expedition travelling to Tibet, sponsored by Himmler, might be interested in plotting against the enemies of the Reich. However, Schäfer and Beger always denied that their work was anything other than scientific. The evidence suggests otherwise. Schäfer went behind the back of the British by illegally crossing into Tibet and negotiating with the Tering Raja, who disliked the British. As war became certain, Schäfer realised that his personal friendships with the Tibetan regent and Lhasa nobility could be of strategic value. The expedition became aware that some Tibetans were very hostile to the British; the Regent even asked if Schäfer could supply him with rifles, a request that was rejected. However, by 1940, that request had been reconsidered. In a letter on 12 January 1940, he wrote: 'The political group has to be equipped with machinery, guns and 200 military fire arms that I promised to the regent of Tibet'. So, either Schäfer dissembled even to his own colleagues, or he contacted the Regent again after September. Either way, it is a damning statement.

Schäfer was aware that there was a long tradition of Germans inspiring indigenous people to topple the hated British Empire. The German government had frequently used 'scientific expeditions' as a cover for espionage. Schäfer called the plot he hatched with Himmler 'The Lawrence Expedition', and this is a clue to the origins of the idea. The Lawrence to which he referred was not T. E. Lawrence 'of Arabia', who had masterminded the Arab Revolt against the Turks during the First World War, but a German Lawrence, a man called Wilhelm Wassmuss (1880–1931). The story of Wassmuss had inspired the novelist John Buchan to write *Greenmantle* and had been recounted by Christopher Sykes in 1937.[36,37,38]

Germany had been conspiring to throw the British out of India since even before the First World War, and the country was aided and abetted in this by a group of Persian exiles who wished to free their own country from both British and Russian control. In 1913, Wassmuss, a 'manly, blond Saxon', arrived in Persia, where he began meeting local tribal leaders. His plan was to incite holy war against the British and pave the way for a German empire in the east. Like T. E. Lawrence, Wassmuss was both a scholar (he spoke fluent Persian and Arabic) and a tough adventurer who had a great deal of experience of the region and its people. His accomplices included men who would play a part in Schäfer's scheme decades later; among was them the geologist Oskar von Niedermayer, who had followed Wassmuss to Persia with a battalion of handpicked men disguised as a travelling circus. The mission was something of a fiasco, but Wassmuss, who split off from the main party, had some success persuading Tangistani, Dashtistanu, and Dastiti tribes to attack the British. His British biographer wrote that Wassmuss believed:

> The flame of war against the infidel power of the British would then have reached the gates of India. Then would the conflagration be at its height and every available man sent from France to the rescue of the Empire.[39]

Schäfer's plot was inspired by the Wassmuss campaign. The idea was to proceed to Moscow, where, with Soviet help, Schäfer would begin preparing a guerrilla campaign enlisting the tribes of Tibet, Kashmir, and Afghanistan in a many-pronged assault on India. He imagined that the Tibetan government or the Regent would agree to an attack on the British, but this was hare-brained; both the Kashag and the Regent would certainly have been interested in acquiring arms to deter the Chinese, but to rise against the British would have been suicidal and pointless, and the Tibetans knew it.

Schäfer's letters refer to leading twenty or so 'commandos', including Geer and Wienert, into Tibet from the north, following a trail across the

Takla Makan. It would be a small party carrying a large amount of cash. He discussed the need to pay heavy bribes in Chinese Turkestan and also to match 'the British bribe'—in other words, paying the Regent to secure his goodwill.

It is possible that Schäfer was thinking about recruiting the warlike Ngoloks, whom he had encountered in eastern Tibet in 1935 and then again in Lhasa during New Year celebrations in 1939. In 1941, Schäfer coordinated a bigger military force of 200 or so that would advance into Sikkim; Wienert's hard-won data would surely prove very useful, as would Filchner's from the northern regions of Tibet. Another of Schäfer's letters contains a cryptic reference to seeking Soviet 'assurances' about territory in Tibet and Sikkim, presumably to make sure they would not become part of the Soviet empire.

From the start, little went well for Schäfer. He discovered that there were several other similar plans in preparation and that he was part of a power game between Himmler and von Ribbentrop, who had his own favoured adventurers. In the end, all these men were outmanoeuvred by Alfred Rosenberg, who went directly to Hitler to pour scorn on any idea of using Tibet as a staging post to invade India. In any event, the Nazi invasion of the Soviet Union ended any thought of working with the Soviets, and so the plans came to nothing.[40]

Tibetan Fighters

Things may not have gone as Schäfer had hoped, but that was not the last we were to hear of the Tibetans. During the Second World War, fighters volunteered to join with the Nazis fighting the Soviet forces on the Eastern Front. The Tibetan brigades were attached to the anti-Soviet Cossack regiments and were renowned for their endurance of sub-zero temperatures and refusal to surrender, making them some of the Axis's toughest fighters. They were exceptional horsemen and staged some of the last cavalry charges in history. It was the remnants of these brigades that the Soviet Army found in the ruins of Berlin, having fought to the last.[41]

Tibet provided a safe haven to escaping Nazis as the Third Reich collapsed at the end of the war. One such refugee was Heinrich Harrer. Harrer first met the Dalai Lama, Tenzin Gyatso, in 1948, when the Austrian had taken sanctuary in Lhasa after escaping from an Anglo-Indian prison. Tenzin was clearly taken by Herrer, amused by his good humour and descriptions of life in Europe; the two met regularly each week.[42]

Icelandic Sagas:
Germanic Myths and Legends

A man's language is no full and certain proof of his parentage. Much bad anthropology has been made by thus carelessly taking language and race as though they went always and exactly together.[1]

Himmler had a personal fascination with Iceland, and the Nazis elevated it to mythical proportions, believing that it was a surviving link to their ancestral homeland of Thule.[2] This idea dates to the fourth century BC journey of the classical explorer and geographer Pytheas, who describes the land of Ultima Thula, the ultimate destination of his voyage.[3] The precise location of Ultima Thula has been much debated, but Rudolf von Sebottendorff (also known as Adam Alfred Rudolf Glauer), the occultist and originator of the Thule Society, was convinced that Pytheas's Ultima Thula was Iceland.[4] The importance of Iceland therefore was that it was the last link to the birthplace of the Aryan race.

The Nazis believed that the Aryans were separate from the rest of the human race. Where others were descended from monkeys, the Aryans had descended from heaven.[5] They found support for this theory in runic inscriptions, such as the *Mensch* and *Hagal* runes, which they believed were symbolic of a 'descent from heaven' of the real '*Menschen*', or Aryan Man.[6] Himmler also believed that the story of Aryan (and thus Germanic) origins was contained within the historic Icelandic *Eddas*.[7] Thus to him, and members of the Ahnenerbe, the *Eddas* were a sacred text. Iceland, like Tibet, was considered a holy land and so within the Ahnenerbe an Institute was established to study the *Eddas*. Other clues were to be found in the caves, prehistoric monuments and dolmens that are scattered across Iceland, and as a consequence the Nazis wanted to send an expedition to study Icelandic artefacts, and as they had in Tibet, perform 'the recording of human images', by way of photography, and to record measure facial dimensions based on anthropological science.

Himmler was not alone in this fascination with old legends; German ultranationalists were captivated by the ancient epics of the *Eddas* and *The Nibelungenlied*, which told the tale of Prince Siegfried's slaying of a dragon and how when he bathed in its blood he became invincible in battle.[8] Many Nazis considered these ancient myths to be more than just stories, an idea encouraged by the writing of Rudolf John Gorsleben, editor of right-wing Munich newspaper *Deutsche Freiheit*. According to Gorsleben's reading of the *Eddas*, in the past, Aryan men and women had superhuman abilities that they had subsequently lost. He believed they could regain these powers, and in 1925 he founded a study group—the 'Edda Society'—to consider how this might be brought about.[9]

Gorsleben's articles created something of a stir and even influenced Hitler, who incorporated some the ideas into his own thinking. In January 1942, Hitler observed:

Legend cannot be extracted from the void, it couldn't be a purely gratuitous figment. Nothing prevents us from supposing, and I believe, even that it would be to our interest to do so, that mythology is a reflection of things that have existed and of which humanity has retained a vague memory. In all the human traditions, whether oral or written, one finds mention of a huge cosmic disaster … In the Nordic legend we read of a struggle between giants and gods. In my view the thing is explicable only by the hypothesis of a disaster that completely destroyed a humanity that already possessed a high degree of civilisation.[10]

Himmler was just a receptive to these ideas. When he was a child, his parents had read German and Norse legends aloud to him, and he returned to these stories as an adult. He reread *The Nibelungenlied* in 1923, noting its 'incomparable eternal beauty in language, depth and all things German'.[11] Now he was able to share his interest with Karl-Maria Wiligut. The two frequently dined together and chatted for hours, and in time, Himmler came to take a particularly literal view of the *Eddas* and other ancient legends. Under Wiligut's influence, Himmler created a department in the Ahnenerbe called 'The Teaching and Research Centre for Folktales, Fairytales and Sagas'. The work of the department was to collect ancient Germanic tales:

Fairytales, sagas and comic fables are all varieties of stories that flow from the soul of the German people … These folktales are to be understood as they are told, without false glorification, in essence to remain true to their words and sounds.[12]

Himmler believed they comprised a history—greatly fragmented, but still intelligible—of northern Europe as it once was, before the arrival of Christianity. More importantly, he believed that the Aesir—the old gods of the Norse legend, such as Odin, Thor and Loki—were in fact beings of pure, undiluted Nordic essence, the earliest Aryans. As such, they were the possessors of superior knowledge.

With the help of the Ahnenerbe scholars, Himmler hoped to recover the lost Aryan lore of the *Eddas*, which seemed to span everything from superior weaponry to potent medicines.[13] He was particularly intrigued by stories of Thor and his lightning-like throwing hammer, Mjollnir, which was described as the strongest and most accurate weapon in the world. In a surviving letter to the Ahnenerbe, Himmler spelled out his particular interest in Thor and his hammer, without a touch of embarrassment or self-consciousness, as if it were a rational scholarly pursuit:

> Have the following researched: Find all places in the northern Germanic Aryan cultural world where an understanding of the lightning bolt, the thunderbolt, Thor's hammer, or the flying or thrown hammer exists, in addition to all the sculptures of the god depicted with a small hand axe emitting lightning. Please collect all of the pictorial, sculptural, written and mythological evidence of this. I am convinced that this is not based on natural thunder and lightning, but rather that it is an early, highly developed form of war weapon of our forefathers, which was only, of course, possessed by the Aesir, the gods, and that it implies an unheard knowledge of electricity.[14]

If this advanced knowledge of electricity could be pieced together again from the old sagas, then German scientists could use it to develop a weapon capable of smashing the enemies of the Reich.

There was no telling what other pearls of Aryan wisdom might lie buried in the *Edda, The Nibelungenlied*, or other ancient legends of northern Europe. The *Eddas* were therefore important to the mystical side of Nazi thought, and their Aryan, northern aspects integrated admirably with the World Ice Theory and National Socialist efforts to revive Nordic mythology as a surrogate religion to replace Christianity (as set out in publications such as Wilhelm Aspendorf's *The Edda as World Ice Theory*, which appeared in 1933).[15]

The *Eddas* themselves are therefore worthy of more detailed consideration. They are a body of ancient Icelandic literature contained in two thirteenth-century books known as the *Prose (Younger) Edda* and the *Poetic (Elder) Edda*. The derivation of *Edda* either means 'the book of Oddi', 'song', or 'poem', depending on whose interpretation you take. The

Prose Edda was written by the Icelandic Chief Judge, poet, and historian Snorri Sturluson, who lived from 1179 to 1241. He was among the most learned men of his time and a person of great influence, eventually becoming President of the Legislature. He wrote his book around 1220 as a text for instructing young poets in the complicated metres of early Icelandic skalds (court poems) and to provide a Christian age with an understanding of earlier mythology.[16]

Skaldic verse forms are thought to have originated in Norway in the ninth century.[17] They differ fundamentally from traditional Germanic and *Eddic* forms in that the syllables are strictly counted and lines have to finish in given ways. Such rigorous requirements made corruption difficult. On the other hand, the complicated syntax and makes interpretation harder. The skalds utilised a complex alliterative system together with internal rhyme and consonance. Their strophes normally comprise eight lines and these are divisible into half-strophes of four lines. Norwegian and other Scandinavian chieftains were frequently the objects of skaldic poetry, but this also dealt with myths and pagan worship. Snorri was an enthusiastic lover of the past and folklore as well as poetry.

In the north, there were special rules for poetic composition and a special language of 'kennings' (*kenningur*), periphrases.[18] For example, a battle was a 'storm of Odin', a ship 'a steed of the billows' and the earth was 'flesh of Ymir', a giant created when the ice of frozen streams (*Elivagar*) from the frost region (*Niflheim*) melted in warm air and life stirred through the power emitting the heat. Life kindling in melting ice is reminiscent of the World ice Theory.

The *Prose Edda* begins with a discussion about kennings and then includes a poem exemplifying 102 forms of verse known to Snorri and addressed to Haakon, the young king of Norway, and his uncle Jarl Skúli. These two parts—*Skáldskaparmál* and *Háttatal*—are mostly interesting to students of Norse and Germanic literature. However, the third part is of general interest and is the most widely read today. This is the *Gylfaginning*, the beguiling of Gylfi, and is made up of a dialogue describing the visit of King Gylfi of the Swedes to Asgard, the citadel of the gods. His questions are answered by them by myths regarding the beginnings of the world, the adventures of the gods, and the fate awaiting all in the *Ragnarök* (the twilight of the gods). Snorri is supposed to have written other important works, including the *Heimskringla* (orb of the world), a history of the kings of Norway from the beginning to the mid-twelfth century. In the first part of this, the *Ynglinga* Saga, they are said to descend from the royal house of Sweden, the *Ynglingar*, itself descended from the gods. Snorri certainly visited Norway twice and Sweden once, so he may well have authored the stories, including tales that he had heard in both of these countries.[19]

The *Poetic Edda* is later, dating from the second half of the thirteenth century, but it has much older mythological poetry in it, hence it is sometimes called the *Elder Edda*. Its second section is devoted to traditional German heroes and many of its stories are known from continental Germany and England, but the earlier Norse sources preserve them in a purer form. The *Codex Regius* version of the Royal Library in Copenhagen comprises twenty-nine poems, and another manuscript, in the Arnamagnaean collection, includes six of these, and a seventh, *Baldrs Draumar* (*Baldur's Dreams*), which is lacking in the former. In this latter text, Odin descends to the underworld to arouse the sibyl so that she may explain Baldur's evil dreams. Some of the legends contained in the *Codex Regius* may have been derived from the Goths, and one, the *Atlakvida* (*Lay of Atli*), describes events occurring in fifth-century western Germany, *Atli* (Attila) having been King of the Huns from AD 434 to 453. Many of the lays are associated with *Sigurd* (Siegried) and his love for Brunhild.[20]

The *Poetic Edda* contains only a small part of Iceland's poetry from the Middle Ages; most has been lost. Other fragments appear in thirteenth and fourteenth-century sagas such as the *Hlödskvida* (*Lay of Hlöd*) in the Heidriks saga, and may have been known to the author of the old English epic poem *Beowulf*.[21] The cycle commences with the sibyl's prophesy (*Völuspá*, *Volva* meaning seeress, who was raised from the dead by Odin, to whom she seems to speak) embracing the whole of time from the birth of the world to its destruction and the destruction of the gods themselves. After that comes the 'Worlds of the High One' (*Hávamál*), Odin himself, disconnected fragmentary poems embodying the wisdom of this warrior god, allegedly in his own words and in the form of cynical, moral precepts probably reflecting a lawless age. Later, this narrates how Odin obtained the magic powers of the runes by hanging himself from the famous World Tree (*Yggdrasil*, meaning 'Odin's horse') and enduring hunger and thirst for nine months. In *Völuspá*, Odin is called 'All Father', living through the ages and fashioning Heaven, Earth, and all things in them. This seemingly unequivocal evidence of Christian influence does not appear to have prevented the survival of antique poetry or traditions apropos the old pagan gods and their adoration. Indeed, although twelfth-century Icelanders were great travellers, and perhaps the most literate people in Europe who translated the lives of the saints, by the next century, they had again became interested in the practices of their ancestors, which is when Snorri wrote the *Prose Edda*.

In the fourteenth century, legends about the old gods and heroes were being incorporated into the heroic sagas (*fornaldar sögur*). Earlier, some of these were included in a Latin book forming a part of the nine-volume work on Danish history written by a Dane, Saxo Grammaticus, the secretary of Archbishop Absalom, who died in 1201.[22] The nine books covered the prehistory of the Danes and are particularly concerned with pagan gods, whom Saxo considered to be the kings and magicians of earlier days. He mentioned Othinus (Odin), also called Uggerus (Norse, *Ygg*). Other deities are Frey, the satrap of the gods, whose seat was in Uppsala, where Adam of Bremen described a sanctuary containing images of Thor, Wodan, and Fricco (Frey), in addition to Baldur, Freya (Frigg), and perhaps Loki, who may be represented by Ugaarthilocus (Utgard-Loki). These are very old deities and many of them were given alternative names by the Romans. Thus Tacitus spoke of Wodan as 'Mercury', Thor perhaps as 'Hercules', and Tyr as 'Mars'. Saxo probably drew on Danish traditions, but he seems to have also obtained information from vagrant Icelanders, about whom he wrote respectfully.

The heroic sagas narrate the adventures of heroes who supposedly lived in Scandinavia or on the continent before Iceland was populated. Some of the gods, particularly Odin, are often reported as intervening in human affairs. As their objective was entertainment rather than instruction, their usefulness as sources is limited. They may be compared with a collection called *The Book of Heroes*, written about the same time and including tales about Theodoric the Great, a popular hero in southern Germany.[23] *Yggdrasil*, the evergreen ash, was cited as having cosmic significance, the welfare of mankind depending upon it. It was believed to have three roots, one extending to the world of death and the others to the worlds of frost giants and men. However, it is described as rotting it is stated that it will fall when *Ragnarök* occurs.

The *Eddic* picture of the universe's origin starts at a time when there was no heaven or Earth and neither gods nor men. Instead, there was a colossal abyss called *Ginnunga-gap* (Yawning Chasm), this perhaps encompassing the ocean surrounding the Earth. North of it lay *Niflheim*, and in that was a well called *Hvergelmir* (Cauldron rushing) from which flowed a number of rivers. To the south was *Muspell* or *Muspelheim*, light and glowing and ruled over by Surt. The streams from *Niflheim* became ice, spread into *Ginnunga-gap*, and were melted there by warm air from *Muspell* to quicken life. Snorri wrote a poem about it based on lost sources and stanzas from *Völuspá*, *Grimnismal*, and *Vafthrudnismal*. *Völuspá* says: 'In time's morning lived Ymir, there was no sand, sea nor cool waves, no earth was there, no Heaven above. Only a yawning chasm, nor grass anywhere'. Snorri's principal account embodies the conception that everything, including giants and gods, is traceable back to the union of fire and water (ice and mist). Incidentally, giants are regarded as having preceded the gods to become their antagonists.

The fire and ice conception is reminiscent of Hörbiger's World Ice Theory, in which great emphasis is placed upon the universal role of ice.

Grimnismal also contains cosmic statements. Odin, as Grimnir, is set between two fires by King Geirrod and gives information to the King's son Agnar, ultimately vanishing while Geirrod dies on his own sword. Following the words of the High One is the Lay of Thrym, recounting how the giant Thrym stole the hammer of Thor, the thunder god, and demanded the goddess Freya in marriage for its return. It is a very humorous work because Thor is portrayed as journeying to Thrym disguised as a bride; he shows astonishing manners at the wedding feast by eating an ox and eight salmon as well as drinking three vessels of mead. Needless to say, Thrym came to a sticky end; Thor slew him with the stolen hammer.

The second half of the *Poetic Edda* incorporates lays about Germanic heroes, and all but one—the *Völundarkvida*, about Wayland the Smith of English tradition—allude to Sigurd (Siegfried), his youth, his marriage to Gudrun, his death, and the tragic fate of the Burgundians (Nibelungs) supposedly destroyed in AD 437. They are the oldest surviving poems of this Germanic legend, the core of the medieval epic called the *Nibelungenlied*, but they are much more cruel, violent, and stoical. Exactly where the *Eddic* poems were written and by whom is unknown. It is likely that many belong to the pagan period prior to AD 1000, but none was composed before AD 800 and only a handful came as late as the twelfth century AD. Some think that the authors were Norsemen in the Western Isles of Britain and under Celtic influence. Others believe that most are based upon stories heard by Norsemen from Irishmen and Englishmen, these perhaps originating in Graeco-Roman mythology and Judeaeo-Christian records. Yet others regard Norway as their place of origin, and it may be that Iceland was involved as well. Two of the best-known heroic poems, *Atlamal* and *Atlakvitha*, were ascribed to Greenland in the thirteenth-century manuscript.

Odin is a prominent figure in some of the poems, and in the *Vafthrudnismal*, he mentions his queries to the giant Vafthrudnir, who answered them by giving him a sort of cosmic encyclopaedia. He says:

> *Out of Ymir's flesh was shaped the earth, the mountains out of his bones,*
> *The heaven from the ice-cold giant's skull,*
> *Out of his blood, the boisterous sea.*[24]

In other poems, Thor is the main protagonist, and both gods appear in *Harbardsljod*, a poem called a 'flyting'—an abusive dialogue between them. Each boasts and insults the other, but Thor is unaware that he is confronting Odin (as Harbard). In *Lokasenna*, the evil Loki is the main speaker and suffers rebuke from Thor, who compels him to stop slandering gods and goddesses. *Rigsthula* describes how the god Heimdall (or 'Rig') came to Earth and begat the first thrall, the first *karl* (peasant) and also the first *jarl* (noble warrior). From the last stock, there came one who is a future king. This poem praises kingship and is most likely Norwegian in origin, but it was composed by someone who had acquired a good deal of Celtic speech and culture.

The Icelandic sagas provide insight into both religion and folklore. They comprise biographical and historical stories, although these are often fictitious. Before they were written down, such works were a favourite form of entertainment on festive occasions, when told by a skilled teller of tales or wandering minstrel (*spielmann*). However the chief source of northern mythology remains the *Eddas*. They include many nature myths, and the meanings of some of them are immediately obvious. Indeed, efforts have been made to explain all on the basis of natural phenomena. This is rather a questionable procedure because nobody can be sure that such antique myths had any of the meanings attributed to them. It is probably imprudent to endeavour to use tales of the distant past in order to support a modern ideology. Ironically, the 'northern' preoccupation so popular in the Third Reich may not have reflected the views of most Nazis as regards the Scandinavians of their day. Alfred Rosenberg expressed a general Party opinion in his diary entry for 5 June 1934, in which he generalised that:

> Things have gone too good for the Scandinavians who have become both sated and lazy. The Vikings left and only the ordinary citizens remain. Only a dire fate will induce the old blood again to become rebellious.[25]

Hans S. Jacobsen agreed, and in 1938 he claimed that modern Scandinavians were suffering from uniformity, indifference (especially about foreign political problems), self-consciousness manifesting itself in a 'small-country' psychosis, and enjoyment of life coupled with lack of nationalism and feeling of strength dating back to before the First World War. According to Hans-Jürgen Lutzhöft, many other Germans had the same view of the Scandinavians, whose behaviour they considered to have changed radically from that of their Viking forebears.[26]

Brugg provided a thoroughly Nazi interpretation of the *Eddas*, which he regarded as embodying Horbiger's concept of the universal conflict between heat and cold in the form of *Muspelheim*, 'light and glowing', and *Niflheim*, 'ice'.[27] Brugg thought that the *Eddas* were much older than others believe, thus permitting him to try to associate events of the last ice age with some parts of them. He introduced the great flood and connected its retreat with the *Ginnunga-gap* or 'yawning chasm', which might have referred to an *Eddic* ocean encompassing the Earth. The melting of the southern faces of glaciers when the ice age terminated was envisaged as producing enormous quantities of meltwater and humidity generally, through which the sun shone fitfully. The phenomenon might have been the basis of the proposed *Niflheim,* which was said to be located to the north of *Ginnunga-gap.*

Brugg considered this in detail, including sections on *Edda und Welteislehre, Edda und Eiszeit, Edda und Sintflut,* and *Edda und 'Goldenes Zeitalter'* (covering the *Eddas* and the World Ice Theory, the *Eddas* and the Ice Age, the *Eddas* and the Great Flood, and the *Eddas* and the 'Golden Age' respectively). As the titles suggest, he was keen to link World Ice Theory to Icelandic legend, noting a legend that describes how Odin entered the underworld and pledged one of his eyes to Ymir in exchange for permission to drink from the spring of wisdom. Thereafter the god was one-eyed, the single orb representing the sun. A parallel in Egyptian mythology characterised the god-king Re as having two eyes—the right one functioned as the sun and the left would descend to Earth as a snake to kill mankind, which had become evil. An ensuing battle plunged the planet into darkness, and Brugg correlated this both with Odin's missing eye and with the break-up of the Tertiary moon, which he thought was recounted in the *Eddas* as the death of Ymir. The flood was described there as the streaming out of his blood after he was murdered by his son, Borr.

Brugg argued that all races recall the flood in their folktales. Amongst these are tales of a tree of life, which he thought might have started if a few trees survived the rise in sea level. It is included in the *Eddas* as Yggdrasil. The sea level later fell and a large island appeared that extended southwards from the west of Gibraltar; this was Atlantis.

According to Brugg, Atlantis was important because without it science was unable to explain the clear relationship between the old and new worlds. Atlantis was also significant in the origin of the 'northern race', the soul of which was born after the last ice age, when the prototype of the strong, heroic warrior emerged between the demolition of the Tertiary Moon and the great flood. Only such a 'valorous people' could have fought and overcome the annihilating effects of the flood, and, after it ended, continued to colonise milder climates. Their descendants went west to discover the fruitful island on which these cool-headed 'northern seafarers' and their children developed, of course, a high-level culture. This idea accorded with that of Alfred Rosenberg, who believed in Atlantis as a 'northern cultural centre' whose children had travelled everywhere as sailors and soldiers.

Brugg declared that wondrous past memories are stored in the *Eddas,* with powerful cosmic influences from the past remembered in folklore. Although science had long objected to superstitions, deeply rooted in *völkisch* traditions and stories, some had begun to think again about the matter. The countryman, closely connected with nature, still sows and harvests following the waning and waxing of the moon. Brugg maintained that people are influenced by the moon—especially sensitive individuals who cannot sleep when it is full, even in completely darkened bedrooms. Some sleepwalk, and epileptics suffer also. He continued with superstition about bad luck ascribed to Fridays, advising that no work should be done or journeys started on that day, nor should couples marry. He concluded that the Fatherland, ancestors, nature, and the cosmic constituted a foundation on which everyone should construct their lives. The World Ice Theory was held to embody these views. It was held to offer guidance for technology and economics and new approaches for locating fresh reserves of ores and predicting earthquakes. It also supported a 'northern' outlook on life and was in accord with the old Aryan, Teutonic picture of the universe drawn from the *Eddas* and the folklore of 'northern' progenitors.

Horbiger's theory was regarded as scientifically supporting the meaning of the *Eddas* and the northern conception of the struggle between fire and ice, light and darkness, and good and evil. Once consequence was that it had reawakened the 'immemorial northern inheritance still slumbering in folklore' to allow old Teutonic thoughts about fate to reassert themselves in association with an 'iron-hard attitude to duty and responsibility' characteristic of 'their' ancestors, who had no need of repentance or reward. Indeed, they knew neither heavenly humiliation nor fear of hell. World Ice Theory was directed at the self-sacrificing heroes who find victory even when defeated by destiny.

Brugg's book is a combination of a little science, much pseudo-science, some misapplied *Eddic* mythology, and Nazi racist ideology, with its constant references to the pre-eminence of the Aryan *Herrenvolk*. Despite this, Brugg was able to cite a number of high-profile academic supporters of World Ice Theory, including: Edgar Dacqué, Professor of Geology and Palaeontology at the University of München; Professor Bärtling, a geologist at the University of Berlin; Professor Dr Grosse, Director of the Bremen Observatory; Professor Franzius of the Technical High School in Hannover; and Professor Dr Briefs, University of Berlin.[28]

They followed the Nazi line that the surviving Aryan race was represented by the people of Scandinavia, England, and Germany, from which emerged the idea of a Germanic pan-Nordic Aryan union. Historically, the Teutonic peoples spread southwards from their prehistoric homes in Denmark and Scandinavia. They had occupied much of central Europe north of the Rhine and Danube rivers by the early Christian era. In the fourth, fifth, and sixth centuries, some of their tribes began to migrate, ultimately seizing the Roman Empire. There were three main groups—the High Germans (in middle and upper Germany, Switzerland, and Austria), the Low Germans (including north Germans, Flemings, Dutch, Frisians, and Anglo-Saxons), and the Scandinavians (in Denmark, Sweden, Norway, and Iceland).

Iceland was colonised from Norway in the ninth century, when Harold the Fair won a victory over the Norse nobles, which gave him control of the whole country.[29] Thus an intellectually lively and vigorous civilisation developed, stimulated by overseas links engendered through the roving habits of the Teutonic peoples. Their religious beliefs are not well-known, but they were probably similar everywhere. The literature of Scandinavia, particularly Iceland, reflects two interesting characteristics of the social and cultural background of pagan Europe and Iceland. Names like Siegfried, Brunhild, and Attila occur repeatedly and confirm the dissemination of legends and traditions common to the early Germanic tribes. Another noteworthy feature is the accuracy with which Scandinavians described the geography of northern Europe. This is no doubt related to explorations by the Norsemen, who discovered Iceland when their ships are said to have blown off course in about AD 860. In the next century, the Vikings pushed west to Britain and Ireland, later travelling down to France and Spain, through the Mediterranean, to North Africa and as far east as Arabia. Across land they reached the Black Sea, they reached the White Sea by sailing north, and at last turned westwards again to find America— long before Columbus.[30]

The Germanic pan-Nordic Aryan union was encouraged through the formation of the *Nordic Gesellschaft* (Nordic Society), which had the personal support of many in Hitler's inner circle, including Reichsleiter Alfred Rosenberg, the leading Nazi racial theorist.[31] The Nordic Society was based in Lübeck had members in Finland, Norway, Denmark, and Iceland. Each year, the Society held a congress at which speeches were given stressing the unity of the Nordic people based on their common race and ancestry, warning them of the threat to the 'white race' coming from a combined Soviet, Jewish, and Masonic threat.

Something of the flavour of these meetings was captured by *Völkischer Beobachter*, the official Nazi newspaper, which reported on a meeting of the Nordic Society attended by both Rosenberg and Darré, a founder of the Ahnenerbe:

> The conclusion of the fifth Reichs-Convention of the Nordic Society in Lübeck gained special importance from a grand speech by Reichsleiter Alfred Rosenberg ... the first speaker, National Librarian Dr Gudmundur Finbogason of Rekjavik, presented a lecture about Icelandic-German cooperation in the field of Nordic Science.
>
> Subsequently State Council Johann E. Mellye, the president of the Norwegian Peasantry Association, spoke concerning the Norwegian

Peasant Movement. Protocol Secretary Carl Patric Ossbahr, Stockholm, then spoke concerning Sweden's North-European mission ... Reichsleiter Alfred Rosenberg heartily greeted the German and Northern country participants and then began to speak ... The Reichsleiter reminded us ... of the grave military and revolutionary events taking place in the Far East, the Near East, and in Spain. If the Scandinavian north and the Baltic states have been spared to some extent from political earthquake tremors, such signifies no more than a temporary reassuring moment for these people and for Europe altogether, and is not to be understood as a sign that these people and these nations themselves are able to escape the larger problems forever. The struggle between Tradition in its various forms and another Breed coming forth for a New Era shall become everyone's destiny.

'Germany stands since 1933', so the Reichsleiter drove home, 'before the question: whether historical survival has come to an end or if the gravity of these events directly constitutes the makings for a renaissance.

After a great struggle within the soul of the German people the entire nation finally agrees about the personality of the Führer ... In only a few years Adolf Hitler's Germany has reaped the harvest of an entire millennium.

This historical fact is big enough to demand attention. It must naturally extend widely beyond political limits because German problems, the first of which are the immediate social-political ones, are also the problems of the remaining peoples. The evolution of the other nations might go more gradually since they are not under an immediate force of destiny; still these problems are also theirs.

We all stand under the same European destiny, and must feel obliged to this common destiny, because finally the existence of the white man depends altogether upon the unity of the European continent! Unanimous must we oppose that terrible attempt by Moscow to destroy the world, that sea of blood into which already many people have dived!' [Strongest applause!][32]

The *Nordic Gesellschaft* appointed the founder of the Institute for Race and Hygiene, Dr Alfred Ploetz, as an honorary member a year before his death.[33] This action seems to have been an attempt to join the scientific and mystic together, as Ploetz was the foremost race theorist. His appointment therefore gave scientific credibility to the Nazi policies of *Lebensraum*, their 'drive to the East', and also helped them justify the extermination of the indigenous populations of those Eastern countries. The Nazis did this by linking the 'scientific racism' of social-Darwinist eugenics to anthropology and mystical Nordic paganism. The Nordic Society was a key supporter of the idea of a new, state-organised, pan-Nordic, pagan religion that was designed to replace Christianity. Himmler's personal interest lay more toward secret esoteric communities rather than organised mass religion; however, he shared the society's interest in the pagan, and it was this that ensured his approval of Ahnenerbe missions to Iceland in search of pagan relics.

In 1936, Otto Rahn led the first Nazi expedition to Iceland, detailing his travels in his 1937 book *Luzifers Hofgesind*.[34] This expedition set off with high hopes, proudly flying a blue Swastika on a white flag—similar to that of the Finnish Air Force at the time. However, the mood changed as the expedition progressed, and Rahn began to send back correspondence to Himmler complaining that the Icelandic people had abandoned traditional crafts such as forging, wood-carving, spinning, weaving, and dyeing, and that they had also forgotten the traditional myths and legends that the Ahnenerbe held so dear. Quite what the Icelandic people made of this quiet German invasion can only be imagined. The idea of Nazis roaming the countryside, making racial measurements, photographing monuments, and significant museum pieces for later 'acquisition', cannot have gone down well. Judging by the actions of the SS elsewhere, they would have considered anything 'Aryan' fair game for removal to Germany for further study of Aryan history.

The justification and rationale for these missions was outlined by Dr Bruno Schweizer in a document addressed to the Ahnenerbe dated 10 March 1938. He proposes a research expedition to Iceland later that year:

Plan for an Iceland Research Journey

From year to year it becomes more difficult to meet living witnesses of Germanic cultural feelings and Germanic soul attitudes on the classical Icelandic soil uninfluenced by the overpowerful grasp of western civilisation. In only a few years has the natural look of the country, which since the Ur-time has remained mostly untouched in stone and meadow, in desert and untamed mountain torrents, revealed its open countenance to man and has fundamentally changed from mountainsides and rock slabs to manicured lawns, nurseries and pasture grounds, almost as far from Reykjavik as the barren coast section, a feat accomplished by the hand of man; the city itself expands with almost American speed as roadways and bridges, power stations and factories emerge and the density of the traffic in Reykjavik corresponds with that of a European city.

... the people forget such ancient techniques as ... the forge- and woodworker's art, the methods of grass- and milk-cultivation, spinning, weaving, dyeing: they forget the old legends and myths that were once narrated on long winter evenings, the songs and the art of the old verses; they lost the belief in a transcendent nature ... Their innate Germanic sobriety becomes cold calculation; pure material interests then step to the foreground; the intelligentsia migrates to the capital and from there swiftly assimilates international tendencies. Genuine Germanic vigour in Iceland is also often transformed into speculation and not at all through real trade; excessive pride of homeland drives them to want to be 150% more modern and progressive than the rest of Europe. This then often permits the present-day Icelander to appear in an unfavourable light and thus cannot usually avoid giving a good German visitor a bad first impression.

These situations determine our research plan.

Every year that we wait quietly means damage to a number of objects, and other objects become ruined for camera and film due to newfangled public buildings in the modern style. For the work in question only the summer is appropriate, that is, the months of June through August. Furthermore, one must reckon that occasionally several rainy days can occur, delaying thereby certain photographic work. The ship connections are such that it is perhaps only possible to go and from the Continent once a week.

All this means a minimum period of from 5–6 weeks for the framework of the trip.

The possible tasks of an Iceland research trip with a cultural knowledge mission are greatly variegated. Therefore it remains for us to select only the most immediate and most realisable. A variety of other tasks ... should be considered as additional assignments.

Thus the recording of human images (race-measurements) and the investigation of museum treasures are considered to be additional assignments.[35]

Schweizer was already an old hand, having travelled to Iceland on three previous trips, but what he proposed this time was on a much larger scale. The expedition was to be all-encompassing, taking in not just the recording of Icelandic folk stories and music, along with traditional dances and a study of architecture, but also the study of ancient farming practices and the collection of soil samples for pollen analysis. He also hoped to discover shrines to the Norse gods Odin and Thor. In order to cover such a range of diverse topics, he was to take no less than seven specialists with him.

The expedition was given the go-ahead by Himmler, whose interest in Icelandic culture was well-known. Unfortunately, news of Schweizer's expedition got out, and his plan to research Icelandic heritage through a study of historic church records made headline news in Scandinavia in February 1939—not least because the records had been lost. Himmler was furious, not so much because of Schweizer's lack of basic historical knowledge (for which he was ridiculed in Iceland), but because he had attracted negative international publicity to the Nazis in general, and the SS in particular. Enraged, Himmler immediately cancelled the trip.

Icelandic cultural history was so important to the SS that, after calming down, Himmler reconsidered. He decided to reinstate the expedition on the strict condition that all future planning was to be conducted in the utmost secrecy. Planning therefore continued, but once again quickly ran into trouble. This time, the difficulty surrounded providing the expedition with sufficient local currency to cover day-to-day expenditure. Iceland's currency, the crown, was in short supply in Germany, and try as they might, Himmler's personal staff were unable to source sufficient money in time for the expedition to take place in 1939, as had been planned. The trip was therefore rescheduled to take place during the summer of the following year. However, before they had chance to depart, events took a further unexpected turn. At the outbreak of the Second World War, the Icelandic government declared its neutrality.

In the early hours of 10 May 1940, British forces launched Operation Fork, the invasion of Iceland.[36] Fearing that the Germans would invade, giving them control over the vital strategic shipping and supply lines across the north Atlantic, Britain carried out a pre-emptive invasion themselves. This effectively halted any plans the Ahnenerbe might have had for further research in Iceland, although, in practice, the planned expedition had been effectively shelved at the outbreak of hostilities.

After taking Reykjavík, one of the first missions for the invading forces was to arrest the German consul, Dr Werner Gerlach.[38] During his residency in Iceland, Gerlach had been assiduously courting the local population, trying to win their support for the Axis powers. He argued that the Icelanders, as Aryans, should join the Nazis in the pursuit of racial purity and domination of inferior peoples. In doing this, he was following orders given to him from the highest level of the German foreign ministry. The longer that Gerlach stayed on the island, and the more locals that he came into contact with, the more his disappointment grew. As a good official, he kept meticulous records, many of which have survived and are stored at the National Archives of Iceland. These 'memos' show that he found 'nothing left of the noble nation and its pride, but servility, lack of decency, toadying and humiliation'.

Reading through his records gives a chilling insight into the nationalistic attitudes of an important Nazi official. He writes:

It's nothing short of arrogance, that these 117,000 souls, one third of them degenerate weaklings, should desire to be an independent state. Add to that that the cultural level is as not high as they say. Icelanders are a great disappointment. The upbringing of children is pathetic. Schools are beyond the pale. The only school considered remotely acceptable is the Catholic school. In the others, the children learn only to argue. Lack of discipline. The director of educational affairs is a communist. The youth has no longer any idea of the sagas or Iceland's history, no sense of family or race.[38]

The stories of Iceland told in Germany had described it as the Aryan homeland, and thus Gerlach expected the country to be a Germanic paradise, a brave 'Aryan nation'. This is not what he found. He wrote home:

We need to reconsider our position on Iceland completely. We need to have scientists do what can be done, but other than that, this grovelling, which meets no kindness, must stop. Modern Icelanders do not deserve us, neither for their temperament, nor their significance, with the exception of a few.

The reason for this was in part due to what he considered laziness:

Earlier than ten in the morning, there is no possibility of waking anyone, and women not earlier than twelve. Men work irregularly. Unemployment. Men do not use their energy for working, but rather to not go to the dogs. Everything, which for us is unimportant, becomes a goal for them (swimming, table tennis). All Germans, that have stayed here long, are not all there, or are apathetic and dumb.[39]

Culturally, they also disappointed him:

Films are almost exclusively American spy films of the lowest sort. The theatre company performs Sherlock Holmes for a whole month. Here, the dramatic subjects from the sagas lie untouched in the gutter ... The theatre company performs a German farce by the Jewish pornographers Arnold and Bach. The police banned the play because of its corrupting influence. Then they stage another premiere in front [of] a full house, where a committee of experts and members of parliament are given access and it's sold out. The press goes mad. Overwhelming enthusiasm and applause ... Musical life is of a very low standard here. There are one or two quite good painters, but there is a lot of pretence and junk. Sculpture—Einar Jónsson is half-mad but very Icelandic. Then there's

Ásmundur Jónsson, who is called a cosmopolitan. Clearly Jewish degenerate art. A book has been published on him.[40]

Nor did he find the Icelanders to be anti-Semitic:

Views on Jews—completely uncomprehending. An Icelandic student was asked by his fellows, when discussing the Jewish matters: 'Would you marry a Jewish woman?' And he answered: 'Yes, why not?' Even the director of the national museum will hand an ashtray to a Negro in a red coat.[41]

The idealised Iceland of German writers such as Dr Bernard Kummel, which described a paradise of 'spiritual treasures', was a far cry from the reality Gerlach encountered. This led him to note: 'One thing is certain and must be clearly stated—there is nothing left of the noble nation and its pride, but servility, lack of decency, toadying and humiliation'.

The British also arrested Bruno Kress, an Ahnenerbe researcher who spent the war in internment on the Isle of Man, from where he was able to correspond with academics in Germany, including Sievers. Kress's *Grammar of Icelandic* was eventually published after the war in 1955, by which time he had returned to live in East Germany, where he later worked for the East German *Staatssicherheit* (Stasi).[42] Kress's obvious connections with the East German secret police suggest that his work for the Ahnenerbe may have involved more than academic research. There is a clear implication that he was operating as an SS spy on Iceland, giving some support to Britain's concerns that had they not invaded the island, the Germans soon would have.

Reading the Runes in Scandinavia

The time is now past when science believed its task was to search for the truth, such as it is. Now the task of science is to proceed with its prophecy, to awaken. Like the morning dawn, it will light a new day.[1]

One might not immediately associate runes, the ancient Nordic alphabet, with plans for world domination, but that is just how they were deployed by the Nazis. When German nationalists, often linked with the Pan-German movement, looked at runes, they saw tangible relics of an ancient legacy, landmarks of Nordic historical accomplishments.

The aim of the Pan-German movement was to unite all the German-speaking peoples of Europe into a single nation. In order to justify these political ideas, a historical precedent was needed that would show that much of what is now Europe was once part of a greater German Reich, even if it was in the remote, prehistoric past. If the Nazis could prove that Europe, from Ukraine to the Atlantic, was at one time part of an ancient Teutonic Empire, then the German people would have historical justification and a rational excuse for taking up arms against their neighbours. To provide the evidence they needed, they looked to the disciplines of archaeology and linguistics; in this, runes played a central role.

Runes are simple alphabetic symbols.[2] They have distinctive shapes based on straight lines, designed to make their carving into wood, stone, or metal as easy as possible. The words formed by the runes were in one of the Nordic languages, and thus belong to the class of purely Teutonic, pre-Christian, and German things prized by the Nazis. The appeal of runes to the Pan-Germans, anti-Semites, and Aryan mystics lay in their clean simplicity and bare prose. To people living with the day-to-day reality of 1930s economic dislocation, the runes offered the comfort of a saner, more honest time, when life's questions were few and the answers clear.

Runes are also tangible relics of an ancient legacy, landmarks of historic accomplishments. Unlike words printed or written on paper, runes were inscribed with deliberation, using iron implements on solid rock; these were serious messages from the past that were intended to survive for centuries. The effort required to carve each word was quite different from the ease with which a pen slides over paper. The implication was that each runic word had been placed after careful consideration, in contrast to the superficial phrases that flowed so easily from the pen.

Significantly, if archaeologists could identify runic inscriptions on stones buried or standing in such faraway places as Minsk or the Pyrenees, then the Nazis could justifiably claim that Minsk and the Pyrenees were once German territories. What is more, if linguists could hear the sounds represented by the runic symbols in place names from other parts of Europe, it would follow that German people had once colonised and settled in those places. This linguistic approach was much more convenient than having to rely on archaeologists actually finding runic petroglyphs *in situ*.

The Pan-Germanist enthusiasm for runes is therefore quite understandable—runes were the physical expression of people of German blood.[3] The swastika is an ancient symbol in many parts of the world; once it had been incorrectly identified as a 'rune', the Nazis were well on their way to proclaiming the entire globe as German territory.

Himmler and his staff in the Ahnenerbe also saw the value of ancient runic writing when looking for evidence of an alternative pagan religion to replace Christianity. The following gives a taste of their thinking:

> Now in conclusion, it remains only to clarify a final symbol. Whence comes this 'Soul' that belongs to the Earth-Mother which, according to the ancient Aryan myth becomes the Heaven-Son, the 'joy of Man'? What is the origin of those' Red Hearts' which later become prominent on images of the Virgin Mary, the Mother of the Son of God Jesus Christ whose festival the Roman Church only decided in the Fourth Century AD to celebrate on 25 December, the ancient Aryan Winter Solstice festival?... We must turn our gaze back to that Ur-time when our Nordic, peasant ancestors of the New Stone Age erected those mighty clan dolmens three to four millennia before Christ: the 'Giants' Beds' of which only a few in north Germany have survived the irreverent vandalism and brutal profiteering of the past two centuries.[4]

At first glance, this reads similarly to many New Age or pagan-influenced books set alongside healing crystals and polished-stone talismans in high-street shops. However, as we read on, the tone changes, reminding us of the Nazis' particular take on mythology and the occult:

Long ago our ancestor, the noble Nordic wife and mother, guardian of her family and of the meaning of the Homeland, was sacred; she to whom one could go, Seeress and Race-Mother, in order to know what was fit and proper. 'We bow in reverence before the image of the German mother,' said our Reichsführer Heinrich Himmler on the last Reich's Peasantry Day in Goslar. And so a German doctor once recognised the most-sacred images of our ancestral legacy, Earth Mother and Race-Mother, the miracle of the love of the Nordic Mother-Soul: that the sacred and eternal Homeland is renewed from her womb, embracing life, as she preserves and protects unsullied the most sacred spiritual and mental values of Family and Race.

> *And Frigga, Isis, Mary are merely names,*
> *Transient veils of the hallowed womb.*

> *The stars, suns and men's souls ...*
> *No mortal lips can praise your Majesty enough.*
> *O incline, Mother, your divine countenance*
> *And guide us to our sweet home in the Eternal Light.*
> *We but wish to stand in faithful watch on the soul*
> *Of the Homeland, on the Living Tree of our Race,*
> *And by its Führer.*[5]

In this, and other texts like it, the Catholic Church was presented as a corrupt institution poisoned by the Jewish Satan, Jehovah. The Church had lost the purity of the Aryan version of the ancient diety, Krist. Himmler, like many other prominent Nazis, had begun casting about privately for a system of spiritual beliefs that could eventually take the place of Catholicism and Protestantism in the Reich.[6] He found Christian doctrine immensely troublesome. Its origins were traced to the deserts of the Middle East rather than to the forests of northern Europe. It presented the tribes of Israel, not the tribe of Germania, as the chosen people. It described Christ as a Jew. It advocated charity, compassion for the weak, the brotherhood of men, and the equality of all in the eyes of God. Himmler found all this abhorrent. He had attended mass faithfully from childhood until his early twenties, but he had lost his faith at about the same time that he joined the NSDAP.[7] Since then, he had openly avowed Nazism as his new creed. 'Our business,' he explained to the readers of the party newspaper *Völkischer Beobachter*, 'is to spread the knowledge of race in the life of our *Völk* and impress it upon the hearts and heads of all, down to the very youngest, as our German gospel.' [8]

Nazism needed a state religion with a god, or perhaps several gods, as well as suitable rituals to take the place of mass and other Christian services. Himmler saw no better place to look for replacement gods and rituals than in the history of Germany's ancestors, the Germanic tribes and their Aryan forebears. He believed that the old pagan gods would be capable of weaning SS men from their Christian faiths. Indeed, as he later confided to his personal physician, he intended to make every *SS-Mann* drop his traditional church affiliation. 'After the war,' he said, 'the old Germanic gods will be restored.'[9]

The trouble was that scholars knew very little about these old gods. Germany's tribes had left few written records of their sacred beliefs and practices before they converted to Christianity, and their Roman neighbours, who possessed a much earlier written tradition, took scant interest in the old Germanic religion. To recover its beliefs, Himmler realised that he needed to find new sources of information. The key to this untapped ancient wisdom was to be the scholar Herman Wirth, who claimed to have discovered the ancient sacred texts of the Nordic race and intended to decipher them through science.

Herman Wirth

Herman Wirth (1885–1981) was an eccentric Dutch-German spendthrift with immense reserves of personal charm. His background was remarkably similar to that of Himmler; his father had also been a schoolteacher and university lecturer who took great pride in his Teutonic ancestry, drumming a love of German culture, history, and language into his son.[10] Wirth applied these ideas to his doctoral research, which lamented the disappearance of traditional folk songs in the northern Netherlands. He believed these songs were portals into the very soul of the ancient Nordic race.[11] The extreme German nationalism that permeated Wirth's life ensured that he naturally gravitated towards Nazi politics.

Like many others, Wirth was disillusioned by the defeat of the First World War. Taking his cue from the historian Oswald Spengler, he concluded in the early 1920s that all Western civilisation was teetering on the brink of collapse. The only hope for the future, as he saw it, lay in recovering the truths of the past. It was at this time, while travelling through the northern Dutch province of Friesland, that he saw something that would change his life. On the gables of many old, neatly painted Frisian farmhouses, inhabitants displayed small wooden folk sculptures consisting of an assortment of carved shapes—curlicues, crescents, crosses, shamrocks, swan necks, stars, hearts, diamonds, and crowns.[12]

To most people, they were little more than folk art, but Wirth was looking with enthusiasm for hidden, secret meanings in the world around him. In these shapes, he thought he saw remnants of an ancient Nordic civilisation.

He concluded that the farmers' wooden carvings of hearts and diamonds and crowns were symbols from an ancient Aryan system of writing, a type of northern hieroglyphs.[13] Their significance, he concluded, had been all but lost to time. Not even the folk artists of the Frisian countryside realised what their carvings truly meant. More bizarrely still, he inferred that the different shapes were remnants of the earliest writing system in the world and therefore the mother of all scripts, from the Egyptian hieroglyphs to the Phoenician alphabet.[14]

These ideas flouted Western science and scholarship. For more than a century, linguists had examined ancient stone inscriptions from around the world, deciphering scripts and delving into the origins of writing. By the 1930s, they had made substantial progress tracing the earliest appearance of the written word to one of two regions in the world—Ancient Egypt or Mesopotamia. In 1938, the editors of *Encyclopaedia Britannica* noted the following of the inscriptions in both places:

> [they went back to] an extremely early date; it is at present uncertain which is the earlier, but both show before 3500 BC and possibly much earlier, a complete organised system of writing which implies many centuries of developments behind it.[15]

By comparison, the inhabitants of northern Europe were late bloomers when it came to writing. They had developed letters for a system of writing known today as 'runes'. The oldest rune alphabet consisted of twenty-four letters, and is known as *Futhark*. However, runic script evolved considerably over time and place in Europe. Anglo-Saxon rune-masters, for example, added new letters, bringing the total to over thirty, while Scandinavian writers reduced the number to just sixteen. Runes were a type of script that blended letters of the Roman alphabet with several new inventions, and most experts in the 1930s agreed that the earliest runes had appeared around AD 250.[16] None of this, however, sat very well with Wirth and other nationalist scholars. If Nordic men and women were truly superior to all others, then it stood to reason that they had founded the world's first civilisation in their ancient boreal homeland. It also stood to reason that they had invented the art of writing there. Since Nordic men and women were, in Wirth's opinion, the world's 'intellectual sourdough starter', they had to have carried their writing system with them on their great migrations to Africa and Asia, thereby passing on the idea of writing to others, who devised cuneiform scripts, hieroglyphs, and the alphabet.[17]

Researchers had failed, however, to detect any proof of a primeval Nordic civilisation in the north, one predating ancient Egypt and Mesopotamia. They had uncovered no ancient cities, no pyramids, and no ziggurats of the north. 'What are the facts?' asked prominent British scientist Julian Huxley in his famous book *We Europeans* in 1935:

> The fundamental discoveries on which civilisation is built are the art of writing, agriculture, the wheel and building in stone. All these appear to have originated in the near East, among peoples who by no stretch of imagination could be called Nordic.[18]

In the absence of evidence, Wirth let his imagination run loose. He proposed that the Nordic, Aryan race had evolved in an arctic homeland 2 million years ago, and then founded a civilisation on the lost continent of Atlantis in the North Atlantic.[19] He even argued, without any particular evidence, that strong Nordic women who possessed 'all seeing capabilities' had ruled this empire as a matriarchy for thousands of years, until a great cataclysm drowned their lands, sending survivors fleeing to northern Europe and North America.[20]

Wirth realised that other scholars would be hard to persuade, given that his thesis challenged the entire foundations of world history. He needed evidence to anchor his ideas in fact. To pursue the matter, he moved his young family—his wife, Margarethe, and his three children—to Marburg, which had a good library and a university willing to give him a teaching position. In 1925, he took out a membership in the NSDAP and began collecting a coterie of attentive young assistants—artistic, idealistic young men fascinated by Wirth's learned patter, his boundless enthusiasm, his knowledge of the ancient world, and his quest to revive ancient Nordic religion and culture. Wirth later brought some of these young acolytes with him into the Ahnenerbe, including Wolfram Sievers, Otto Plassmann, and Otto Huth. They modelled themselves after him, dressing in short trousers, as he often did, and addressed him affectionately as 'Dear Father' and Margarethe as 'Dear Mother'.[21] He frequently invited his young disciples to stay for dinner, and it was not unusual for fifteen people to crowd around the family table.[22]

In private, Wirth rifled through the scientific literature, determined to prove that the Nordic race had evolved in the Arctic. He also pored over Plato's legend of Atlantis. He believed it to be an accurate description of the fate of his imagined Nordic empire in the North Atlantic, and he set about trying to prove this theory.[23] All his talk of Atlantis and a lost Nordic civilisation stirred a great deal of public interest. In the northern city of Bremen, Ludwig Roselius, the wealthy inventor of decaffeinated coffee, drew up plans for a stunning new building in honour of Wirth.[24] The edifice, dubbed '*Haus Atlantis*', would take visitors on a metaphorical journey of rebirth, from the dark-blue depths of the ocean, where Atlantis languished, to the soft glow of the Sky Hall on the top floor. As part of the original design, Roselius created a lecture hall and exhibition space for Wirth.[25] He also displayed his own impressive collection of ancient artefacts, bronze swords, golden vessels, bronze musical instruments, fine jewellery, and casts of ancient rune stones.[26]

With the backing of such influential men, Wirth was propelled onto the national stage, much to the horror of many serious German scholars. His first major book was released in 1929; it was a huge, rambling, inchoate study of the origins of the Nordic race and their later migrations, all heavily larded with invented jargon. The publication aroused intense criticism. Gero von Merhart, a prominent German prehistorian, observed:

> Only the feeling that the author has been taken by an almost holy insanity and the fact that he inspected a considerable mass of literature with unusual eagerness and diligence to support his delusions, which he considers science, restrain me from responding to this book … with rudeness.[27]

Others were less charitable. Taking firm aim at Wirth's risible powers of reasoning, another critic noted that the Dutch scholar was 'unable to distinguish between probable, certain, possible and impossible'.[28]

Outside Germany, discerning archaeologists were quick to pick up the extremist political tenor in Wirth's work. In Sweden, for example, archaeologist Nils Åberg published a warning about Wirth after attending one of his public performances in Germany. Wirth, he wrote, seemed harmless enough, but his visions of the murky past were intended to seduce unwitting Germans into dangerous dreams of racial superiority and national aggrandisement—dreams that could fan the flames of war in Europe. As such, his lectures were a thinly disguised call to action in which Wirth 'the magician, the Hitler of German scientists, captures his public'.[29]

This was the man that Himmler had placed in charge of the Ahnenerbe in 1935 and made SS-Hauptsturmführer in RuSHA. This was the man who set about mounting, with the blessing and financing of the SS, the brain trust's first major expedition abroad. Wirth's destination was the remote granite hills of Bohuslän, in southwestern Sweden. Along the slopes of these hills lay tens of thousands of ancient engravings. Wirth believed these were the sacred texts of the ancient Nordic race.

Bohuslän, Sweden

The story of the expedition began on the evening of 19 February 1936, when Herman Wirth gathered with a group of friends and like-minded souls to show them a film about his recent visit to Bohuslän, Sweden.[30] He waxed lyrical about the famous rock art, explaining his interpretation of these ancient markings as the glyphs of an ancient writing system. His key point was that they were evidence for the world's oldest writing system, invented more than 12,000 years ago by Nordic scribes inhabiting a lost North Atlantic homeland, predating those of the ancient Mesopotamian civilisations.

Wirth had filmed the carvings during an exploratory trip to Bohuslän. For nearly a month in the autumn of 1935, he and a fellow SS officer, Wilhelm Kottenrodt, had bumped and scraped along the roads of Bohuslän, driving a shiny new Adlerwagen purchased by the Ahnenerbe.[31] They had roamed the countryside, sliding down ridges and trekking through shady forests of oak and elm, searching out the largest and most accessible rock-carving sites. Kottenrodt, who had trained as a sculptor, had assisted Wirth in making plaster casts of selected engravings, the beginning of what Wirth grandly hoped would become the world's most important collection of primeval Nordic symbols and the nucleus of future museum exhibits on the superiority of the Nordic race.[32]

The autumn trip to Bohuslän had merely wetted Wirth's appetite. The scholar desperately wanted to return to Sweden this time at the head of a major Ahnenerbe expedition. He was keen to broaden his studies and put more men to work on the arduous task of collecting casts. For this, he needed the approval and financial assistance of the superintendent of the Ahnenerbe, Himmler.

Wirth's presentation captured the imagination of Himmler, the most influential of the select audience. He considered the potential benefits to the SS and his own personal ambitions. He had been disappointed that Hitler had taken little interest in the Ahnenerbe.[33] In fact, the Führer continued to complain about Himmler's passionate enthusiasm for northern European prehistory. He complained to Albert Speer:

> Why do we call the whole world's attention to the fact that we have no past? It's bad enough that the Romans were erecting great buildings when our forefathers were still living in mud huts, now Himmler is starting to dig up these villages of mud huts and enthusing over every potsherd and stone axe he finds.[34]

Although he admired Hitler as a genius, Himmler believed that on the matter of the Germanic past, the Nazi leader had yet to see the light.

Himmler sought new ways of changing Hitler's mind, and it must have occurred to him that a professional film production of Wirth announcing his discovery of the world's earliest writing system in Scandinavia might succeed where Himmler's other arguments had failed to spark Hitler's imagination.[35] Such a film would also be an invaluable weapon in the SS educational offensive, greatly bolstering Nazi claims of Aryan superiority. The casts would become important assets in themselves. The Ahnenerbe could put them on public exhibit, and Himmler could use them himself as props in the speeches he gave to senior SS officers.[36] He could also present copies as gifts to NSDAP bosses. The previous autumn, Wirth had made a cast of an ancient swastika, a symbol long associated with the Scandinavian god of thunder, Thor, in Bohuslän.[37, 38]

Himmler therefore gave the go-ahead for a larger return expedition to the region of Bohuslän, in southwestern Sweden. This was to be the first official expedition financed by the Ahnenerbe, and Himmler was keen that it should be a success. Wirth, although valued as an intellectual, had proved himself to be spendthrift, and earlier he had had to be bailed out by Himmler in order to avoid public embarrassment.[39, 40, 41, 42]

The expedition departed on a three-month long journey on 4 August 1936. The team would have a number of goals. It would study and make casts of ancient rock-art symbols in Sweden and along the western coast of Norway, from Stavanger to Trondheim.[43] It would also stop *en route* at local museums to photograph and make casts of old farm implements and household goods decorated with old patterns and designs.

The first port of call was the German island of Rügen. From there, they continued to Backa, whose significance lay in it being the first recorded rock-art site in Sweden. Amongst the rock carvings of warriors, animals, and ships were also lines and circles; it was these that Wirth believed formed a prehistoric alphabet. Looking at the markings carved into the rock, Wirth's imagination allowed him to read far more into the symbols than a more objective scientist would allow. Thus a simple marking, a circle bisected by a vertical line, was to Wirth the representation of a year, and a man standing with raised arms represented 'the Son of God'.

Establishing a pattern to be repeated throughout the expedition, the team proceeded to prepare materials and then make casts of what Wirth deemed the most important carvings. Once dry, the heavy plaster casts were manhandled back to camp, where they were carefully packed and shipped back to Germany. Satisfied with their work at Backa, the team set out for Bohuslän, eventually trekking across Sweden to the island of Lauvøylaudet, Norway.

As they travelled, Wirth developed his interpretation of the meaning of the carvings in line with the notion that Norway had been the centre of a rich Aryan culture. According to him, the carving of a standing man with raised hands was to be interpreted as 'the son of God'. That of a circle crossed by a vertical line was to be understood as the symbol for a year. These, along with other divinations, owe more to his imagination than scientific deduction.

In 1936, Bohuslän was a rugged land of small farms and fishing villages, isolated from the rest of Sweden by poor roads. Its residents were a stubborn, self-reliant people who possessed little that seemed to interest the outside world. Even in its poverty, Bohuslän possessed one thing in abundance—an astonishing wealth of primeval rock carvings. Northern Bohuslän counted more than 5,000 rock-art panels that teemed with images of the ancient world: ships, warriors, ploughmen, horsemen, acrobats, bulls, snakes, ducks, cranes, fish, trees, carts, axes, spears, battles, hunts, and rituals.[44] Their makers had engraved them in hard granite by pecking or grinding the rock surface to create furrowed lines. Some of their work was remarkably beautiful, expressive, and mysterious; other figures were far rougher and cruder. However, nearly all dated to the Bronze Age, the era when bronze came into vogue as a material for weapons, tools, decorations, and jewellery. In southwestern Sweden, the Bronze Age began in approximately 1800 BC and ended 1,300 years later.[45] Swedish archaeologists have managed to date the rock carvings of Bohuslän by a variety of painstaking methods. They have compared certain distinctive objects portrayed in the engravings, such as spectacle broaches, with real examples found in graves that can be accurately dated. They have also studied superimposed images on the rocks to determine which styles are the oldest, and have examined changes in shorelines for additional dating clues.[46]

The carvings were a point of pride among the farming and fishing families of Bohuslän. The inhabitants of Bohuslän had long been intimately familiar with the carvings, but they first took a serious interest in them during the nineteenth and early twentieth century, when scholars from the outside began to study these remarkable works of ancient art.[47] For nearly 200 years, Scandinavian scholars who studied Bronze Age art had beaten a path to the region, scrambling over hills and across fields to record the art and decipher its meaning. They had drawn careful sketches of the most important panels and published them in fine illustrated books, proving Bohuslän to be one of the world's great rock-art repositories.[48] No other part of northern Europe could touch it in terms of the sheer number of carvings or the immense range of motifs.[49]

Herman Wirth, who was captivated by ancient symbols wherever they might be found, read about the carvings of Bohuslän with enormous fascination. In his office on Brüderstrasse, he pored over the enigmatic shapes and furrows of the illustrations. He was astonished and extremely excited; he felt certain that he was looking at the script of an ancient Nordic holy text. He got down to work, hammering out plans for the expedition with Sievers. Working together, they estimated that the Scandinavian expedition would take two months and require a team of six. Wirth wanted to bring Kottenrodt, the SS sculptor who had accompanied him to Bohuslän the previous year. He also intended to recruit four other men for the expedition—two technical assistants to help make and transport the casts, a driver who could double as a photographer, and an experienced cameraman to shoot the SS documentary on the work in addition to two cultural films for the Ahnenerbe.[50]

Wirth drew up lists of necessary expedition gear, from workmen's clothing and rain boots to tents, steel-pipe beds, sleeping bags, folding chairs and gas stoves. With the assistance of Bruno Galke, one of Himmler's most trusted aides, Sievers scrupulously budgeted the expedition costs down to the last pfennig, pegging the final tab at 12,590.76 RM, the equivalent of $65,000.[51, 52]

By late July, Sievers had succeeded in solving nearly all the most pressing organisational problems. He had located a suitable cameraman for the expedition—thirty-three-year-old Helmut Bousset, an SS-Untersturmführer.[53] He had obtained an export visa to ship more than 20 tons of plaster of Paris to Scandinavia and arranged for a small convoy of vehicles for the trip—most notably an Opel-Blitz truck from the SS.[54, 55] He had laid hands on the necessary foreign currency, which was no easy matter as Germany had quietly focused its economy on the rearmament of the Wehrmacht and dispensed with many of the exports that had once brought in foreign exchange.

However, Wirth and his team still lacked something essential to the expedition—an official archaeological permit from Stockholm. Without this crucial piece of paper, they would be unable to conduct any research or make any casts of the Swedish rock art. Meanwhile, antiquities officials in Stockholm were in no hurry to issue the permit; they were furious with Wirth.[56] The previous summer, he had physically damaged some of the ancient engravings and neglected to clean others when he was done with them. At one site, an assistant he hired left several plaster casts still attached to the rock. This bizarre oversight had given grave offence.

Wirth swiftly penned a letter of apology, well aware that the entire expedition depended on making prompt amends.[57] Nevertheless, the Swedish officials dragged their heels on the question of the permit. Finally, on 29 July, halfway through the summer field season, they notified Wirth that they would issue a permit, but only for the work he wanted to do in northern Bohuslän. They did not want him ruining sites in lesser-known areas that had barely been recorded. Wirth had little choice but to accept their decision, but he stubbornly held out hope that he could still persuade the Swedish officials to relent.

Just before the team departed, Sievers received a list of detailed expedition rules drawn up by Himmler himself.[58] All participants, he instructed, were to conduct themselves in a comradely manner and leave behind all personal disagreements. Moreover, the expedition was to stay focused on the work at hand; its members were not to talk politics to outsiders or make any public display of the swastika, nor were they allowed to drink or smoke during working hours. They were to spend expedition funds sparingly. So insistent was Himmler on this last point that he refused to give Wirth, the expedition leader, access to the team's funds. Instead, he put another team member in charge of both the account books and cashbox.

The Ahnenerbe's first major expedition was to be all business. Germany's Reichsführer-SS wanted no embarrassing mistakes, no troublesome rows, and no international incidents. Some three weeks later, on a soft, green August morning, Wirth clambered up a gentle ridge of exposed granite known as Backa, not far from the Swedish village of Brastad, in northern Bohuslän. On the slope below, his team started to unload the dusty trucks, carrying bags of plaster of Paris, wooden planks, water buckets, and burlap to the base of the ridge. Settling down their loads, they stopped to watch as Wirth climbed up and down the rock, scouring its surface for ancient markings. In the early morning light, deep shadows accentuated the lines of the engravings; it was one of the best times of the day to search for weathered furrows.

Wirth went about his work at a whirlwind pace, bursting with energy and exuberance. The previous summer, at a training camp for Dutch youths, a newspaper reporter had observed him in action and marvelled at his vitality:

> No effort was too much for him. During those days, he was busy from nice in the morning until one at night. He didn't take any time for a meal. This man has the holy fire of a missionary in him.[59]

After the first two weeks of the expedition, Wirth and his team had already covered an impressive amount of ground. Departing on 4 August, just three days after the spectacular opening of Berlin's Olympic Games, the convoy had headed north to the Baltic coast and boarded a ferry for Rügen, a rugged island of white chalk cliffs and dark forests much-loved by German holidaymakers. Over the next two days they cast an inscribed standing stone; they then boarded a fishing surveillance cutter bound for the remote Danish island of Bornholm, some 60 miles to the west. Wirth believed that primordial Nordic migrants had chosen Bornholm as a stepping-stone on their journey south to Germany, and he was keen to find evidence of their passing. Under Wirth's direction, the team cast carvings at two sites on the island. Then they packed up and pressed on to Sweden. Lodged with friends in the village of Brodalen, Wirth was anxious to resume work at the famous site of Backa.

The scent of juniper rose in the morning air as Wirth bent down over the rock. Along one side of the outcrop, water trickled down in a thin, dark ribbon, slicking the stone. Between clumps of heather and patches of pale-green lichen, dozens of engraved figures jostled across the rocks. A 5-foot-tall warrior, clearly a man of power, brandished a large, erect penis and waved a giant battle-axe in his hand—in victory or menace, it was difficult to say. Off to one side, a tribe of lesser figures looked on. On the rock above, a fleet of sleek wooden ships rode invisible waves.

Backa was the first rock-art site in Sweden to be recorded by scholars. In 1627 a Norwegian university lecturer, Peder Alvsøn, passed through Bohuslän in a carriage and heard word of Backa's carvings. The ancient images so intrigued him that he made a freehand painting of some of the most obvious figures. It was a fine piece of early scientific illustration, but Alvsøn seems to have been a prudish man. He bowdlerised the largest and most obvious figure at the site. In place of the large man in proud tumescence, he modestly painted a large woman with small breasts.

Alvsøn's liberty was eventually corrected by more meticulous illustrators in the nineteenth century. It was their work that stirred the first real scientific interest. What, wondered researchers in Stockholm, had the Bronze Age artists intended to portray? Why had they gone to so much trouble to engrave these figures in granite? In 1927, Oscar Almgren published a landmark book on the subject entitled *Rock Carvings and Cult Practices*. Inside, the Swedish researcher proposed two main points; firstly, he suggested that the strange jostle of figures on the Bohuslän rocks was the work of an ancient fertility cult that prayed for healthy children and abundant harvests, among other things.[60] Secondly, Almgren suggested that the rock-art panels often represented scenes of ancient sacrifices and fertility processions, in which people carried or pulled their great wooden ships.

Wirth had read and apparently admired Almgren's work, but he was temperamentally incapable of following in anyone else's footsteps.[61] What riveted his attention at Backa and at other sites in Sweden was not the scenes of human beings dragging or carrying boats, but the far more mysterious engravings of circles and lines, the ancient holy script of his imagination.[62] He believed that the key to reading this script lay in the far northern origins of the Nordic race. In Arctic lands that were shrouded in darkness for months each winter, Nordic men and women had felt a deep, abiding affinity for the sun, or so Wirth supposed. The movements of the sun across the horizon had eventually given rise to the awareness of a god, and the Nordic race had founded a great cult to worship this heavenly divinity. To mark the dates of their religious festivities and other events in the solar year, they had devised ideograms, Wirth believed, that evolved into a writing system.[63]

At Backa, Wirth scoured the rock for the symbols he believed he could read. He saw carved circles, disks, and wheels as ideograms for the sun and the annual cycle of life. He interpreted the figure of a man standing with raised arms as a symbol for a primeval divinity he called the Son of God, predating Christianity by thousands of years.[64] He believed the image of two circles linked by a vertical line represented the rebirth of life at the winter solstice, while a circle bisected by a vertical line indicated a year.[65] So it went; Wirth's research had long ago abandoned reality and solid ground. It was soaring in a dense, impenetrable fog, no longer containing even the slightest fraction of science.

Wirth insisted that his team cast the panels he found most important.[66] Whenever he found something suitable, he outlined its furrows in chalk, and Bousset, the team cameraman, filmed the engraving. An assistant then hammered together a wooden frame to be fitted down upon the rock. With wads of damp clay, team members sealed gaps between the bottom of the frame and the uneven rock surface and brushed a thin layer of soapy lubricant onto the engraving. They hauled heavy buckets of plaster of Paris up the slopes and tipped the contents into the frames, then adding a layer of burlap and iron bars for strength.[67] When the cast finally hardened, the team began the tricky work of prying it loose. They levered it upward with iron bars and mallets, praying that they would not break either the cast or the granite below.

However, that was the easy part. A sweaty trek followed. Many of the casts were nearly 10 feet long and weighed several hundred pounds. They were heavy and awkward to convey on trails over broken ground and through gnarly forests.[68] In a letter to Swedish officials, Wirth explained:

> The rock art does not just lie off the side of the road, but is often in hard to reach areas, where the work material (plaster of Paris, wood, iron, water etc.) had to be taken over quite a distance in a small cart or slid [on the ground] or carried on the back, and the plates had to be transported back with great difficulty.[69]

Later, at camp, team members packed the casts in sturdy handmade crates and hauled them by car to the nearest port, where they could be shipped to Gothenburg, and from there to Germany. It was not an expedition for shirkers.

Some local residents watched the goings-on with fascination, and two young men even went so far as to join Wirth's team as assistants, but others adopted a more jaundiced view. The region was well-known for its socialist sympathies, and most farmers and fishermen did not have much use for Nazis.[70] They were rather dismayed to see flocks of German tourists turning up in increasing numbers to visit the rock carvings in the area. One newspaper rather pointedly stated:

> This is mainly due to a German professor declaring in Munkedal that he never felt more reverent than when standing in front of a rock carving. He must never have sat in front of the Führer then, for that is surely the greatest happiness for a Nazi.[71]

Wirth was well-aware of the region's politics. He was pleasant and charming to the farmers and tried his best not to make enemies. From Brodalen, he and his team headed north up the Bohuslän coast. Pitching camp wherever they could, they toiled on sites from Askum to Tanum, collecting truckloads of casts. When they were done, they crossed the border into neighbouring Østfold County in Norway, another region blessed with rock carvings. Wirth seemed tireless. In a final report, he wrote:

> As soon as work got under way at a site, I had to immediately arrange things for the next. In between material had to be brought and transported, sleeping quarters had to be found, local offices had to be dealt with and casts had to be done, which I did in work groups...[72]

By the first week of September, the team had completed fifty-five massive casts. Wirth was in fine fettle. He believed that he and his team were doing something the Swedes could not be bothered with, making replicas of the engravings before quarrymen destroyed them. He couldn't resist crowing about this in a report from the field to Himmler. He boasted:

> This will be a collection that has no equal and never will ... whoever wants to study the Nordic race in relation to the rock art will have to come to Germany, to the '*Deutsches Ahnenerbe*', because it is only there that the main monuments will be collected together. No one in Sweden could see them for themselves because they are strewn far and wide. Soon the *Deutsches Ahnenerbe* will have rock carvings that don't exist anymore in Scandinavia because they are being destroyed.[73]

Wirth was greatly exaggerating the situation. Swedish officials guarded the rock art vigilantly, well aware of their responsibilities to protect a national treasure. Still, the German scholar knew he had to put the best possible face on his research for Himmler. On 5 September, midway through the expedition, Wirth journeyed to Oslo to meet with Norwegian officials. He was eager to obtain advice and assistance for the next leg of the trip. He planned to lead the team northward, along the western coast of Norway, in order to cast several small, scattered rock-art sites, with one located just short of the Arctic Circle. He also planned to engage in some fundraising in Oslo, although he did not mention this in his field report to Himmler. Specifically, he intended to sell replicas of the team's Norwegian casts to the antiquaries museum at the University of Oslo, a transaction that would undermine his claims about the exclusive nature of the collection he was compiling. In the museum offices, he met one of Europe's most respected archaeologists, Anton Brøgger.

At fifty-two, Brøgger was at the peak of his career. A generous, urbane man who was fond of the theatre and music, Brøgger was a passionate advocate of Norwegian culture.[74] He had played a leading role in the excavations of the Oseberg grave mound, the richest Viking burial site ever found, and had written extensively about its many beautiful treasures. He had edited a popular journal, *Oldtilden* (*Ancient Times*), and inspired a generation of archaeology students in his lectures at the University of Oslo. He had also helped to host meetings of the International Archaeological Congress, which had recently brought 500 archaeologists from around the world to Oslo.[75]

Brøgger knew a great deal about German attitudes towards prehistory. He had watched with alarm the way in which the NSDAP had twisted and distorted the past to advance its political agenda. A few months later, he wrote:

> These days, prehistory and archaeology have become popular sciences across the entire world. Excavations, particularly those which take place on a grand scale, speak immediately and often dramatically to a nation's emotions and passions. Fantasy is set in motion ... Therefore, one must be cautious. These days, archaeological artefacts and results have an important meaning for nations. They are part of a people, a nation's spiritual capital. However, they should not be misused for nationalistic propaganda.[76]

Few were as guilty of misusing science and scholarship for political ends as Wirth, but Brøgger did not seem to know this, and Wirth, who was under strict orders from Himmler to avoid political discussions with outsiders, likely refrained from making his own position clear. By the end of the meeting, the two men had struck a deal. In exchange for what he hoped would be 1,000 crowns, he agreed to provide the University of Oslo with a selection of casts of Norwegian rock art for its own research collections.[77]

Satisfied, Wirth went back to work, leading his team up the west coast of Norway. They journeyed along the winding highway north of Trondheim, past steep fjords and rugged cliffs, and stopped to make twelve casts of rock art at Bardal and another two at Østre Tessem.[78] It was spectacularly beautiful country, but the nights were growing increasingly cold and they could no longer camp out, so Wirth hunted each evening for whatever lodging he could find. In the darkness, after a long day of driving or casting, he found a farmer to give them shelter in a hayloft or looked for rooms in a local youth hostel.

At Mosjøen, a small fishing village just 500 miles south of the Arctic Circle, Wirth and two assistants boarded a small boat bound for Rødøya.[79] The tiny island boasted a famous engraving of a very rare subject; it portrayed a human figure on skis, and was thought to date back 4,000 years.[80] Wirth was keen to cast it for the Ahnenerbe collection, so on a stormy day in mid-September, he and his team put out into the cold coastal waters. Rain and heavy wind lashed at the windows, and spray from the fierce grey waves drenched the deck as they crossed to Rødøya, but Wirth was not about to let the weather dampen his spirits.

He was closer than he had ever been to the Arctic, the imaginary birthplace of the Nordic race he loved.

Finland:
In the 'Land of Heroes'

*A magnificent blond nation is born in the North. Its overwhelming
fertility spreads in waves to the South. Each migration is a conquest,
each conquest enriches the customs and civilisation of the conquered.*[1]

While Wirth was exploring Sweden and Norway, collecting casts of rock
carvings, a second Ahnenerbe-financed expedition was underway in
Finland. This second expedition was led by a young Finnish scholar, Yrjö
von Grönhagen, who had gone in search of the sources of the Finnish
national epic *The Kalevala*, meaning '*The Land of Heroes*'.[2] The expedition
had come about as the result of an article about *The Kalevala* that
published in a Frankfurt newspaper in 1935, which Himmler happened
to read. Himmler believed that the old legends and myths of Europe were
full of clues to the prehistoric religion and technology of the Aryans,
and he firmly believed that the old songs of Karelia, a remote wilderness
straddling the Russian-Finnish border, contained valuable leads. They
merely needed to be studied and deciphered. Keen to rediscover the lost
Aryan wisdom—and, if possible, put it to use in the Reich—he contacted
Grönhagen, who quickly agreed to meet Himmler.

Yrjö von Grönhagen, a handsome young Finnish nobleman, was a
romantic idealist who roamed eastern Finland to record and film ancient
magical rites. He believed they were religious rituals handed down through
the centuries from the Aryans. He was born on 3 October 1911 in St
Petersburg, during a time when Finland was a grand duchy of the Russian
Empire. His mother, Zine von Holtzmann, was a doctor of jurisprudence
who traced her ancestry to Finnish and Russian nobility.[3] His father,
Karl von Grönhagen, was a Finnish officer and journalist whose family
origins extended back to the Swedish, German, and Dutch aristocracy.
Grönhagen grew up during a turbulent period in Finnish history.

When the Russian Revolution began in 1917, Finnish patriots seized the moment and declared Finland's independence, unleashing bitter political rivalries. A bloody civil war followed, pitting Finnish communists and socialists against conservatives in the Finnish upper and middle classes. Grönhagen's family sided firmly with the conservatives. His older half-brother fought as an officer for the White forces in Russia and was captured and executed in Moscow in 1920. All this made a lasting impression on Grönhagen. He grew up loathing communism and despising the Soviet Union.[4]

By his late teens, Grönhagen was a handsome lad of 5 feet 7 inches, with delicate, even features, a pair of luminous eyes, a mop of thick, dark hair, and a ready grin. He possessed fine manners and an aristocratic air. He dreamed of conducting anthropological fieldwork in India, but one of his professors suggested that Europe would be a better place for such research. Grönhagen heeded the advice.[5]

In the spring of 1935, he hatched a plan to travel by foot from Paris to Helsinki, studying 'practical sociology' on the road.[6] He bought a journal so that people he encountered could write something they fancied in it— an old proverb, perhaps, or a poem. He departed on 27 June, crossing eastern France and trekking across the rolling hills and valleys of Belgium. He entered the Third Reich on 1 August and immediately felt at home.[7] He had learned German as a child and was favourably disposed toward the Nazi government, which seemed to loathe communism and Bolsheviks almost as much as he did. The first person to sign his journal in Germany was a leader of a Hitler Youth group.

Soon afterwards, Grönhagen met the editor of the *Frankfurter Volksblatt* newspaper, who agreed to publish his article on *The Kalevala*.[8] *The Kalevala* consists of 23,795 verses divided into fifty *runot* (songs) and was the work of a nineteenth-century country doctor, Elias Lönnrot, who believed that the old songs of Karelia were actually fragments of a lost northern epic that dated back thousands of years.[9] He set about collecting these songs, journeying across Karelia by boat and sled, writing down the words and knitting them together with snatches of his own writing to form a flowing narrative. He first published this text in February 1835. *The Kalevala* played an instrumental role in the development of the Finnish national identity, which ultimately led to Finland's independence from Russia in 1917.

While a few Finnish intellectuals complained about the liberties that Lonnrot had taken, most Finns loved *The Kalevala*. They particularly adored the hero of this boreal epic, a great sorcerer named Wäinämöninen. At least one of these Finnish critics set aside his objections, however, after learning that the famous German linguist and story collector

Jacob Grimm praised *The Kalevala* highly, ranking it as highly as the Greek myths.[10] In *The Kalevala*, Wäinämöninen and his assistant magically transform a treeless northern land into a vast, verdant forest. With his many enchantments, the sorcerer warms the sun and cleanses the land of pestilence by awakening the magical heat of a sauna. Indeed, at nearly every twist and turn of the plot, Wäinämöninen and his fellow characters rise above adversity with the help of their powerful spells. As one nineteenth-century English translator of *The Kalevala* observed: 'Here as in the legends of no other people, do the heroes and demigods accomplish nearly everything by magic'.[11]

On 1 October, the young Finn sat down in a meeting with Himmler. The two men had an amicable discussion. Afterwards, Himmler wrote an entry in Grönhagen's journal. It read: 'Germans and Finns shall never forget that they once had the same fathers'.[12]

Himmler took a personal interest in the affable young anthropologist from the beginning, drawn to his refined manners and Germanic pedigree. Moreover, Himmler obviously relished the conversation that he had with Grönhagen on the ancestry of the Finns. For many years, European scholars had puzzled over the origins of the Finnish people. The Finnish tongue bore few similarities to German, English, French, or any other member of the Indo-European language group. Indeed, along with Hungarian, Estonian, Sami, and a group of lesser-known languages from Russia and Siberia, linguists had placed Finnish into a separate linguistic family, the Finno-Ugric languages.[13]

This linguistic classification raised a large red flag in the minds of many nationalist Germans. If the Finns didn't speak an Indo-European tongue, how could they possibly by Aryans? Some scholars suggested that they descended from the ancestors of the Hungarians; others speculated wildly that they sprang from the loins of Mongol invaders.[14] The short, round skulls of Finns, they observed, resembled those of Asians, and the reserved, reticent character of Finns seemed more Eastern than Western.[15] Furthermore, they were fond of linking the Finns to an enigmatic tribe described by the Roman historian Tacitus, the *Fenni*, who had once lived somewhere in the northeast Baltic region.[16] Modern scholars have been unable to determine exactly who Tacitus was referring to when he mentioned the *Fenni*. It is possible, for example, that he was relating stories he had heard of the *Sarni* in Scandinavia and Russia.[17] The *Fenni*, noted Tacitus, lived in 'unparalleled filth and poverty'.[18]

Grönhagen did not believe for a moment that he or his countrymen were of Mongol origins or that they were in any way members of an inferior race—quite the opposite. He was convinced, as he later wrote, that the prehistoric Finns arose from a vast wildland that stretched from

Scandinavia, in the north, to the Black Sea, in the south.[19] He had also persuaded himself that the Finns were blood brothers to the Aryans and therefore the two shared a common ancestry—a suggestion that would have shocked and dismayed most Finnish scholars of the day.[20] Grönhagen wasn't above offering his own racial observation as evidence. He later noted:

> Even the outer appearance of the Finnish person is telling. Blond and tall, on average taller than the Germans, with mostly blue eyes or grey eyes, they belong racially to western or northern Europe.[21]

Himmler also relished what Grönhagen had to say on the subject of *The Kalevala*. As Grönhagen pointed out, the people of Karelia, whose songs were immortalised in *The Kalevala*, still preserved many of their ancient customs and religious beliefs.[22] Indeed, as Finnish folklorists had discovered, the remote territory was a refuge of paganism, a land where traditionalists still practised an ancient form of shamanism. In Karelia, seers still recited magical spells to call upon spirits and gods, who in turn might help divine the future, cure chronic diseases, assist in childbirth, and protect families from harm. Many rural Karelians still revered and feared these magicians. Grönhagen later observed:

> The entire life of the peasants is still filled with pagan customs, the use of magic and chants. It is especially the power of the healing knowledge, which is full of secret chants, that is ingrained in the beliefs of the people.[23]

Himmler was so impressed by these ideas that he sent the young Finn to see Wiligut, who was working in an office in RuSHA and whose relationship with Himmler had by then become the subject of much talk in the SS. One story doing the rounds described an outing that Wiligut had taken with Himmler in his private car, which had the number plate 'SS 1'. As the two men were talking, Wiligut suddenly slumped in the leather seat, foaming at the mouth. Himmler immediately ordered his driver to stop. As the car screeched to a halt, Wiligut bolted from the seat and ran headlong into a field, his arms stretched out like wings. Himmler followed. Eventually, the old man dropped to his knees in the wet barley, instructing Himmler to dig at his feet. Himmler purportedly obeyed, dispatching a team of excavators to the site; they were said to have discovered an early historical settlement there.[24]

Himmler seems to have wanted Wiligut to assess the young Finn and his intriguing claims. The two men met several times—one paunchy, puffy-faced, and prone to psychosis, and the other alert, curious, and eager to make a good impression.[25] Wiligut obligingly channelled memories and tales from his ancient ancestors and recited what he claimed were Gothic proverbs from the Black Sea region that had been handed down in his family for centuries. Grönhagen listened attentively. After one such session, he reportedly told Wiligut, 'Oh I know this too. I learned the same thing from my father.'[26] Grönhagen passed muster, and soon afterwards Himmler offered him a job with the Ahnenerbe. The young anthropologist started work on 1 November 1935.[27]

His first assignment was to return to Finland to conduct research in the folklore archives of the Finnish Literature Society in Helsinki, which held the original field notes of Elias Lonnrot in addition to the manuscripts of many other prominent folklorists and experts on *The Kalevala*.[28] He was also to lead an expedition through the Karelia region of Finland to record pagan sorcerers and witches. There was some uncertainty about whether the Karelians would allow photography, and so Finnish illustrator Ola Forsell accompanied the team, along with musicologist Fritz Bose, who took along a Magnetophon in the hope of recording the pagan chants. Himmler and Wiligut seem to have hoped that his would serve several purposes; it would prepare Grönhagen for future fieldwork in Karelia, collecting and recording ancient myths and magical chants, and it would also assist Wiligut in researching ancient Aryan religious ceremonies for the SS.

Himmler was immensely keen to replace Christian rites with rituals he deemed more Aryan. He believed, as Herman Wirth did, that the sun played a central part in the primordial religion of the Nordic race. In keeping with this idea, he wanted to create an SS summer solstice festival to celebrate life and a winter solstice festival to remember the dead and honour the ancestors.[29] He asked Wiligut and Professor Karl Diebitsch, a cultural advisor in the SS, to research and draw up suitable rituals.[30] The two men had already developed an SS naming ceremony to replace the traditional christening ceremony for a baby.

The team departed for their expedition in June 1936. Grönhagen corresponded with both Himmler and Wiligut, keeping them posted on his work.[31] The two men sometimes passed his letters back and forth and discussed his progress. On 19 April 1936, Himmler wrote a chatty letter to the young anthropologist, inquiring solicitously after his health, Grönhagen had recently suffered a bout of jaundice, and Himmler instructed him to extend his stay in Helsinki until the summer.[32] As soon as the weather permitted, he wanted Grönhagen to take a journey through Karelia to photograph the sorcerers and witches and record their songs and incantations for study.

Grönhagen must have been delighted, but he could see potential problems. He was uncertain whether the elderly Karelians would agree to see him and pose for pictures, so he proposed to recruit a Finnish illustrator, Ola Forsell, for the journey.[33] A more serious problem lay in Grönhagen's lack of musical training. The fieldwork really required an ethnomusicologist familiar with diverse folk music traditions in Europe and abroad. For this, Wiligut recommended Dr Fritz Bose, a musicologist from the University of Berlin.[34] Bose was a member of the NSDAP and a self-described expert on music and race.[35] He firmly believed that the world's diverse musical styles reflected racial traits rather than cultural influences.[36] It was a theory that appealed greatly to the new Nazi regime, and Bose capitalised on it whenever he could. In 1934, at the age of twenty-eight, he became head of the Berlin Acoustics Institute after his mentor was sacked for being Jewish.[37]

Himmler must have hoped that Bose, with all his theories on race and music, could determine whether the ancient chants and incantations of Karelia were Aryan or something very similar. Bose, for his part, seems to have been delighted with the assignment. He joined the SS, being assigned to RuSHA and Himmler's personal staff.[38] He then set about preparing for the trip, searching for suitable recording equipment. While other scholars of the day generally employed disc cutters (devices that captured sound on acetate-coated metal discs), Bose hunted for more sophisticated equipment. He chose a piece of audio gear that had debuted only a few months earlier at the Berlin Radio Fair.[39] It was the magnetophone, a prototype of the modern tape recorder.[40]

In June 1936, Grönhagen, Bose, and Forsell set out from Helsinki by rented car to Viipuri, the principal city of Karelia. Viipuri was a busy cosmopolitan port on the Gulf of Finland, a place that comfortably mixed old medieval stone churches and a thirteenth-century castle with modern theatres and cafes. It was a far cry from the northern wilderness that Grönhagen yearned to explore, so he and his companions soon set off to the east. Along the north shore of Lake Ladoga, they found a land of dark fens and gentle ridges topped by pine forests. There, among scatterings of small log cottages, they began scouting out sorcerers and witches to record and photograph.

For weeks, Grönhagen and his two companions journeyed to rustic log cabins, tape-recording elderly men and women as they chanted magical incantations, communicated with the dead, and sang songs of ancient wizards. Karelia, as one team member later observed admiringly, is a 'land of witches and sorcerers'.[41] Karelia certainly clung stubbornly to the old ways. Blanketed by dense forest and threaded with dark bogs and cold lakes, the region was buried beneath thick drifts of snow for much of the year.

For many centuries, the extreme winter cold, the summer clouds of mosquitoes, and the rugged terrain had tended to discourage economic enterprise and other contact with the outside world. Then, in the late nineteenth century, forestry companies arrived to size up Karelia's timber. Loggers followed, thinning some of the dense stands of spruce and fir, while railway lines from the east and west began slicing through the taiga, transforming small towns into small cities. Still, modern life had yet to invade all corners of the remote fishing villages along the larger lakes. In these isolated hamlets, some elders still passed the long winter nights singing songs of enchantment and casting ancient magic spells.

Their first success was with a traditional singer, Timo Lipitsä. It was so close to midsummer that the sun hardly set, and they often worked late into the evening. One day, in the woods that stretched beyond the small village of Suistamo, they visited Lipitsä, a traditional singer who was well-known among Finnish folklorists.[42] On their arrival, they saw an elderly man dressed in a snowy white tunic and dark work trousers. Lipitsä's hair was white and his eyes, as Grönhagen later wrote, gleamed with 'a far away look'.[43] He had never attended school. He could neither read nor write, and he had never so much as laid eyes on a train. Grönhagen was delighted. Lipitsä, he later recalled, '[knew] nothing of civilisation or technology'.[44]

Grönhagen introduced himself and his teammates, explaining that he was collecting material for a department of Finnish folklore he planned to establish in Germany.[45] After gaining the old man's confidence, he asked if the man could sing some verses from *The Kalevala*. This rather confused Lipitsä, for he did not know what *The Kalevala* was, but he offered to sing for his visitors just the same. He called over his son, and the two men sat across from each other by the hearth. Holding each other's hands so that the 'power [became] stronger' they began to rock back and forth.[46] As they moved, they sang an old story about the creation of the world, a story that closely resembled one published in *The Kalevala*. This amazed Grönhagen:

They sing the language of *The Kalevala* without even suspecting the existence of a scientific collection of song.[47]

Bose diligently recorded the songs, fussing over the dials to get the best sound.[48] He was fascinated by the performance. The old man, he later noted, seemed to enter a trance state:

His focus is fixed out into the beyond and he no longer sense his environs [*sic.*]. It is almost impossible to interrupt him. He does not take kindly to any attempt to halt his sacred singing which is also an enormous and difficult artistic effort.[49]

Finally, at the end of the recording session, Grönhagen asked the elderly singer to pose for a photograph in the bright sunlight outside his cabin. Lipitsä graciously obliged, squinting into the light.

The trio resumed their travels. In the small village of Tolvajärvi, they photographed and recorded a prominent Karelian musician, Hannes Vornanen.[50] Vornanen was a master of the kantele, a traditional Finnish string instrument made from birch wood. The kantele and its murky origins interested Bose greatly. Some scholars of the day speculated that the kantele traced its roots to Asia. They observed that it had originally possessed just five strings and bore a resemblance to an old Chinese zither known as the *guqin*. Intriguingly, the *guqin* was also reputed to possess magical powers, making snow fall in summer and flowers blossom in the cold and darkness of winter.[51]

Bose discounted the Asian theory, pointing to a myth in *The Kalevala*. According to one ancient song, the wizard Wäinämöinen had created the first kantele from the jawbone of a common species of fish in Finland, the pike. Other clues he noted pointed to the Finnish origin of the instrument. The kantele shared a tonal system with the songs of *The Kalevala*, which suggested that their histories were intertwined. Moreover, Bose believed the kantele was far older than its Asian counterpart. Its tonal system was more primitive and its overall construction was much simpler, lacking the arched cover of the 'guqin'.[52] Based on this, Bose concluded that the kantele was a thoroughly European instrument—a scholarly opinion that must have pleased Grönhagen, who was anxious to refute any suggestion that the Finns were of Asian origin. Scholars continue to debate the origins of the kantele today, pointing out its resemblance to instruments as diverse as the Russian *gusli* and the Arabic *quanun*. However, one of the world's greatest historians of Eurasian stringed instruments, Bo Lawergren, suggests that the kantele likely developed from the lyres of Europe: 'To convert a lyre into a zither [like the kantele], all one needs to do is fill the hole in its upper part'.[53]

One of the trip's final successes was in finding Miron-Aku, an elderly soothsayer living in the woods near Salmi, who was believed by locals to be a witch. The locals advised against meeting her. When Grönhagen arrived at her hut, it was empty, so he waited for her to return. In the distance, he heard someone talking; it was ninety-two-year-old Miron-Aku. She was picking mushrooms. She looked up at him and stared into his eyes. Grönhagen was riveted by her first words; she told him that she had dreamed about him three days earlier. 'You came to me in my sleep and wanted to take away my secrets. Since then I have been sick and will die soon. What do you want of me?'[54]

Grönhagen tried to befriend her: he wanted to learn more about her reputed ability to see into the future. He paid her several visits.

She brewed him a bitter drink from local plant roots and talked of an old god that people in the region had once worshipped before they embraced Christianity. She also described how the spirits of her ancestors resided with her in her hut.[55] By summoning them ritually, she could divine future events. This information fascinated Grönhagen and Bose. After a long negotiation, they persuaded her to perform the ritual for the camera and tape recorder.[56] She reluctantly gave them the demonstration, but she was terribly dismayed when Bose later played back the tape. She told him that 'she would never be able to practice magic again' because she had committed a sacrilege by performing a spell simply to satisfy the curiosity of others.[57] Worse still, this error of judgment was now preserved on the tape.

The team moved on to the next village, and as the summer stretched on, they broadened their research. Grönhagen diligently recorded all the folklore he could concerning an ancient Finnish tradition, the sauna. Karelian healers believed that the sauna's combination of water and fire-warmed rock generated a powerful force capable of warding off many forms of sickness.[58] To better avail themselves of the mystical powers of steam, healers often took the sick into their own saunas, where they performed sacred ceremonies

Bose, for his part, kept adding to the collection of tapes. He recorded old Karelian dance songs with titles like 'Boys Travelling' and 'Children on a Cliff'.[59] He recorded ancient lullabies, work songs, and patriotic tunes. He also recorded women's songs of lamentation, which impressed him greatly. He later observed:

> As a kind of magical priestess, the mourning singer helps the souls of the dying and the dead to cross from this side to another.[60]

In total, the team taped more than 100 songs, chants, and instrumentals, and by the end of the summer, Bose was convinced that he had successfully adduced the racial origins of the otherworldly songs that made up *The Kalevala*. The impoverished nature of the lyrics suggested to Bose that these songs were very old—much older, in fact, than the earliest relics of Nordic poetry. '*The Kalevala*', he suggested, 'must be a very early Nordic cultural level', possibly even dating back to pre-Aryan times.[61]

Back in Berlin, Grönhagen sent Himmler a note about the trip and a copy of the photograph he took of Timo Lipitsä, the old man who had sung about the creation of the world. He then set to work writing a short article for *Germanien*, a monthly archaeological and anthropological magazine partially owned by the Ahnenerbe. The Ahnenerbe had entered into an agreement to publish this magazine together with the Society for the Friends of German Prehistory. The first joint issue rolled off the press in March 1936.[62] Grönhagen chose Karelian magic chants as the subject of his article; with journalistic flair, he described the age-old rituals that Karelian women performed to fend off evil spirits in cemeteries and heal the sick in the cleansing heat of the saunas. The editors of *Germanien* quickly published the piece, listing the author as Georg von Grönhagen.[63] The change of name made the young Finn sound more German and therefore a good deal more acceptable to the magazine's nationalistic audience.

In Helsinki, Finnish researchers were growing suspicious of the Ahnenerbe team. Grönhagen had met several important folklorists the previous winter in the Finnish capital, and some, such as Martti Haavio, had received reports about his field activities from Karelian friends.[64] Haavio, the director of the folklore archives at the Finnish Literature Society, was greatly concerned about the use that Grönhagen's work might be put to.[65] He was loathe to see Finnish folklore falsified or manipulated in some fashion in order to advance the Nazi cause, so in the autumn of 1936, he advised at least one of his trusted Karelian sources against cooperating any further with Grönhagen.[66]

Grönhagen seems to have been oblivious, however, to the controversy he was stirring in his homeland. On 27 January 1937, he and Bose attended a private meeting at Himmler's home in Berlin.[67] The two researchers were ushered into a study, and as they glanced around, they were startled to see their photo of Timo Lipitsä hanging like a treasured icon above Himmler's desk.[68] They had arrived bearing other mementos of their travels, which made quite an impression. Himmler and his wife, Marga, flipped through the photographs together, before Bose produced the kantele and gave Himmler a short impromptu lesson on it. Himmler was so delighted with the instrument that the two researchers ended up giving it to him. He immediately placed an order for ten more for the SS.

The SS leader was keen to hear Bose's tape recordings, and he wanted to know how old the Karelian songs were and whether they were related to music of the ancient Germanic tribes. After listening intently to Bose's replies, he mentioned the possibility of a grant for further research on these subjects. He and Wiligut, it transpired, were planning to use ancient Nordic musical instruments in SS solstice ceremonies, and they hoped to find examples of authentic ancient Nordic music.[69] In one of the primary SS training slideshows on German history, *Das Licht aus dem Norden*, one of the slides depicted two men playing lurs during an ancient summer solstice celebration. The accompanying text noted:

A tree with a decorated wreath, a symbol of the sun, is placed on a cliff. Next to it burns the bonfire, which is still customary today, and the lur players greet the sunlight with celebratory sounds.[70]

Bose's ideas on the origins of European music impressed Himmler so much that he later asked the scholar to help cast replicas of another ancient Scandinavian instrument, the lur. The lur also figured in an important German debate at the time over the origins of polyphony, a style of musical composition that juxtaposes two or more melodies in harmony. German nationalists claimed that ancient Germanic tribes had invented this sophisticated style of composition on their own. As evidence, scholars cited the fact that archaeologists usually found lurs in pairs. This, they claimed, proved that Germany's ancestors had always been drawn to consonance and avoided the atonal music deemed typical of Jewish people.[71] Bronze Age artists had depicted this wind instrument in their rock carvings in Sweden.

Grönhagen also shone that evening with his colourful stories of Timo Lipitsä and the old seer, Miron-Aku.[72] Less than a month later, Himmler named the young anthropologist head of the Ahnenerbe's brand-new department of Indo-Germanic-Finnish studies, a prestigious appointment for a young Finn of twenty-six who did not possess a graduate degree.[73] The mission of the new department was to search for parallels between the Aryans and the Finns in order to 'establish their shared origins'.[74] Two months later, Grönhagen expanded this work plan and gave it a more academic-sounding tone, likely at the insistence of Walther Wüst.[75] The top two priorities were studies on the metaphysical meaning of *The Kalevala* and research on magic, witches, and rune singers.

Himmler intended to make use of this Finnish lore, too. Grönhagen's description of the mystical healing powers of the sauna, with its combination of fire and water, had particularly aroused his interest. He suggested to Dr Ernst-Robert von Grawitz, the chief physician of the SS, that SS men would benefit from using traditional Aryan methods of body cleansing. Grawitz's staff dutifully launched a joint study with the Ahnenerbe on 'Germanic bathing' in 1937.[76] As part of this project, Sievers instructed Grönhagen to share his research on Finnish saunas with the SS medical staff.

Having 'proved' both the superiority and northern origin of the Aryan race, expeditions were next planned to establish the dispersal of the Aryans to the south and east, where they established the cultures of Ancient Rome, Greece, and Mesopotamia.

Spies in the Caves

The conflict of races is now about to start openly within nations and between nations, and one can only ask oneself if the ideas of fraternity and equality of man were not against nature ... I am convinced that in the next century people will slaughter each other by the million because of a difference of a degree or two in the cephalic index.[1]

Following the success of the expedition to Bohuslän, the Ahnenerbe agreed to finance an expedition to study the rock carvings of the valley of Val Camonica in Italy the following year, 1935. The expedition was led by the archaeologist Franz Altheim, who was accompanied by the photographer Erika Trautmann. Their aim was to study prehistoric rock inscriptions, looking for similarities between them and those identified in Scandinavia; this would support the theory that culture had originated in the Aryan north from where it had dispersed.[2]

According to Nazi belief, the Aryan race had originated in the Ice Age, the relics of whose people were found across Europe by archaeologists such as Otto Haufer, who had located many skeletons in the Dordogne and Beziers areas as well as graves and cult symbols such as 'Venus' figurines. The most celebrated of these had been found in Willendorf, Austria, just after the turn of the century; since then, however, many more had been unearthed at sites all over Europe. The Venus figurines are small carved stones representing generously proportioned females with large breasts, swollen stomachs, and distended thighs.

These figurines had fascinated Himmler; he was particularly entranced by their prominent rears, which he thought reminiscent of the similarly well-endowed African 'Hottentot'. Following the Tibet Expedition, Himmler instructed Beger to study the figurines from an anthropological point of view to prove his theory that the Venus figurines represented an older people who had been expelled from Europe when the superior (presumably more modestly proportioned) Aryans had appeared. Himmler also observed that many Jewish women had comparable endowments; he thought this meant that Jews and Hottentots were the living representatives of the prehistoric people who created the Venus figurines, and that that Jews were the primitive relatives of Hottentots. Beger enthusiastically endorsed Himmler's ideas, as quoted in Pringle's *The Master Plan*:

> The racial similarities between the Hottentots, the North Africans, and the Near Eastern peoples are unmistakable. Among the Jewesses it is noticeable that they have very well-developed bottoms which could be linked to the fat bottomed lineage seen amongst Hottentots and bushmen.

Beger and his colleagues in the SS realized that the camps and ghettos created by resettlement were an outstanding opportunity for science. Beger enthusiastically recommended the following:

> The RuSHA, when they assemble foreigners and the women are mustered together and undressed, might pay special attention to how fat the women's bottoms are, and perhaps some photographs could be taken. It would be possible for the RuSHA to examine a line-up of Jewish women from the Polish ghettos with strong evidence of highly developed fat content in their rears. This would allow us to establish that this fat development comes from the same inherited factors as can be seen in Hottentots and Bushmen, allowing us to prove that this race existed in Europe as well.

Beger's involvement in Himmler's Venus project was a turning point. As so often with Himmler's hobby-horse assignments, little was really achieved, but Beger had accepted that as an anthropologist, he could go much further than simply endorsing the race theories of the Reich. As a scientist, he could exploit the human booty of conquest. At this time Beger also travelled to Norway, which Hitler had conquered in 1940. Here, he used a new technique to get metrical data. X-rays (radiography) could see beneath the skin, just as anthropologists had always wanted to do. When he saw the results, he told Himmler of an ambitious plan to use X-rays to produce a directory of Nordic types. 'Very good,' replied Himmler. This was a first step to his participation in the holocaust. Beger was sent to Auschwitz in 1942 to begin selecting suitable subjects for his skeleton collection. Sievers and Hirt understood that this would involve the murder of the selected individuals, and documents show that Beger did as well; if not at the outset, he certainly became aware of this during the process.

Archaeologists R. R. Schmidt and Assien Bohmers were also busy at work. They had discovered red ochre, a pigment used by the Cro-Magnon for cave painting at the Mauern Caves, in the southern Jura mountains of Bavaria.[3] Bohmers (1912–1988), a Frisian nationalist and member of the SS-Ahnenerbe, had taken over the excavation in the autumn of 1937, after which he unearthed burins, ivory pendants, and the skeleton of a woolly mammoth, in addition to the remains of a Neanderthal who was buried with what appeared to be spears—a technology thought to have been developed by the Cro-Magnons.[4] Bohmers interpreted this to mean that Cro-Magnons had left these stones in the caves over 70,000 years before, and that this was therefore the oldest Cro-Magnon site in the world. To validate his claims, Bohmers travelled to France, meeting Abbé Henri Breuil, Europe's foremost expert on cave art, at the Parisian Institute for Human Paleontology.[5] Breuil arranged for Bohmers to visit Trois Frères, a site whose owners allowed only a small number of visitors. First, however, Bohmers took a quick trip to London, followed by a tour of several other French points of interest—La Fond de Gaume (a site featuring Cro-Magnon cave paintings), Teyat, La Mouthe, and the caves of Dordogne. Then Bohmers moved on to Les Trois-Frères, 'where Himmler and where so many other Nazis had long dreamed of standing—in the shrine of the ancient dead, in the dark embrace of the ancestors' (Pringle, *The Master Plan*).

The remains of the Cro-Magnon and Aurginacian people unearthed by these excavations were taken to be the tribal fathers of the northern race. Leo Frobenius, one of the most celebrated European anthropologists of the day and founder of the Research Institute for Cultural Morphology, organised annual field expeditions to record the Paleolithic cave art of France and Spain.[6] One of the artists that he took with him to make these recordings was Trautmann, who had participated in the institute's 1934 expedition.[7]

Trautmann was 'a very striking blond woman with whom you could have an intelligent conversation', recalled her cousin Walther Nehring.[8] The daughter of a once-wealthy estate owner in eastern Prussia, she had impeccable Nazi connections. Hermann Göring had attended cadet school with her older brothers, and according to one story, he had fallen in love with her as a young woman and asked to marry her—a proposal she declined.[9] She possessed a talent for sketching and enrolled in the state arts and crafts school in Berlin in 1933.[10] She then took a job as a scientific illustrator at Frobenius's Institute, which specialised in the study of ancient art.[11]

She was considered to have had a fine, observant eye for detail and a knack for discovery. This impressed Frobenius, who had made her a regular on the summer expeditions. She seemed at ease crawling on her stomach, going down narrow subterranean passageways and painting by the flickering light of lanterns.[12] What she and her colleagues recorded revealed that the 'Aryan' Paleolithic people had been skilled artists, portraying animals beautifully in their cave art as well as in horn and bone engravings and wood-carvings. The Nazis thought this proved that they could not be the descendants of apes. No stone weapons or tools have been found, stated Hörbiger, because they lived in 'tropical paradises free of stones'. He added that dragons abounded everywhere'. World Ice Theory described how a great flood had followed the slow ending of the Ice Age, prior to which the Tertiary moon had approached the Earth, looming ever-larger, causing sea level to rise, and forcing the surviving people to take refuge near the North Pole.[13]

Hörbiger's theory included sufficient reference to racist ideas as to link it with Nazi ideology in a supportive role. The World Ice Theory described the northern ancestors of the Teutonic peoples surviving the disintegration of the Tertiary moon, the last Ice Age, and the great flood. These were tough people who survived adverse conditions, which fitted well with the wish of Richard Walther Darré, originator of the Nazi blood-and-soil doctrine, to introduce selective breeding on a voluntary basis in order to create a new, 'Nordic' German aristocracy. Both Himmler and Darré had studied agronomy and knew something of the breeding of livestock, and so they attempted to turn the SS into the desired new German stock.

In August 1936, Frobenius dispatched Trautmann and two others to Val Camonica, northern Italy, under the direction of Franz Altheim, a classical scholar whom he had befriended and recruited for the Institute.[14] Altheim was an expert on the origins of Roman religion and the history of the Latin language. At the age of thirty-nine, he had already built a major international career as a classical scholar, counting the German historian Oswald Spengler and other prominent intellectuals among his friends. Clever and irreverent, Altheim disavowed conventional armchair research in favour of fieldwork conducted amongst Italy's classical ruins, making a reputation for uncovering weathered inscriptions and worn statuary that others had overlooked.

Spread along the valley of Val Camonica, Italian researchers Giovanni Marro, Paolo Graziosi, and Raffaele Battaglia had discovered extensive panels consisting of some 200,000–300,000 prehistoric stone carvings.[15] Frobenius was fascinated by this art and planned to curate an exhibition of detailed paintings of the new finds. Altheim's interest in the carvings was the potential they offered for revealing the ancient cultic practices of the early Romans. Working in tandem, Trautmann and Altheim spent weeks tracing the outlines of the weathered carvings. Separated from her engineer husband and her conventional life in Frankfurt, she grew closer to Altheim; a few months after her return to Germany, she obtained an official separation from her husband.

On their return to Germany, the couple worked to interpret all that they had seen at Val Camonica, which resulted in a joint paper published in a German historical journal.[16] They claimed to have found traces of Nordic-style carvings of deer, chariots, carts, warriors in battle, and sacred rituals that looked similar to the Bronze Age engravings Wirth had studied in Sweden.[17] The couple argued (incorrectly, as it turned out) that the carvings of Val Camonica were several centuries younger than those of Bohuslän in Sweden, which suggested that ancient Scandinavians had developed this art in the north and carried it south to Italy, an interpretation quickly adopted by the fascist Italian archaeologist Marro.[18]

This discovery solved a question that had troubled the Nazis for some time—why was it that Romans from the south of Europe were able to conquer the known world and forge an empire? In order to fit Nazi ideology, the Roman Empire had been given a Nordic pedigree, which traced the Romans back to blond-haired migrants from the north.[19] After visiting Rome in 1937, Himmler wrote to Wüst, requesting that he establish a new department in the Ahnenerbe to 'find proof that the Romans ... stem from Aryan Indo-Germanic groups who migrated from the North'.[20]

Trautmann, well-aware of the importance of their article to the Third Reich, passed a copy to Göring, who proceeded to introduce the couple to Himmler.[21] The SS chief was delighted with the pair's research, and particularly with its connection to the Swedish rock art that Wirth had studied. He quickly agreed to fund a further expedition. In the summer of 1937, Altheim and Trautmann departed for Italy and the Adriatic coast of Dalmatia, in what is now Croatia, to find more evidence of Nordic migrants. They travelled from Berlin to Munich, Vienna, Zagreb, Split, Cattaro, Dubrovnic, Mitropica, Keztheley, Trieste, Venice, Val Camonica, Bologna, Florence, Rome, Syracuse, and Enna, and then returned to Berlin.[22] They dispatched regular reports from the field, outlining their new finds; this must have impressed Himmler as he instructed Sievers to recruit them into the Ahnenerbe on their return.[23]

While travelling, Altheim and Trautmann had plotted a more ambitious expedition that would travel from central Europe to and then through western Asia. Altheim was careful to describe the project in racial terms when presenting it to the Ahnenerbe. The purpose of the trip, he explained, was to examine evidence for a great power struggle that wracked the racially diverse Roman Empire during the third century AD. This struggle pitted 'Indogermanic peoples of the North' against 'the Semites of the Orient' for control of the empire.[24] Such an examination, he added, would break important new scholarly ground. American and British scholars had viewed this tumultuous period largely from a Marxist point of view, focusing on class warfare within the empire.[25] Altheim, however, favoured a very different approach. He and Trautmann proposed to study the conflict 'between peoples and races', and determine how it was that the Nordic race triumphed in the struggle for power over the empire.[26] This, they promised, would be a significant contribution. 'Here we have a great opportunity to present the meaning of race in the writing of history'.[27]

Wüst read the proposal with great interest, noting 'Agree very much' at the top of his copy.[28] It was precisely the kind of research that he wanted to encourage in the Ahnenerbe, and so he agreed to match the 4,000 RM (the equivalent of some $20,900 today) that Trautmann's old friend Hermann Göring had offered to provide.[29]

Quite possibly it was Wüst who saw the potential of using Altheim and Trautmann as spies. Wüst was an informer himself, and he may have been instructed to keep a look out for suitable agents by Himmler. The Ahnenerbe, with its bright young staff and its expeditions and research trips to foreign lands, was an obvious place for Himmler to look for potential spies. A few of its researchers undoubtedly possessed the necessary resourcefulness, intelligence, and discretion for a good agent. Their proposed itinerary to the Middle East took them through several areas that were strategically important due to their oil. Germany possessed very little crude of its own, relying for much of its supply on the Ploesti fields in Romania.[30] 'Without Romania,' Göring was reported to have declared in 1937, 'we cannot start a campaign.'[31] Romanian oil producers made a considerable fortune from their exports to Germany, but the political situation in Bucharest had become unstable with the emergence of a new ultranationalist movement. Turmoil in Romania needed careful watching as nothing could be allowed to disrupt German oil supplies.

The other major European powers were equally dependent on foreign reserves. Great Britain had turned Iraq into a virtual colony after the First World War and helped develop its vast reserves. Iraq joined the ranks of the world's major oil producers in 1934, shipping its own to the Syrian port of Tripoli, on the Mediterranean, *via* a new pipeline. From there, tankers ferried much of the production to Britain. It was a long, tenuous supply line, and it would become even more so in the event of a war in Europe. If German forces could seize control of the oil fields near Kirkuk or sabotage the pipeline, then they could sever one of Britain's vital arteries.

Adolf Hitler was a fervent nationalist, racist, and anti-Semite. He was less interested in the occult than Heinrich Himmler, but he saw the potential of deploying myths from the Germanic past in order to create a twentieth century Germanic empire. (*Bundesarchiv Bild 183-S62600*)

A still from one of the infamous Nuremberg rallies, at which Hitler galvanised the people of Germany through his mesmerising oratory. (*Private collection*)

Fɪɢ. 197.—Tabernacle from the Balâwât Gates. (B.M.) (P. & C.)
Date, ʙ.ᴄ. 859 to 824.

Above: The Ark of the Covenant—also known as the Tabernacle—in which the Ten Commandments were housed. (*J. Ward*)

Left: The bust of the Egyptian queen Nefertiti housed in Berlin; Hitler refused to return it to Egypt. (*Private collection*)

A mugshot of Wolfram Sievers (1905–1948) taken by the American authorities after his arrest. Sievers was the Executive Secretary of the SS-Ahnenerbe. He was sentenced to death on 7 August 1947, during the Doctors' Trial, for crimes against humanity; he was hanged on 2 June 1948. (*US National Archives and Records Administration*)

A 1910 portrait of Guido von List. (*Bundesarchiv Bild 183-2007-0705-500*)

An 1875 portrait of Madame
Helena Blavatsky.
(*De Bienvenida en portal*)

Stage design for Act III of Wagner's *Parsifal* by stage designer Paul von Joukowsky
(1845–1912), *c.* 1882. (*Paul von Joukowsky*)

A portrait of Arthur de Gobineau.
(*G. Crés, Nouvelles Asiatiques, 1924*)

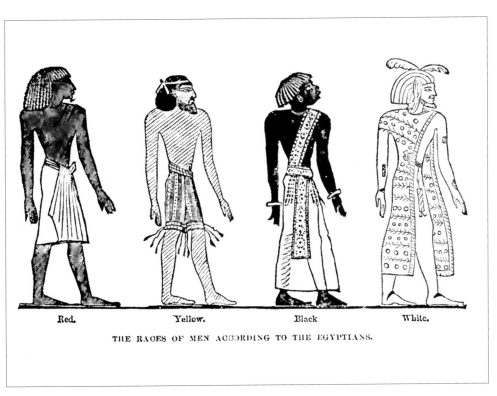

Red.   Yellow.   Black   White.

THE RACES OF MEN ACCORDING TO THE EGYPTIANS.

'The races of men according to the Egyptians'.
(*I. Donnelly, The Antediluvian World, 1882*)

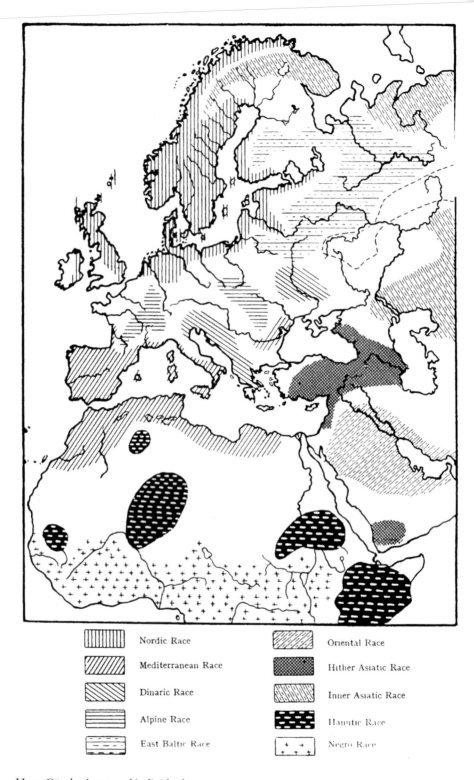

‖‖‖ Nordic Race		Oriental Race
Mediterranean Race		Hither Asiatic Race
Dinaric Race		Inner Asiatic Race
Alpine Race		Hamitic Race
East Baltic Race		Negro Race

Hans Günther's map of individual races.
(*H. Günther, The Racial Elements of European History, 1927*)

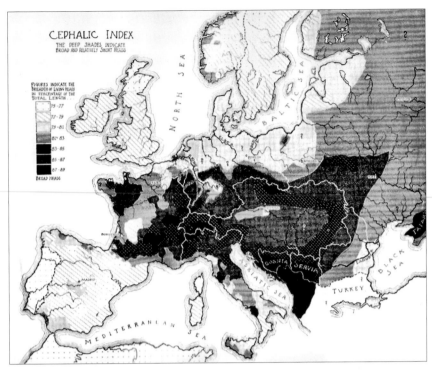

A map representing the Cephalic Index for the peoples of Europe.
(*W. Z. Ripley, The Races of Europe, 1975*)

Arthur Posnansky poses against an ornamental gateway at Tiwanaku, Bolivia. (*E. Kiss, Das Sonnentor Von Tihuanako Und Hoerbigers Welteislehre, 1937*)

Above and below: The Gateway of the Sun at Tiwanaku before and after restoration. (Above: *E. Kiss, Das Sonnentor Von Tihuanako Und Hoerbigers Welteislehre, 1937.* Below: *private collection*)

Above: The surviving remains of the ruined city of Lubaantun, Belize, where the crystal skull was said to have been found. (*Private collection*)

Right: The crystal skull. It was highly prized by the Nazis, who believed that whomever possessed it would have access to supernatural powers. (*Private collection*)

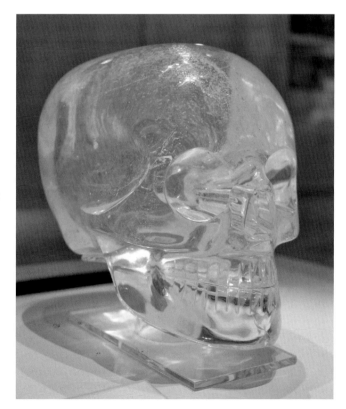

Emmanuel de Rougé's translation of the north wall of the mortuary temple of Ramesses III at Medinet Habu, Egypt, led him to coin the term 'Sea Peoples'. This famous scene shows what is known as the 'Battle of the Delta', when an attack by the 'Sea Peoples' was repulsed by the Egyptians in 1192 BC. (*E. de Rougé, Inscriptions Hiéroglyphices Copiées en Égypte Pendant la Mission Scientifique de M. le Vicomte Emmanuel de Rougé, 1877*)

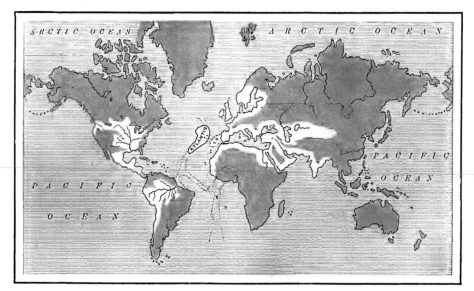

THE EMPIRE OF ATLANTIS.

Ignatius Donnelly (1831–1901) took Plato's account of Atlantis seriously and attempted to establish that all known ancient civilisations were descended from its high Neolithic culture. In this map, he showed the presumed location of the lost continent of Atlantis. The unshaded areas of Europe, North Africa, Asia, and North, Central, and South America represent the areas settled by Atlanteans, forming the 'Atlantean Empire'. The dotted lines connecting Atlantis to South America and Africa show a presumed 'connecting ridge' that linked the continent with the rest of the world (*I. Donnelly, The Antediluvian World, 1882*)

ANCIENT COINS OF TYRE.

Ancient coins from the city of Tyre, depicting the Pillars of Hercules.
(*I. Donnelly, The Antediluvian World, 1882*)

Aryans Entering India 3500 BC. (R. B. Ogle, Hutchinson's History of the Nations, c. 1910)

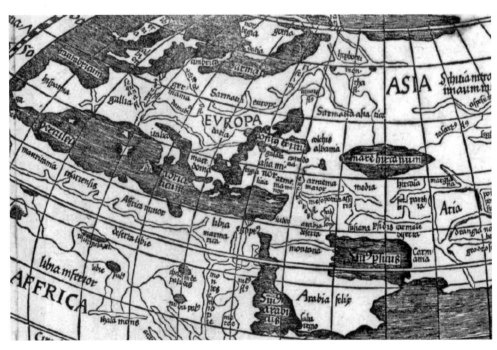

A map dated 1507 that shows the extent of the then known world; this includes the land of 'Aria' (centre-right), home of the Aryans. (*Waldseemuller 1507*)

A portrait of the author
of World Ice Theory, Hans
Hörbiger (1860–1931).
(*Smithsonian Digital
Collection*)

Sven Hedin in Tibet in 1900.
(C. Alberti-Stittenfeld, 1909)

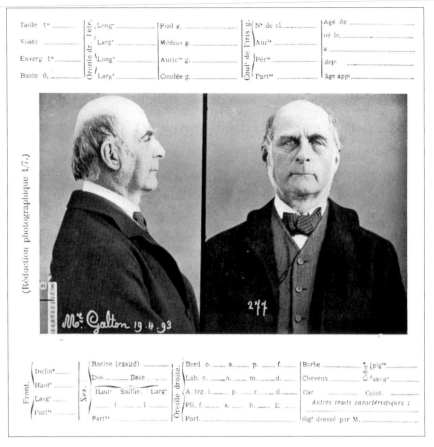

Francis Galton, the British originator of eugenics and a pioneer of anthropometry. He subjected himself to measurements, as this image shows; it was taken in 1893 at Alphonse Bertillon's Paris laboratory. (*http://galton.org/*)

The Norse god Odin. In the Icelandic Old Norse texts, he is depicted as having one eye and a long beard, frequently wielding a spear and wearing a black or blue cloak and a broad hat. He is often referred to as the founding figure of the Germanic peoples of Scandinavia, England, and the Langobards. (*A. S. Murray, Manual of Mythology: Greek and Roman, Norse and Old German, Hindoo and Egyptian Mythology, 1897*)

Right: The Nazis were keen students of Nordic mythology, believing that it offered a unique insight into the origins of the Aryan people. This image shows the Norse cosmology, which centred on the tree *Yggdrasil* (the World-Ash); the tree embraces the origin, life, and death of the Earth and its generations. (*A. Weller, Esoteric & Occult Art, 2011*)

Below: Examples of the prehistoric rock carvings. These are from Lokeburg, Bohuslän, in Sweden, and they were recorded by Herman Wirth. (*Private collection*)

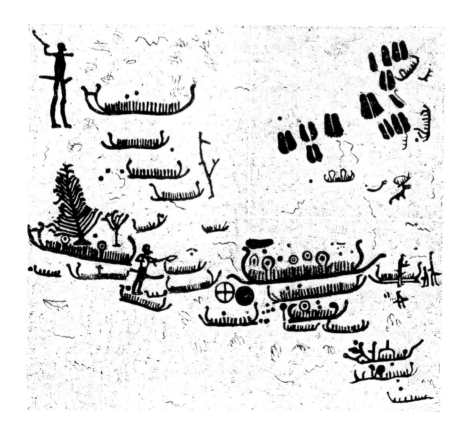

House gables showing supposedly ancient Nordic motifs.
(*H. Wirth., Die Ura Linda Chronik, 1933*)

The Finnish anthropologist Yrjö von Grönhagen in 1935.
(*Frankfurter Volksblatt 1935*)

KANTELE PLAYERS

An 1897 photograph of Kantele players in Finland.
(*Alec Tweedie, Ethel Brilliana, Through Finland in Carts, 1897*)

Left: An example of the rock carvings at Val Camonica, Nadro, Italy. They were studied by the expedition led by the archaeologists Franz Altheim and Erika Trautmann.
(*Luca Giarelli*)

Below: Erika Trautmann sketching rock carvings at la Cova del Cavalls, Spain.
(*Frobenius Institut, Frankfurt*)

The Behistun Inscription, Iran, which dates to the Achamenid period and formed the focus for Wüst's planned archaeological expedition. (*Private collection*)

Preparing to bury the large Sounion Kouros statue.
(*National Archaeological Museum, Athens*)

Above and below: The pit dug beneath the floor of the National Archaeological Museum in Athens; the museum's finest statues were buried within to prevent capture by the Nazis. (*National Archaeological Museum, Athens*)

Above and right: Wewelsburg Castle. The dining room (above) contained the round table at which Himmler's SS-Knights would dine. The chamber directly below (right) held an ornamental swastika set into the ceiling, and a ritual hearth was set into the floor. (*Private collection*)

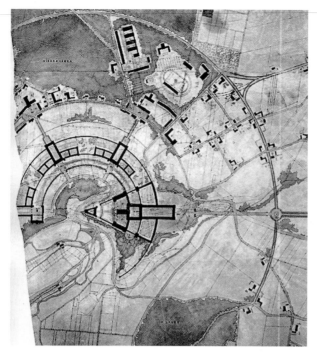

An architectural plan for the development of the Wewelsburg complex. The castle forms the triangular point at the centre of the ring of planned buildings. (*Bundesarchiv Bauplan der Wewelsburg*)

An example of the Third Reich's pagan 'religion'. Himmler was keen to develop an alternative to Christian ritual and created a new Nazi ceremony. (*Bundesarchiv Bild 146-1969-062A-62*)

Fig. 311.—Greek Carved Fret.

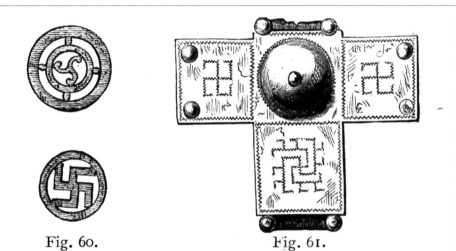

Fig. 60.   Fig. 61.

Figs. 60 and 61.—Metal Mountings from Thorsberg. *(Danish Arts.)*

Top and middle: A Greek carved fret with swastikas and Danish metalwork decorated with the swastika motif. (J. Ward, 1897)

Right: An English Anglo-Saxon cinerary urn decorated with swastika motifs. (*Private collection*)

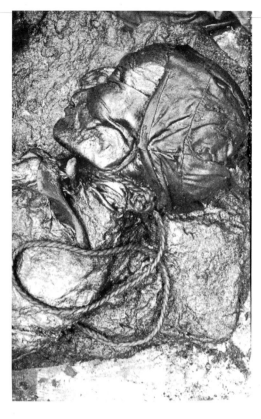

The 'Tollund Man' in the process of being excavated from the site at Tollund Fen, Denmark. (*P. V. Glob, The Bog People, 1971*)

The cover of the popular Nazi magazine *Germanien*, celebrating Germanic history and culture. (*Germanien, September 1937*)

The *Heiligenberg Thingstätte*, part of the Nazi reinvention of the Germanic institutions of the past. (*Private collection*)

The dramatic natural rock formations of Externsteine. Known as 'Germany's Stonehenge', Externsteine had ancient spiritual meaning for the Nazis. (*Private collection*)

Herbert Jankuhn's excavations at the Viking site of Haithabu/Hedeby, Denmark.
(*Private collection*)

Coronation of Harold. (Bayeux Tapestry.)

The Coronation of the Saxon King Harold from the Bayeux Tapestry.
(*J. Ecclestone, An Introduction to English Antiquities, 1847*)

Heinrich Himmler (seated) with cronies during a tour of Franco's Spain. The aim was to bolster political and military ties between the countries, drawing Spain into the war on the side of the Axis powers. The Nazis failed to achieve this in part due to Franco's ardent Catholicism; as such, he was opposed to the mysticism that so gripped Himmler. (*F-3428-02-4-1*)

The Altar of Veit Stoss, St Mary's Church, Krakøw, Poland. Peter Paulsen commanded a team ordered to steal this fifteenth century altar. Aware of the plot, the Poles dismantled the altar into thirty-two pieces, each of which was shipped to a different location. However, Paulsen was able to locate each piece. (*Private collection*)

The prehistoric site of Biskupin, Poland, first excavated by the Poles and then claimed by the Nazis. (*Private collection*)

The spoils of war; cultural treasures and works of art looted by the Nazis were found stored at Schlosskirche Ellingen, Bavaria, at the end of the war. (*Private collection*)

Above: The monastery of Montserrat in Spain, said to be the home of the Holy Grail, the cup from which Christ and his disciples drank during the last supper. (*Private collection*)

Right: Otto Rahn. (*O. Rahn, Luzifers Hofgesind, 1937*)

The Spear of Destiny (also known as the 'Holy Lance'), which was reputed to have pierced the side of Christ whilst he was on the cross. (*Private collection*)

St Dominic de Guzman and the Albigensians by Pedro Berruguete (*c.* 1450–1504).
The painting portrays a dispute between St Dominic and the Cathars in which the books
of both were thrown onto a fire. St Dominic's books miraculously survived, whereas the
Cathar teachings were destroyed. (*Private collection*)

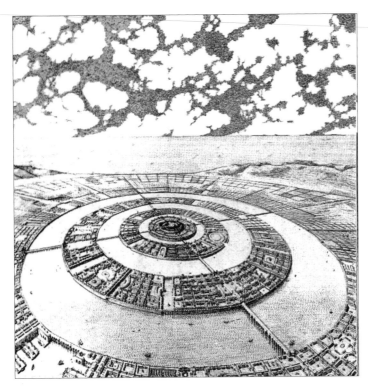

A hypothetical reconstruction of the lost city of Atlantis, showing a series of canals. (*E. Kiss, Frühling in Atlantis, 1933*)

Adolf Hitler digging for victory—a publicity stunt by the Third Reich. (*Bundesarchiv Bild 183-R27373*)

Altheim and Trautmann, with their easy *entrée* into academic and government circles, could be extremely valuable intelligence assets. The two could readily locate and befriend Nazi sympathizers, individuals who could later be recruited as local agents. In trains and restaurants, hotels and museums, the witty scholar and the statuesque blonde could easily glean useful bits of intelligence from casual conversations with foreign nationals and local inhabitants. Moreover, they might even succeed in contacting Bedouin leaders on the excursions they planned into the deserts of Iraq and Syria, gathering valuable information on their predisposition toward Germany.

European scholars had a proven track record as secret agents; the most famous of them was T. E. Lawrence, who had been among the British archaeologists that had excavated site of Carchemish in Syria.[32] Lawrence had passed himself off as nothing more than a keen student of the past, but in reality, the future 'Lawrence of Arabia' was maintaining surveillance for British intelligence on a German railway line under construction from Berlin to Baghdad. Later in life, Altheim spoke with great admiration of Lawrence of Arabia, and it may be that the supposed glamour of espionage blinded him to the repression and brutality of the Nazi regime.[33]

The pair spent several days searching for the remains of the Dacians, a warlike Nordic people who had founded a magnificent kingdom in the Transylvanian hills.[34] During their fieldwork, they met Constantin Daicoviciu, Director of the Institute of Classical Studies in Cluj-Napoca, who they considered potentially useful to the Reich. Daicoviciu was one of Romania's leading classical scholars, and he had kindly taken the Germans on a personal tour of one of his Dacian excavations. They had found him 'an impressive personality'.[35] In their report, they noted:

> ... his political position is neutral. However, he is a former reserve officer in the Austrian-Hungarian Empire, has an encompassing grasp of German scholarship and possesses one of the most capable minds.[36]

Altheim and Trautmann arrived in Bucharest, the 'Little Paris of the Balkans', in August 1938.[37] There they met Grigore Florescu, the director of the Municipal Museum, to discuss not just Romanian archaeology and history, but also politics and the activities of the Iron Guard. 'Everything', noted Trautmann and Altheim in a later secret report, 'was overshadowed by the events regarding the Iron Guard and the government'.[38]

The paramilitary Iron Guard was the creation of the anti-Semitic Corneliu.[39] Corneliu admired Hitler and dressed in a white peasant costume. He travelled the countryside on a snowy white horse, preaching a blend of Christian mysticism and rabid nationalism.[40] The success of Corneliu in rallying the people had so alarmed Romania's king, Carol II (a grandson of Queen Victoria), that in the spring of 1938, he had felt forced to assume dictatorial power and arrest the charismatic Corneliu. The result had been unrest.

Altheim and Trautmann began their research, poring over museum collections of old Roman inscriptions and texts, and chatting with high-ranking museum officials. They took a keen interest in the aristocratic director of the Municipal Museum. Grigore Florescu was a member of Romania's privileged class, the *boyar*; his wife's kin included two prominent leaders of the Iron Guard, General Cantacuzene and Prince Cantacuzene. Altheim and Trautmann found him fascinating. Later, in their report, Altheim and Trautmann noted:

> We learned an excellent series of facts from Florescu. He described the adventurous flight of the two Cantacuzene in disguise. He told us of the battle between the Iron Guard and the role of the Jewish Madame Lupescu. Not only does she possess the 'heart' of the king (many have followed after her), but she still has an inexplicable hold on him and determines his political actions. The position of the large Jewish banks in Bucharest is more powerful than ever.[41]

The two scholars then went on to evaluate Florescu's future usefulness to the Reich:

> Mr Florescu speaks fluent German, is related to almost all the big Romanian families (Bratianu, Bibescu, Ghika, Cantacuzene, *etc.*), and because of this and his access to the court and other high positions, he is full of information. Should his position become endangered, then he would like to flee to Germany, where he owns land because of his German relatives. We would like to point out that through him, we could win 1.) a supporter of the Iron Guard, 2.) a friend of Germany, 3.) a sharp and well-informed mind.[42]

It seems that Altheim and Trautmann had slipped into the role of spy with alacrity. In the late summer they travelled by rail from Bucharest to Istanbul and Athens, from where they sailed to Beirut. Loyal to their assignment, they quickly identified the Northern Irish Nazi sympathiser James Jacques. Jacques was an active fascist who was deeply engaged in German politics. Described as 'A constant companion and loyal helper', they reported back to Germany that:

> The Irishman JAMES H. JACQUES, (Belfast, Ireland, 35 Haddingtons Gardens) ... is an enthusiastic supporter of the NSDAP, knows *Mein Kampf*

and the most important publications, and has them constantly with him. He arranges for these works to be distributed in his home, Ireland, and on his worldwide trips.[43]

No doubt they were happy to formally recruit Jacques into the Nazi secret state, taking advantage of his knowledge of the strategically important Northern Irish ports to gather useful intelligence for the Third Reich.

It is likely that it was Jacques who helped them make arrangements for the next stage of their trip to Damascus, the Syrian capital. The cosmopolitan souks were alive with local Arabs, tribal Bedouins, Kurds, Turks, Circassians, and Armenians. Syria's largely Muslim population opposed the colonial rule of the French, creating opportunities for foreign powers to stir unrest. The whole region was ripe for revolt; as in neighbouring Palestine, the Muslim population felt under threat from an influx of large numbers of Jewish immigrants who had fled Nazi persecution. The British had proposed dividing Palestine into two states—one Jewish, one Arab—a prospect which enraged much of the Middle East.

The French were aware of the sensitivity of the situation in Syria and clearly suspected that their Nazi visitors were up to no good. According to Altheim and Trautmann's secret report, the local police kept a watchful eye on them: 'The constant surveillance of the *Sûreté Géneral* limited our movement. We did not make any connections with French scholars'.[44] Ordinary Syrians, however, offered the two Germans a warm welcome, with many regarding Hitler as a natural ally against the Jews:

> The conflict in Palestine resulted in a deeply felt reaction, and each word of the Führer on this subject made a great impact, reaching from Syria into the deepest corners of Iraq. A flyer was given to us by a Mr George I. Saad (Firma Ibrahim I. Saad & Fits, Beirut, Post Box 66) with ten commandments against the Jews written on it. He brought it back from Iran, where thousands of examples are distributed. (We will be sending an original one in the next few days.) Herr Saad and his wife (a Belarussian) are, like all Syrians, strongly anti-French and anti-Jewish.[45]

Sami al-Joundi, one of the founders of the ruling Ba'ath Party, later recalled:

> We were racists. We admired the Nazis. We were immersed in reading Nazi literature and books.... We were the first who thought of a translation of *Mein Kampf*. Anyone who lived in Damascus at that time was witness to the Arab inclination toward Nazism.

However, it was clear to Altheim and Trautmann that their presence attracted too much attention, both welcome and unwelcome. So, travelling by rail, they crossed hundreds of miles of desert, punctuated by oases and date palms, to Baghdad, a city of some 400,000 people. After centuries under the yolk of the Ottoman Turks and then the British, Iraq had only become fully independent in 1932. The German envoy Fritz Grobba was already busy cultivating relations with the government and spreading Nazism through a daily newspaper—*The Al-Alim al-Arabi*, which had, among other things, published an Arabic translation of *Mein Kampf*. He had met with some success, founding a fascist-style youth organisation, *Al-Futuwwa*, whose leaders had travelled to Nuremberg to attend the annual Nazi party rally.[46]

Grobba was the perfect host, introducing the two travellers to his wife and circle of friends in Baghdad, which included Dr Julius Jordan, a prominent German archaeologist who had founded a local branch of the Nazi party.[47] With Grobba's assistance, Altheim and Trautmann hired a driver and car and set off to photograph and study southern Iraq's historic ruins, including Ctesiphon, the ancient winter capital of Parthian kings and Persian monarchs (who were considered Nordic by German scholars) and Babylon.[48]

From Baghdad the explorers went north to Assur, where they met Sheikh Adjil el Yawar, the leader of the Shammar Bedouin tribe and commander of the northern Camel Corps. They discussed German politics with him and heard of his desire to duplicate the success of Abd al-Aziz ibn Saud, who had recently ascended to power in Saudi Arabia. Altheim reported: 'For him, it was enough to hear from us that the Führer would never allow a Jewish state in Palestine'.[49] Altheim almost certainly made no mention of certain Nazi racial theories that classified the Arabs as a Semite people, greatly inferior to the Aryan race. Nor did he likely make any mention of the stated goals of his own research—namely to study the great battles of the northern Indo-Germanic people and the inferior peoples of the Orient.

With the support of Sheikh Adjil el Yawar, Altheim and Trautmann travelled to their final archaeological destination—the ruins of Hatra, on the former border between the Roman and Persian empires.

When they had finished their explorations, the two German researchers returned to Baghdad and headed west from there. They stopped at the ancient city of Palmyra, a spectacular place, and chatted to the local people, gleaning what snippets of political information they could. In a later report, they concluded:

> The Bedouins are always ready to attack at any opportunity. They told us that in the event of a European conflict, things would immediately erupt.

In addition to Ibn Saud, they speak the names 'Hitler' and 'Mussolini' as if they are holy ... The routes of the oil pipelines are hidden but every Arab and Bedouin knows exactly where they are. Time and time again we were told that the pipeline ran here or over there.[50]

There is no doubt that this extended journey took in many archaeological sites, and that they were able to claim later that these sites supported their thesis that the success of the Roman Empire was due to people of a Nordic background. However, the circuitous route, choice of informants, and topics of conversation all point to this being less about archaeology and more about political bridge-building and intelligence-gathering in anticipation of the conflagration that was to come.

On their return to Germany, Altheim and Trautmann wrote a detailed secret report by hand, appending several personal recommendations to the end. Among these was a proposal to strengthen their blossoming friendship with el Yawar by a follow-up trip to Iraq:

> The connection to Sheikh Adjil will thereby be maintained.... He himself has urgently invited us. We recommend sending an SS officer along also. There are many possibilities for scholarly studies, as our recent results have shown. A present of a hunting gun and sufficient ammunition would serve to deepen the friendship.[51]

In addition to this, they advised sending the sheikh the requested propaganda material.

Sievers sent the report to be typed and promptly passed it on to Himmler, who in turn forwarded it to the staff of the SS Security Service.[52] On 12 May 1939, two intelligence officers from the service met with Sievers to examine the report's recommendations.[53] The two officers were clearly impressed by the information that Altheim and Trautmann had gleaned, particularly in Iraq; contacts with the restive Bedouins would prove very helpful in the future if Germany needed to cut off British oil supplies in the Middle East. To further this strategy, the two intelligence officers agreed to the couple's plan to cultivate el Yawar, and they approved Altheim's request to return to Iraq. They also arranged to dispatch the requested Nazi propaganda to Baghdad by diplomatic pouch so that it would not be intercepted.

Sievers relayed the substance of this meeting to Altheim, who was at work on a new book, *The Soldier Emperors*, which drew on the new Middle Eastern research and described the clashing empires of East and West during the third century—an important turning point in history. The scholar was delighted by the prospect of a return trip to Iraq.

Again, he and Trautmann did not hesitate to volunteer their services as agents of the Reich. In a letter to the Ahnenerbe, they wrote:

> We plan on keeping a diary for the trip to Iraq and central Arabia that will include not only scientific results, but also everything that is important in the ethnological, economic and political respect. The talks with Sheikh Adjil el Yawar shall be recorded in his characteristic wording as much as possible.[54]

Iran Expedition

Wüst was proud of Germany's tradition of Middle Eastern archaeology. In 1930, Alfred Rust (1900–1983) and a friend had famously cycled all the way to the Middle East in order to study the origin of Palaeolithic stone tools in central Europe. Rust had become interested in prehistoric archaeology as a child, when he had explored the moors and marshes near to his home of Hamburg. In the 1930s, encouraged by the pre-historian Gustav Schwantes, Rust undertook excavations at the sites of Meiendorf, a site belonging to the 'Hamburg culture', dated to the late Palaeolithic about 15,000 years ago, and *Stellmoor* ('marshy place'), a site representative of the Ahrensburg culture, dated 12,700 years ago. This work proved that groups of hunter-gatherers frequented the tundra stretching to the foot of the huge glaciers that covered northern Europe during the Ice Age. He found numerous flint tools—awls, scrapers, chisels for working bone and antlers, pairs of blades for mounting on a pair of scissors, and carved stone, wood, or bone weapons including spears. He also discovered the bones of sacrificed animals (especially deer); they were found intact except for a large stone that was placed intentionally in the thorax of each animal. Among his other notable discoveries were an amber plate with a hole and engraved figures (horse, bird, fish), a finely carved and incised stick, and a baton decorated with a large pair of reindeer antlers.

In order to better understand his discoveries, he had cycled to the Holy Land, where British archaeologist Dorothy Garrod had recently excavated a similar Stone Age culture. Rust was exhausted and ill when he arrived at Nebek, north of Damascus. He took time to recover, exploring and excavating the caves of the *wadi* (valley) of Skifta, near the small town of Yabrud. He discovered, with the help of his friend and some local labourers, one of the most important Palaeolithic sites in the Middle East. The adventurous story of this discovery and the results of his excavations at Yabrud were published between 1931 and 1933 in *Offa*, a journal of archaeology edited by Rust's mentor, Gustav Schwantes, and the archaeologist Herbert Jankuhn.

Wüst was not content to sit behind a desk in Germany while Altheim and Trautmann explored the Middle East. He planned an archaeological expedition of his own to Iran, where he would study the Behistun Inscription and also no doubt gather further useful intelligence for the Third Reich. The inscription was important to the Nazis because it contained a declaration from Darius I that he was of Aryan origin. The inscription, variously spelled 'Behistun Bisotun', 'Bistun', and 'Bisutun', meaning 'the place of god', is multi-lingual and located on Mount Behistun, in the province of Kermanshah, in western Iran. It was written by Darius the Great sometime during his reign (522–486 BC). The inscription begins with a brief autobiography, including his ancestry and lineage, and continues with a lengthy description of the events following the deaths of Cyrus the Great and his son Cambyses II, with whom Darius had fought a total of nineteen battles in the year 521 BC. These battles were to suppress multiple uprisings throughout the Persian Empire orchestrated by several impostors, each of whom proclaimed themselves king during the upheaval. Darius proclaimed himself victorious in all of these battles, allowing him to suppress the uprising; he attributed these successes to the 'grace of Ahura Mazda'.

The inscription is written in three different languages—Old Persian, Elamite, and Babylonian (a later form of Akkadian)—and played a crucial part in the decipherment of the cuneiform script. Although lying near to the ancient road connecting the capitals of Babylonia (Babylon) and Media (Ecbatana), the inscription itself was largely inaccessible, being carved into the face of a cliff 100 metres above ground. The text itself stood 15 metres high and 25 metres wide. The Old Persian version contained 414 lines set out in five columns; the Elamite text was 593 lines in eight columns; and the Babylonian text was 112 lines long. Accompanying the inscription was a life-sized bas-relief of Darius I holding a bow (a sign of kingship) in his hands while his left foot crushes the chest of a figure, reputed to be the usurper Gaumata, beneath him. To the left of Darius stood two servants, and to the right stood nine 1-metre-tall figures, each with their hands tied and with a rope around their necks, representing the people conquered by Darius. Faravahar floated above, giving his blessing to the king. One figure appeared to have been added after the others were completed, as was Darius's beard, which was a separate block of stone attached with iron pins and lead.

Cuneiform writing fell into disuse after the fall of the Persian Empire, and the ability to read the inscription was lost. One thousand years later, a legend began around Mount Behistun. In the version written down by the Persian poet and writer Ferdowsi in his *Shahnameh* (*Book of Kings*) in AD 1000, he tells of a man named Farhad, the lover of King Khosrow's wife, Shirin. The legend states that after being exiled for his behaviour, Farhad was given the task of quarrying away the mountain to find water; he was promised that if he succeeded, he would be given permission to marry Shirin. He found water after many years and excavating half the mountain, but he was then informed by Khosrow that Shirin had died. Farhad went mad, threw his axe down the hill, kissed the ground, and then died. In the book of *Khosrow and Shirin*, it is said that his axe was made out of pomegranate wood and that a pomegranate tree grew where the axe landed. This tree bore magical fruit that could cure the sick. Meanwhile, it transpired that Khosrow had lied and that Shirin was still alive; she went into mourning on finding out that her former lover was dead.

The inscription was brought to the attention of European scholars in 1598, when the English diplomat Robert Sherley saw it during a mission to Persia on behalf of Austria. However, it was left to the German scholar Georg Friedrich Grotefend, using the first published account made by German surveyor Carsten Niebuhr in 1764, to begin the work of translating the inscription. Grotefend had deciphered ten of the thirty-seven symbols of Old Persian by 1802, after realising that unlike the Semitic cuneiform scripts, Old Persian text is alphabetic, and each word is separated by a vertical slanted symbol. In 1835, Sir Henry Rawlinson, an officer of the British East India Company Army assigned to the forces of the Shah of Iran, began studying the inscription in earnest. Despite its relative inaccessibility, Rawlinson was able to scale the cliff and copy the Old Persian inscription. As the Elamite version was across a chasm and the Babylonian version 4 metres above, they were left for later. With the Persian text, and with about a third of the syllabary made available to him by the work of Grotefend, Rawlinson was able to decipher the type of cuneiform used for Old Persian by 1838, presenting his results to the Royal Asiatic Society in London and the *Société Asiatique* in Paris. The translation of the Old Persian sections of the Behistun Inscription paved the way for the subsequent ability to decipher the Elamite and Babylonian parts of the text, which greatly promoted the development of modern Assyriology.

Wüst's interest in the inscription lay in its supposed Aryan connections, which he wanted to study first-hand. When they were first cut, the craftsmen had erected a wooden scaffolding to reach the cliff face, and it would have made sense for Wüst's team to do the same, but they were unable to afford the cost. Instead, in 1938, he proposed that he, along with his wife, an amanuensis, an Iranian student, a photographer, and an experienced mountaineer all floated up the cliff face in a wicker basket suspended beneath a hot air balloon. Perhaps to the relief of his wife, the onset of the war saw the trip postponed indefinitely. Unfortunately, that did not mean that the cliff was left to its own devices; Allied soldiers decided to use it for target practice during their Anglo-Soviet invasion of Iran.

The Ahnenerbe planned similar expeditions in other parts of the world. An expedition was, for example, sent to Kafiristan, a province in the Hindukush region of Afghanistan. Kafiristan takes its name from the inhabitants, the Kafirs Kalash, a fiercely independent people with distinctive culture, language, and religion. These ethnic phenomena attracted the Nazis, especially Walter Wüst. The Kalash spoke a language that is close to ancient Greek, had a pagan religion very similar to the Greek Dodekatheon, and, in the eyes of the Nazis, were much more advanced and refined that their Muslim neighbours. All this was taken as evidence that they were descended from the armies of Alexander the Great, which, in turn, like the other Greeks, were descendants of ancient German migrants.

Greece:
The Gates of Hades and
the Delphi Treasure

*The alleged Aryan origins may be safely compared to the fables about
the origins of Troy, which grew up in Rome in the second century before
our era. That myth survived for a remarkably long time, since it was
adopted by the Franks who, by this means, affiliated themselves to the
Trojans. Let us hope that the Aryan myth, as it is still accepted today, will
soon be replaced by a more reasonable and scientific conception of the
past of European peoples.*[1]

As well as believing that the Kafiris and the ancient civilisations of
Mesopotamia had been ruled by Aryans, the Nazis also believed that
the ancient Greeks were of Nordic stock, which allowed them to claim
ownership of Greek cultural and scientific achievements. In order to
investigate this connection, the Ahnenerbe organised several expeditions
and excavations in Greece. Archaeologists explored Athens, Thebes,
Delphi, Eretria, Rhamnus, Thorikon, Aegina, Korinth, Epidavros, Nafplio,
Argos, Sparta, Megalopolis, Olympia, and Herakleion in Crete.[2] In
these endeavours, the Germans counted on the collaboration of Greek
authorities as well as the German Institute of Archaeology in Athens.

The Nazis idealised the achievements of ancient Greece, which they
claimed as their own, believing that the Greeks were descended from
Germans who had survived a northern catastrophe and migrated to
Greece, where they had evolved a highly developed culture.[3] They pointed
to the city-states of Sparta, which they admired for its 'pioneering eugenic'
policies, and Athens, for its artistic and intellectual perfection, as exemplars
of this Aryan culture. Schliemann had started his excavations at Troy as
early as 1871. The sanctuary at Olympia had also always held particular
significance for the Germans, who had been conducting excavations
there since 1897. When the Olympic Games were held in Berlin in 1936,

Hitler saw them as the perfect opportunity to parade the 'achievements' of the Third Reich before the world. Germany was presented as the cultural successor to the ancient world, with symbols of the classical world (such as the Olympic Torch relay) manipulated to this end.[4]

The Gates of Hades

The Nazis occupied Greece between 1941 and 1944. During this period, Himmler heard stories about an underground system of caves located somewhere in the Southern Peloponnesus. He came to believe that these caves were linked with other underground passages, making an uninterrupted subterranean system that continued all the way to Berlin. Incredible as it may sound to us, Himmler believed that not only had the ancient Germanic people known of the existence of this cave system, but also that they had exploited it to escape Germany when a natural disaster struck, fleeing to safety in Greece. Perhaps Himmler was so quick to accept the veracity of this story because he had already fallen for the *Glazial Kosmology* (Glacial Cosmology) theory of Hans Höbiger. He accepted the notion that in ancient times, Germans had escaped from their northern homeland to avoid disaster, re-settling in the Mediterranean, where they established the culture of classical Greece; as such, it was natural for Himmler to accept a story that explained how this had happened.[6]

As soon as Himmler heard of the cave theory, he immediately instructed the Ahnenerbe to dispatch secret agents to the 'Gates of Hades' (the Greek name for the caves) and establish the truth of the report. Heading the mission was archaeologist Hans Reinerth (1900–1990), a high-ranking official in the office of the Amt Rosenberg. Reinerth had been a member of the nationalist-minded, anti-Semitic *Kampfbund für deutsche Kultur* before joining the NSDAP in 1931. He was very well-regarded; from 1933 until the end of the Second World War, he was the head of the Reich Association of German Prehistory. In 1934, Reinerth succeeded Gustaf Kossinna as Chair at the University of Berlin. Seemingly a loyal Nazi, he wrote in the journal *Volk und Heimat* in 1937:

> ... those who revile or minimise our Germanic ancestors no longer face the scattered ethnic fighters, but the closed front of Nationalsocialist Germans.

However, he was expelled from the party in February 1945 because he had 'maintained friendly relations with Jews'. In reality, it is more likely that he was embroiled in a dispute between the Amt Rosenberg and the

SS Ahnenerbe organisation; Reinerth belonged to Amt Rosenberg, which came off worse.[7]

The first problem that Reinerth had to deal with was locating the Gates. The ancient Greeks believed that Hades lay far to the west, beyond the horizon, where the River Oceanus, which encircled the earth, began. That description was of no help to Reinerth, but there were later stories of dark caverns and long, dim passages that led down to the underworld from the Greek mainland itself. The Gates were therefore thought to lead to the Kingdom of the Dead and Hades. These later accounts were much more promising prospects for the explorer, with candidate caves across the Aegean Sea in Asia Minor at Thesprotia, in Peloponnessos, near Sparta, and at the small village of Tainaro, one of the southernmost points of continental Europe. The latter location was traditionally believed to be the ancient site of the Gates, so this was the site that Reinerth and his team settled on.

For the modern visitor, this 'Gate of Hades' is a less-than-spectacular hole covered with concrete slabs placed there in the name of 'health and safety'. It was not always so. The natural caves form part of a ritual landscape that includes several features imbued with religious significance. Nearby is the Psychomantium of Poseidon, known as the 'Oracle of the Souls'. A psychomantium is an ancient form of mirror used to contact the spirits of loved ones. Near to Poseidon's Oracle there is another enigmatic spot; set in a landscape littered with thousands of rocks of various sizes, there is a circular area devoid of all rocks and pebbles. To complete this ritual landscape, not far from the Tainaro Cape, in the place called Phrearton Inousson, is one of the deepest abysses of the Mediterranean, plunging to a depth of 4,850 metres.[8]

Although Reinerth's mission was shrouded in secrecy at the time, it was subsequently reported in *The Research Report of the Reichsbund for German Prehistory* dated July–December 1941. The report stated that the expedition lasted nine weeks; during this time, Reinerth claimed, he and his team had discovered major new evidence of Indo-Germanic migration to Greece during Neolithic times. Unsurprisingly, there is no reference— let alone a confirmation—of the existence of an underground network of passageways leading from the Gates of Hades to Germany.

Many years later, the famous French undersea explorer Jacques Cousteau heard about this legend and requested permission from the Greek government to dive in the area and explore the underground passageways. The permission was initially granted, but a few days before the French dive was to get underway, the Greek government reneged on the deal and withdrew their permission. The reason given was that this was a 'sensitive military area' and therefore off-limits to exploration by the public. This last-minute change of heart played into the hands of conspiracy theorists, with many taking this as evidence of an official attempt to suppress the 'secrets' of the caves.

The Delphi Treasure

The Ahnenerbe also undertook an extensive search for the fabled treasure of the 'Oracle of Delphi'. According to ancient sources, the Temple at Delphi was not only home to the Oracle, but also a magnificent treasury packed with gold, silver, and precious stones. This treasure had accumulated over many years as valuables were traditionally given to the temple priests in the hope that the Oracle would look upon them generously.

The Nazis were not the first to go in search of the treasure. In 279 BC, the Celtic chief Brennus led 200,000 soldiers into Greece, intent on capturing the Delphi treasure. The Celts were on the point of victory at Parnassus when they suffered a series of natural disasters—lightning storms, falling rocks, hailstones, and heavy snow. As Brennus and his troops tried to defend themselves from the forces of nature, the Oracle offered the townsfolk of Delphi reassurance that Apollo would not allow them to suffer. Meanwhile, the Celtic army suffered heavy losses. From then on, as a consequence, the treasure was considered to be cursed. The Nazis believed that no one had dared attempt to steal the treasure due to this curse, and that it was therefore still in the vicinity of the Temple complex. Like the Celts, the Ahnenerbe were to fail in their attempts to discover the treasure, which—if it exists—is still presumably safely hidden.

The Nazis may have missed out on the treasure of Delphi, but they more than made up for this loss by striping the country's famous museums and private collections of the choicest antiquities and works of art.[9] In various regions, including Thiva, Heronia, and Tanagra, the occupiers stole treasures, chased the Greeks out of the museum, and installed themselves in it. The museum at Knossos was robbed by a German general. He had his men steal 8,500 Minoan, bronze, and stone statues worth (in current values) some £1 trillion. Elsewhere, excavations were undertaken at Aigina, Chalkida, in Nea Acnhialos of Magnesia, and in a cave on the Kopais Lake, all in the hope of finding treasures that could be stolen. Equally disrespectful was the treatment of Greek national monuments by the German occupiers. The Museum of Livadia was turned into a bicycle repair garage; the Lions Gate at Mycenae was used for target practice, while the Parthenon was converted into an anti-aircraft battery in 1941. The soldiers stationed there entertained themselves by taking pot-shots at the sculptures. It is even said that the men relieved themselves against the Acropolis' gateway, the Propylaea.

Fortunately, the archaeologists of the Greek Archaeological Service, acting in accordance with a ministerial decree, had the foresight to hide many of the most famous antiquities before the German invasion, and also had the courage to protect them.[10] In the six months before the German invasion, these archaeologists buried as many of the cultural treasures as they could in caves, ancient tombs, museum cellars, and even under the base of the statue of Hermes of Praxiteles in the Archaeological Museum of Olympia.[11] Most audacious of all, the floor of the National Archaeological Museum was carefully dug up, creating deep trenches into which delicate statues were lifted; sand was then poured around and over them, before a concrete slab was poured on top to seal them from prying eyes. Other items were placed into crates that were then hidden in the museum basement, which was then filled to the ceiling with dry sand.[12]

When the Nazis arrived at the museum in April 1941, they found, much to their anger, that it had been stripped of its contents. The German occupiers created a special military 'service for the protection of art' headed by the archaeologist Hans Ulrich von Seneberg, who held the military rank of Lieutenant Colonel. The function of the service was to locate the missing artefacts so that they could be removed to Germany. Von Seneberg met with the stubborn resistance from the brave Greek archaeologists, but many items were still stolen.

A post-war report by the Greek Ministry of Education lists some of the treasures taken by the Germans: the ancient head of a woman of the fourth century BC was given as a gift to Marshal List. The entire collection of archaeological artefacts from Potidea was stolen, as was a black-figure plate from the Museum of the Kerameikos. A marble statue of the Herakleiotissa was taken by force from the Thessalonike, along with a statue of a woman, a geometric vase, and a late antiquity portrait. Five clay vases and a gold, leaf-shaped earring were taken from the Museum of Chaironeia, and a Roman statue of Aphrodite and other objects were taken from the Gortyna Museum.

As well as stealing from museums, German archaeologists also resumed excavations that had been interrupted by the onset of the war, carrying out illegal excavations in seventeen areas and sending their finds back to Germany. This operation was well-organised; the Luftwaffe photographed classical sites, the Wehrmacht cordoned off the ruins, and the Kriegsmarine salvaged pieces of an ancient frieze that was sunk near Piraeus. Many of the antiquities taken from Greece to Germany during the Second World War have remained there. It is only very recently that the Greek government has begun to actively pursue the repatriation of these stolen objects. In 2014, some 10,600 fragments of clay vessels, stone artefacts, and osteological material were returned to Greece; these objects had been unearthed during Nazi excavations between June and December 1941. The return of this material was marked by a formal ceremony at Pfahlibau Museum, in the German city of Unteruhldingen.

The Nazis continued looting and destroying Greek archaeological sites until their occupation came to an end in 1944; the retreating soldiers used their rifles and bayonets to destroy statues and vases on the Acropolis and in the *Kerameikos* (Ancient Cemetery) in Athens.

Symbols of Power in the New *Germania*

... to see these twelve ... sitting in a circle, all sunk in deep and silent contemplation, was indeed a remarkable sight.[1]

Many of the looted Greek artefacts were destined for the Nazi fortress of Wewelsburg Castle, the ideological centre of Himmler's SS. The medieval stronghold had a sinister history. According to legend, thousands of accused witches had been tortured and executed there, and an inquisition room still survived in the basement. For Himmler, however, the castle, perched high above the valley of the River Oder in Westphalia, governed over a region he associated with the mythic origins of the German nation.[2]

Wewelsburg Castle

The castle was built in the early seventeenth century for the Prince-Bishops of Paderborn. Sited on a tapering ridge overlooking the river, it is a narrow triangle in plan; this triangle points due north, with an immense round tower at the apex. In 1933, Himmler had been struck by this geometry and believed that it depicted the 'Spear of Destiny', an occult symbol. For the Reichsführer, the '*SS School Haus Wewelsburg*' was part monastery, part Camelot, and part fortress—an 'SS Vatican', the centre of the new Aryan world.

The design of the castle was inspired by the legend of King Arthur, and particularly the idea of the Knights of the Round Table. What survives today is but a shell of the building Himmler knew. We can glimpse a sense of his vision in the surviving north tower, where, behind a locked iron door, is a stone-lined room ringed by Romanesque arches. This was the *Gruppenführersaal,* a great dining hall complete with a large oak table capable of accommodating the twelve men who formed the secret chapter of Himmler's new religious order. These men formed the Nazi equivalent of the Knights of the Round Table, and each was hand-picked by Himmler from the senior Gruppenführers. These twelve were the only people permitted entry to the castle, with the exception of the occasional invited guest.[3]

Each of the twelve members had his own armchair with an engraved silver nameplate, while the walls behind were adorned with their coats of arms. For those who lacked armorial bearings (including Himmler), designs were drafted by the genealogist Professor Diebitsch and experts from the Ahnenerbe. When Himmler and his inner circle met, they would engage in mystic communication with dead Teutons and perform other spiritual exercises. These exercises were observed by Foreign Intelligence Chief Walter Schellenberg. He had been allowed into the castle in order to interrogate General von Fritsch, who had been falsely accused of 'moral offences'. Schellenberg recorded the following:

> He [Himmler] assembled twelve of his most trusted SS leaders in a room next to the one in which von Fritsch was being questioned and ordered them all to concentrate their minds on exerting a suggestive influence over the General that would induce him to tell the truth. I happened to come into the room by accident, and to see these twelve SS leaders sitting in a circle, all sunk in deep and silent contemplation, was indeed a remarkable sight.[4]

Embedded in the marble floor was a twelve-spoked *Sonnenrad* (a sun wheel) that was once lined with gold; for Himmler, it represented the 'Centre of the New World'.

Below this was an equally mysterious circular, domed chamber, a 'realm of the dead' where the exposed brick walls resembled those of a torture chamber. The design was inspired by the tombs of the Bronze Age Mycenaeans and a semi-mythical ruler Himmler admired—Agamemnon, the Mycenaean conqueror of Troy. At the zenith of the dome was an ancient symbol that had been found on pottery at Troy and on golden decorations at Mycenae, a symbol the Nazis appropriated for their own baleful ends—the 'crooked cross' also known as the 'swastika'.[5]

The Swastika

For most people in the West, the swastika remains inextricably linked to the atrocities committed by the Nazis in the twentieth century. Today, the swastika immediately conjures images of one of the most horrific periods in modern history; it symbolises all that was most offensive about the Third Reich. For Jewish people, the swastika is undoubtedly a symbol of fear and repression, of the holocaust and of extermination.

The swastika, which can face either left or right, is a universal symbol that exists in every culture in the world. It is based upon the shapes of nature, such as the way a flower blossoms, and in India it is part of everyday life; there, it is found on houses, temples, and even on the front of books. The word comes from the Sanskrit words 'su', meaning 'well', and 'asti,' meaning 'to be'. 'Swastika' therefore means 'wellbeing'.[6]

In the west, Nazi associations have made the study of the swastika something of a taboo subject. However, in recent years there has been a revival in study of pre-Nazi origins of the symbol. Around 100 years ago, there was a noticeable western fad for the swastika; it was a design many western travellers had seen in Asia and adopted enthusiastically when they returned home. It was widely used on public buildings, in advertising, and on bank notes and textiles. Rudyard Kipling used it on his book covers, Carlsberg stamped it on the bottom of their beer bottles, and the RAF even painted it on their aeroplanes as late as 1939. In the United States, Coca Cola used the swastika in advertising at the turn of the twentieth century, while the Boy Scouts also used it. The Girls Club of America even named their magazine *Swastika,* giving away swastika badges as an award for selling copies.[7]

It was in the nineteenth century, while translating ancient Indian texts such as the *Rigveda,* that European scholars first noticed similarities between the Sanskrit and German languages. They concluded that there must have been some ancient link between German and Indian people, which they labelled 'Aryan' (using a term found in the *Rigveda*).[8] German nationalists exploited the idea and turned what was a linguistic connection into something darker. They created the myth of an Aryan super race of godlike warriors from which the Germans were descended. The idea of German exceptionalism fitted with the wider ideas of occultists, who were happy to believe that they were a race apart, members of an Aryan culture. They adopted the swastika as their symbol and wrote for magazines such as *Ostara,* which disseminated the idea of blond, blue-eyed supermen to their readers—including Hitler.[9]

Adolf Hitler appropriated the swastika in 1920, creating the distinctive red-white-black flag of the NSDAP. He is thought to have first seen the symbol at Limbeck Abbey in Austria, and he explained in *Mein Kampf* (1925) that the colouring of the swastika flag was highly significant. The red part symbolised socialist ideas, and the white part reflected the ultranationalist ideas of National Socialism. Interestingly, the swastika actually posed a problem for the Nazis; it hardly seemed right for an ultranationalist movement to adopt an Indian symbol. Hitler was therefore keen to 'Germanise' the swastika, using the word '*Hakenkreuz*' to refer to the symbol; the term 'swastika' was reserved for German ehtnographers. As the Nazis rose to power, the swastika became a tightly controlled tool of propaganda designed to be used everywhere—on banners, armbands, and badges.

For German Jews, the swastika must have been a genuinely menacing symbol. They saw themselves as German citizens, and they must have found it extremely offensive to see this symbol of anti-Semitism become the official flag. Many German Jews had fought for Germany in the Frist World War, and they were shocked when they found themselves relegated to the status of second-class citizens.

People elsewhere ceased using the swastika after the Nazis rose to power. After the defeat of the Third Reich in May 1945, the symbol was banned in Germany and Austria; thus a symbol that had been ubiquitous throughout Germany for twelve years disappeared overnight. The swastika is still banned in Germany, and anyone who displays it is committing a criminal offence. Elsewhere in Europe and North America, the symbol still has the power to shock when it is occasionally paraded by minority neo-Nazi groups. The irony is that according to the *Rigveda*, which mentions Aryans thirty times, the meaning of the word 'Aryan' is 'the one who follows the traditions of his country/one who is faithful to the gods of his country/a good family man praised by everybody'. The Aryan of the *Rigveda* is therefore not the white super race of warriors portrayed by Nazi ideology; indeed, the term is open to anyone—white or black—who is worthy of praise by others.[10]

However, it is also incorrect to see the swastika as an exclusively Aryan symbol rooted in a mystical Indian past. Archaeological finds have long demonstrated that the swastika is a very old symbol and that its geographic origins are by no means limited to India. It is found in ancient cultures from Europe to China, with some of the oldest identified examples in eastern Europe and Russia.[11]

The place that best demonstrates the swastika's long European history is Ukraine.[12] In the National Museum of the History of Ukraine in Kiev is a figurine of a small bird about 10 cm long, made from mammoth-tusk ivory, decorated with the oldest identified swastika pattern in the world (dated to the late Palaeolithic, 15,000 years ago). Engraved on one side of the bird is a large triangle, and on the other is a series of swastikas joined together in a pattern known as a 'meander'. This association of the swastika with the triangle or rhombus on female figurines is a recurring theme in many ancient artefacts, and it supports the idea that the swastika started out as a fertility symbol.

The palaeontologist Valentina Bibikova made a surprising discovery when she examined a cross-section of ivory tusk and saw inside a pattern similar to the swastika meander. The swastika pattern occurs naturally inside ivory tusk, something that prehistoric people might have noted and then deliberately copied as a symbol of fertility and wellbeing.[13]

The swastika may have more than one origin, independently invented several times in different places and at different times, perhaps inspired by nature. Also at Ukraine's National Museum are examples of swastika symbols from many different Ukrainian cultures, showing how the symbol evolved through time. Pots decorated with swastikas were excavated at the beginning of the twentieth century and found to date from the Middle Bronze Age and Late Bronze Age. When Germany invaded Ukraine, the Nazis were particularly interested in these objects because they seemed to fit with their interpretation of history. The Nazi thesis was that the Aryans travelled from the German homeland in the north to Ukraine, taking the swastika with them. According to this line of reasoning, the discovery of the swastika symbol in Ukraine was evidence of an Aryan presence in the Bronze Age. The Nazis therefore gathered the objects together and carried them away to Germany. Unlike many other objects, they were returned at the conclusion of the war.

Also in the museum collection are items from the Greek period. In the seventh century BC, the Greeks founded colonies in Ukraine. Architectural features were decorated with interlinked swastikas that form the distinctive Greek key pattern found on tiles and carpets to this day. There are also terracotta vases beautifully painted with swastikas with curling limbs that resemble unfurling tendrils, and an artistic representation of a goat, under whose belly is the swastika. Swastika-decorated ornaments were clearly very popular in the Greek period.

Kiev Museum houses a remarkable textile fragment of a gold-embroidered standing collar dating to the twelfth century; it was probably the property of a Slav princess. The embroidery has a complex pattern with crosses and swastikas, and some glass inserts. These were worn by wealthy women to ward off evil. Interestingly, it is a practice that continues in China to this day. Beyond Ukraine, the swastika appears on stone seals found in the Indus valley and terracotta figurines from Troy. In Norse mythology, the swastika is a sign of good fortune and luck.

We may never know the full meaning of all the swastikas used by people in the ancient past, but that the swastika appears in so many places, and in so many similar objects, shows a common cultural importance. Nevertheless, it is still most closely associated with the Nazis.

An elaborate swastika design, set inside a concrete ring directly below the *Sonnenrad* ('Sun Ring') in the Great Hall above, dominated the room in the basement of the Wewelsberg Castle. Beneath that, set at the top of ceremonial steps, was a sunken stone circle or well. The skull-head ring of each SS member was to be ceremonially cast into this well in the event of their death. Whenever one of the 'Knights' of the Black Order passed away, their coat of arms was to be ceremonially burned. Ringing the walls of the chamber were twelve stone pedestals that were once lined with the heraldic emblems of senior SS officers and decorated with runes. This was a place of the dead, a *Valhalla* where the 'Knights' of the SS were ceremonially honoured after death.

Within the castle, each member of the inner circle had his own room that was decorated in remembrance of an Aryan hero. Himmler's room was designed to celebrate 'King Henry the Fowler'—Heinrich I, the Saxon king responsible for the first German 'Drive to the East'.[14] Himmler's interest had gone so far as to have his skeleton exhumed from Quedlinburg Cathedral. The royal remains had then been measured and studied by Beger, who was retained on Himmler's *Persönlicher Stab* (personal staff). He had verified that the skull was that of 'Henry the Fowler'. The remains had then been solemnly reinterred beneath the cathedral floor in a ceremony lit by the torches of SS officers. Some commentators have argued that Himmler saw himself as a reincarnation of Henry and that he communed with his ghost. Whether that is true or not, in his memory, Himmler created the King Heinrich Memorial Institute in 1938 in Quedlinburg.

Himmler's vision for the castle was even more grandiose. In 1935, architectural plans were drawn up and models constructed.[15] They reveal that he was intent on transforming not only the castle, but also the village of Wewelsburg, turning it into an SS city. Local villagers would be moved to a new 'model village' several kilometres away. The project cost was 250 million RM. Wewelsburg would be a pagan Vatican City where the SS elite would receive spiritual and *weltanschauliches* ('world view') training. Libraries would be assembled, astronomical observatories constructed, appropriate works of art acquired, special furniture made and decorated with arcane symbols and runes, and in pride of place would be all the archaeological artefacts collected by the SS and Amt Rosenberg from around the world.

To achieve all this, prisoners were brought form Sachsenhausen, the concentration camp near Berlin, and a new camp was built in the Niederhagen Forest nearby. The prisoners were forced to cut stone blocks from a local quarry and drag them to the castle. More than 1,000 were worked to death. Wewelsburg was torn down and put back together again, then sumptuously decorated. Himmler called it an 'ancient Germanic cult centre' and brought in scientists and researchers, who lived in cell-like rooms while investigating the 'foundations of Germanic culture'.

These 'Reich leaders' had to be 'free of any inclination to see science as an end in itself'. They were told, 'We need neither a fossilised scientist nor a dreamer.' Nobody knows how close Himmler came to realising his dream, and nor which artefacts may have been brought there. Deep within the castle lay a secret chamber—Himmler's private vault. However, when American soldiers captured Wewelsburg in 1945, they found it empty, its contents unknown and seemingly lost forever.

We do know something of the deprivations suffered by the concentration camp captives forced to build Himmler's Grail Castle, as they composed the following touching song:

> *And the stones are hard, but our step is firm*
> *As we carry along the picks and the spades*
> *And in our hearts,*
> *In our hearts the sorrows;*
> *O Wewelsburg, I cannot forget you*
> *Because you are my fate ...*
> *And whatever our future is,*
> *Nevertheless we say 'yes' to life,*
> *Because soon a day will come*
> *And we will be free!*[16]

By 1943, some 1,285 concentration camp inmates had gained their 'freedom'; they were buried in the red earth of Westphalia or burned in the crematorium at Niederhagen.

While the forced workers suffered, the Nazi elite at Wewelsburg enjoyed pagan festivals, which were celebrated at each summer and winter solstice, and SS wives were admitted to the *Sippengemeinschaft* ('kinship') of Himmler's order.[17] These ceremonies dispensed with the 'false trappings' of Christianity. The bride was forbidden to wear a veil and myrtle crown since these were 'oriental' customs. Instead, there were 'Sig runes' and swastikas, fir sprigs, holly, and ivy. Ordination rites like these bound Himmler's officers and their families into a community dedicated to obedience and 'hardness'. According to Himmler, 'these inner feelings of the heart, of honour and of a feeling for the most real and profound world view are ultimately the things that give us strength...'

Himmler and the twelve were the elite of the new religion, which all members of the SS were encouraged to join. Having broken from Christianity, the SS were introduced to a series of alternative religious ceremonies. Rather ironically, a winter solstice ceremony was designed to replace Christmas, which had been a Christian replacement for the early medieval pagan ceremonies. The Nazi replacement extended to a 1939 ban on the word 'Christmas' in all official SS documents. Deliberately inverting the Christian Christmas, the Nazis designed a celebration of the summer solstice; from then on, gifts were to be exchanged in summer rather than in the winter. Such was their grip over the new religion that they even built a factory specifically to manufacture appropriately Aryan gifts (*tschochkes*).

The new Aryan ceremonies were spectacular affairs. They often took place at night so that sacred fires and torch-lit processions could be deployed to add drama to the proceedings. The participants were carefully selected, young, blond-haired, blue-eyed Aryan men who would invoke the Teutonic deities before the crowds of onlookers. Weddings and 'christenings' were likewise replaced by pagan SS rituals and liturgy. The Hitler Youth took the lead in educating children about this new religion; a Hitler Youth 'Nazi Primer' was published during the war and contains many examples of pagan ideology and anti-Christian sentiment aimed at a youthful readership.

Germania

The notion of ancient Teutonic Knights may seem to be one of the more harmless of the Nazi beliefs, but it also carried the idea of a prehistoric Teutonic empire and (importantly for Nazi ideology) the justification for their dream of a Greater Germania. Greater Germania was to be the home to people of pure German, Aryan blood. To make this idea reality, Germany not only invaded her neighbours but also set about the mass murder of those they described as being of 'inferior blood'. To their shame, many German historians, archaeologists, and linguists constructed 'evidence' out of nothing to support the idea of the prehistoric Greater Germania, which was then used by the NSDAP to justify Germany's demand of a *Lebensraum*. Meanwhile, their anthropological colleagues created through their measurements the basis for racial laws that cost the lives of millions of people, particularly those of the Jewish faith.

In reality, there had never been an ancient Germanic Empire; the Nazis simply invented one, helped by willing archaeologists and historians. The Danish archaeologist Jørgen Jensen explained how this came about:

Soon after Hitler's takeover in 1933, archaeology and history research became part of the Nazi cultural politics. In Nazi mythology, the idea of the pure Germanic race and its superiority played a central role. It was through that idea that they wanted to justify the policy of expansion. By turning to ancient times, they created a forgery of history without precedent. It was founded on the perception of 'the Germanic people's common destiny', and about a continuous development of particular Germanic virtues ever since the Bronze Age. The vast majority of German archaeologists agreed at the time, that it was the culture of the Bronze Age, which could first be described as Germanic. It was during those years common knowledge that the culture originated as a combination of two older cultures, the Battle Axe culture and the Megalithic culture. At the end of the Stone Age, this *einheitliches Volkstum*, a common Germanic people, should have emerged. It was in reality the same idea that the Danish archaeologist and prehistorian, Johannes Brønsted described in his book *Danish Antiquity*. But in Germany, the idea of 'original' was used to describe Germanic peoples in areas far away from the German borders. Hence, it was instrumental in creating a scientific basis for the German *Drang nach Osten*.[18]

To construct the Greater Germania, historians drew on the work of the Roman Gaius Cornelius Tacitus (56–117) and his description of the Teutons in *De Origine et situ Germanorum* (literally *Concerning the Origin and Situation of the Germanics*), usually shortened to *Germania*, written in AD 98.[19] The book is an ethnographic work describing the Germanic tribes beyond the Roman Empire, beginning with a description of the lands, laws, and customs of the Germanic people (Chapters 1–27). The book then describes the individual tribes, beginning with those living closest to the Roman frontier and ending with those on the furthest shores of the Baltic, among the amber-gathering *Aesti*, the *Fenni*, and the unknown tribes beyond.

Himmler relied upon the words of Tacitus in his attempts to prove that the German people were part of a race of Aryan 'super-humans'. He used Tacitus's descriptions of Germanic society to help shape the Nazi state based upon the principles of warriorhood, and he used the notion of German ethnic purity described in *Germania* to justify the murder of millions of 'non-Aryans'. It was therefore not without justification that Jewish-Italian historian Arnaldo Momigliano described *Germania* as 'among the most dangerous books ever written'.[20]

The Nazis homed in on particular sections that they argued supported their racial and nationalistic theories. For example, in Chapter 2, Tacitus writes that physically the Germanic people appear to be a distinct nation, not a mixture of their neighbours, as nobody would choose to migrate to a land with such a miserable climate:

The population of Germania has not degenerated due to the mixing of strangers, but appears with pure racial descent with an individual distinctive mark without comparison to others. That is also why all of them, despite their great numbers, have the same appearance: Threatening blue eyes, red-blond hair and strong bodies...[21]

This text was used to support ideas of racial 'purity' and the ideal Ayran 'type'. Tacitus also praised the Teuton 'barbarians' for their valiant struggle against the Roman occupiers:

> When it comes to battle, it is disgraceful of the leader to be surpassed in bravery, disgraceful for the army not to be his equal in bravery. And life-long is the dishonour and infamy for he, who survives him by withdrawing from battle. To defend him and protect him and bestow him honour also for one's own deed, that is the army's most noble oath of allegiance. The leader fights to win, but the army fights for the leader.[22]

Tacitus contrasted the 'noble savages' of the text with the 'moral corruption' that he saw in Rome, a city and empire that he considered decadent and corrupt. The Nazis had exactly the same view of the Weimar Republic. They rejected decadent city life and sought to return Germany to a more pastoral way of being that was characterised by the respect of old virtues. This idealised world would be inhabited by decisive, strong men and respectable, fertile women. Women, the subject of Chapters 7 and 8, often accompanied the men to battle, where they would offer encouragement; Tacitus says that the fear of them being taken into slavery helped to motivate the men. In Chapter 18, he explains that the Germans were mainly content with one wife—except for a few political marriages—and compared this favourably to other barbarian cultures, perhaps because monogamy was a value shared with the Romans. He also recorded in Chapter 19 that adultery was very rare, and that an adulterous woman would be shunned by the community regardless of her beauty:

> There are, despite the large population, remarkably few incidents of marital infidelity. The punishment befalls the husband, and is executed immediately. He cuts off the hair of his wife, disrobes her in the presence of relatives, banishes her from the home and drives her with a whip through the entire village. For there is no mercy for the abandonment of a woman's virtue. Neither due to youth, beauty or wealth can she find herself another husband. Nobody smiles overbearingly where immorality is found...[23]

In Chapter 7, Tacitus describes their government and leadership as somewhat merit-based and egalitarian, with leadership by example rather than authority. He also writes that punishments were carried out by the priests. He expands on the Germanic judicial system in Chapter 12:

> Penalities are distinguished according to the offence. Traitors and deserters are hanged on trees; the coward, the unwarlike, the man stained with abominable vices, is plunged into the mire of the morass, with a hurdle put over him. This distinction in punishment means that crime, they think, ought in being punished, to be exposed, while infamy ought to be buried out of sight.[24]

Taking his cue from Tactitus, Herbert Jankuhn (1905–1990), the head of the archaeology department at the Ahnenerbe, argued that this explained the many bodies found preserved in the bogs of Southern Scandinavia. They were, he said, either cowards or men who had taken part in 'perverse sexual offences'.[25]

Archaeologists were, and still are, divided in their explanations of the bodies found preserved in layers of peat. For example, at Borre Fen, Denmark, the well-preserved body of a man was found covered and packed around with heather stems; this pattern has been repeated elsewhere, where bodies have been found covered in branches.[26] Some archaeologists thought these bodies were the corpses of sacrificial offerings made to appease the gods; others thought that they were murdered prisoners of war. Jankuhn put forward a different hypothesis—that these individuals were social pariahs, deserters, and homosexuals who had been put to death for their behaviour according to Germanic law.

Academic 'evidence' that the Germans had once executed their men for homosexuality provided Himmler with the justification he needed to support his own policies. Speaking at the SS officer-training school at Bad Tölz in 1937, he explained:

> Homosexuals were drowned in swamps. The worthy professors who find these bodies in peat, do not realize that in ninety out of a hundred cases they are looking at the remains of a homosexual who was drowned in a swamp along with his clothes and everything else. That was not a punishment, but simply the termination of an abnormal life.[27]

The Reichsführer-SS continued to expand on the theme, explaining that homosexuals were a threat to the Third Reich as they could 'infect' heterosexuals with their sexual preferences. If this happened, the SS would be weakened, destroying one of the cornerstones of the Nazi state.[28] Himmler's views are out of step with modern thinking, but his speech would have been considered unexceptional at the time; homosexuality was illegal in most European and North American countries, and even some of those who contributed significantly to the Allied war effort, such as the British codebreaker Alan Turing, were prosecuted for their sexuality.[29]

With the support of other leading Nazis, Himmler ordered a crackdown on those suspected of being homosexual, with as many as 15,000 men sent to concentration camps; when they arrived, they were marked with a distinctive pink triangle.[30] Some were castrated, while others were subjected to experimental procedures designed to transform them into heterosexuals.[31]

This exemplifies how the Nazis deployed archaeological speculation in order to justify mass murder. In reality, Tacitus never visited northern Europe; all his information is second-hand at best, with large sections copied from the lost *Bella Germaniae* of Pliny the Elder.[32] While Pliny may have been the primary source, he also drew from Caesar's *Gallic Wars*, Strabo, Diodorus Siculus, Posidonius, and Aufidius Bassus, as well as numerous non-literary sources. Much of this was presumably based on interviews with traders and soldiers who had ventured beyond the Rhine and Danube borders, and Germanic mercenaries in Rome.

All copies of *Germania* were lost during the Middle Ages, and the work was forgotten. In 1425, a single handwritten manuscript was found in Hersfeld Abbey in Germany. Named the *Codex Hersfeldensis*, it was taken to Italy, where Enea Silvio Piccolomini, later Pope Pius II, first examined and analysed the book. This sparked interest among German humanists, including Conrad Celtes, Johannes Aventinus, and Ulrich von Hutten.[33]

Inspired by the rediscovered text of *Germania*, the name *Germani,* used to describe the German people, was revived in 1471. Until then, the term had hardly been used during the medieval period. The rediscovered name was adopted to invoke the warlike qualities of the ancient Germans in a crusade against the Turks.

Germania had a significant influence on the development of Pan-German and Nordic ideology, and played a major role in the formation of the core concepts of Nazi ideology.[34] Given the important place that *Germania* held in Nazi culture, and bearing in mind their generally acquisitive attitude to archaeological and artistic 'treasures', it is not surprising that Himmler was determined to take possession of the *Codex Hersfeldensis*. Their first attempt was diplomatic. In 1936, Mussolini made an official visit to Berlin in order to meet Hitler, during which the Führer personally asked Mussolini to give the *Codex* to Germany. It was hard for him to refuse when asked face-to-face, and Mussolini conceded, hoping, no doubt, that Hitler would return the favour at some future date.[35]

Mussolini then found it equally difficult to stand up to the vociferous opposition he faced on his return to Italy. The Italians protested that they simply would not tolerate the gift of national treasures to foreign powers. Mussolini had no option but to change his mind, much to the anger of Hitler and the Nazis.

The Germans did not forget the *Codex*, but merely bided their time. They did not have to wait long, as Mussolini was out of power as soon as 1943. Spies working for the Ahnenerbe had already discovered that the *Codex* was in the possession of an Italian Count, Aurelio Baldeschi-Balleani. Seizing the opportunity afforded by Mussolini's removal from power, a plan was made to capture the book.[36] Acting on the orders of Himmler, the SS-troops attacked the Count's Villa Fontedamo, located on the Adriatic coast of Italy. They broke down the doors and headed for the library, where their intelligence had said the book was kept. They entered only to find no trace of it, and so set about ransacking the villa, searching for the historic copy of *Germania*. The dramatic raid was to no avail as the crack troops were unable to locate the book, leaving empty-handed. It eventually emerged that the noble count had hidden the valuable book underneath his kitchen floor.

The manuscript remained in Italy after the war, and even though it was damaged in a flood in 1966, it remains safely housed in Italy at the *Museo Nazionale* in Rome. Without the surviving book, the Germans had to make do with reprints of later editions; as it was the bedrock of Nazi ideology, copies were sold in large quantities and taught in all German schools throughout the 1940s. At this time, *Germania* was widely celebrated as a comprehensive account of the ancient Germanic people. Although Tacitus's description of the early Germanic tribes was not universally positive, the Nazis liked the description of their ancient ancestors as simple, brave, loyal, and pure. In *Germania*, the citizens of Germany found a description of people they were proud to call their forbears.

Claiming the Past

These stones are linked with one of the most significant phenomena of history, the birth of Indo-Germanism! That this German territory, this Germany should have been the homeland of the race which has been called to the highest cultural achievements cannot leave us, who are its heirs, indifferent. We cultivate a heritage which is indeed our own, which did reach us from elsewhere, and did not come to us from the Orient. It was here that it was founded and here that it developed throughout the millennia.[1]

Externsteine

Wewelsberg Castle lay close to the famous battleground in the Teutoburg Forest where Hermann (also known as Arminius) of the *Cherusci* made his last stand against the Romans. The imposing castle's auspicious location is further emphasised by its proximity to the famous stone monument Externsteine, which is as significant to the Germans as Stonehenge is to the British. Consisting of a distinctive natural rock formation, Externsteine is located in the Teutoburg Forest in North Rhine-Westphalia, not far from the city of Detmold at Horn-Bad Meinberg. The formation consists of five sandstone pillars, the tallest of which is 37.5 metres (123 feet) high, forming a wall several hundred metres in length. In a region that is otherwise largely devoid of rocks, the pillars are particularly impressive—as their name, which means 'star stones of the ridge', suggests.[2]

Himmler was heavily influenced in his understanding of Externsteine by the work of Wilhelm Teudt (1860–1942) who had done much to popularise the site since the mid-1920s. Teudt's interest in searching for an ancient Germanic civilisation, and his book *Germanische Heiligtümer*

(1929), served as an inspiration to the Third Reich. He captured the public's imagination by calling Externsteine the 'Germanic Stonehenge'. Teudt suggested that Externsteine was the location of a Saxon shrine, the location of *Irminsul* and an ancient sun observatory. It was even rumoured that the Nordic World-Tree (*Yggdrasil*), had its roots in the region, perhaps at Externsteine. Like many who were drawn to the NSDAP (and embraced by its members), Teudt was an occultist; he believed that he had a paranormal ability to receive the 'vibrations' of his ancestors, which he said helped him to visualise the ancient landscapes of the sites he was researching. According to Teutonic legend, Externsteine was also a destined to be central place in the nation's future, when it form the location of the apocalyptic 'Battle of the Birch Tree' between the forces of East and West. Himmler believed these stories and trusted he would have a ringside seat when the Eastern army was defeated (as the legend foretold).[3]

The area had been of interest to archaeologists since the enquiries of Hermann Hamelmann in 1564. In 1932, August Stieren was given permission to undertake excavations—the third at the site—but he failed to discover any 'cultural remains'. The following year, the *Externsteine-Stiftung* (Externsteine Foundation) was established, headed by Sievers and with Himmler its first president. The foundation organised for the Ahnenerbe to study the formation, and properly funded excavations of the site began in 1934–35 under Teudt's direction. He appointed Julius Andrée to head the day-to-day work.[4]

Andrée (1889–1942) had studied both geology and prehistory under Kossinna, and he taught 'Racial History' as Professor of Prehistory at the University of Halle. He postulated the existence of a high culture in Germany 250,000 years ago that then spread across the globe. These ideas fitted neatly with those of Himmler and the Nazi regime, although they were critiqued by Alfred Rust. In addition to his academic research, teaching activities, and work at Externsteinein, he later joined the staff of the Amt Rosenberg, where he identified prehistoric finds in the occupied territories of Belgium and France.

Teudt's research showed that Externsteine may have been a centre of religious activity for the Teutonic peoples and their predecessors prior to the arrival of Christianity in northern Europe. There may even be a reference to the site in the *Eddas*.[5] Analysis of the rock carvings showed that the site was first occupied by the Celts 2,000 years ago, then being adopted by Teutonic tribes in the Roman period. Remains from this time include, at the top of the tallest rock, a chamber containing an altar stone that may have once been used for sacrifices before later being Christianised. Directly above the altar stone is a circular hole cut into the wall. This hole faces the direction of sunrise at the summer solstice, and it was interpreted by Teudt as a solar observatory. More recent astro-archaeological research by Professor Schlosser of Bochum University has suggested that the observatory was established between AD 1 and AD 50.[6] Teudt believed that the observatory had been destroyed by Charlemagne, which is possible given analyses of Frankish historical records and Christian carvings that confirm he disapproved of the site.[7] After conquering Eresburg in 772, Charlemagne is reported to have ordered the destruction of the Saxon Irminsul. The earliest evidence for Christianity is that of a monastery, possibly founded in AD 815.[8] In addition to his excavations, Teudt also forced Serbian prisoners of war to landscape the area, creating a *Heiligtum* (sacred grove). In the process, the prisoners demolished various cafés, hotels, and even a tramway that had sprung up to serve the tourists visiting Exernstein.

Himmler took inspiration from the pagan associations of the site in the development of his new Germanic religion. He drew on the long tradition of summer solstice celebrations, some of which had been recorded in the middle years of the nineteenth century:

> [They are] like giants from a prehistoric world which, during the furious creation of the Earth, were placed there by God as eternal monuments ... Many of our *Volk* are known to have preserved pagan beliefs and their rituals, and I remember that some sixty years ago, in my earliest childhood days ... the custom was to undertake a long, continuous journey that lasted for whole days and which only ended on St John's Day, to see those ancient 'Holy Stones' and to celebrate there, with the sunrise, the Festival of the Summer Solstice ... Goethe says, 'Nobody can overcome the impressions of his earliest childhood,' and I have also, despite a long and costly journey, often since celebrated the summer solstice on those very stones.[9]

In an article from the monthly magazine *Lower Saxony*, An 'A. E. Müller' goes on to tie the prehistoric monument of Externsteine to twentieth century Aryan mysticism:

> Especially included for your consideration are the sculptures found on the reverse of the Externsteine on which were thus originally discovered the image of the tree *Ydragsil* [*sic*.], the World-Ash, whose melancholy myth embraces the Origin, the Life, and the Death of the Earth and its generations.

He then describes how images of a human couple seen within the form of the root of the World-Ash, '*Ydragsil*' (*sic*.), and embraced by the Serpent,

Nidhögur (the symbol of a devouring Death), were used by the Catholic Church to support its own creation story—the Biblical-Babylonian legend of Adam and Eve and their fall from grace. Müller complains that the pagan iconography and images of Externsteine were co-opted by the Church and exploited to support the conversion of the pagan population of Lower Saxony to that Semitic interloper, Christianity.

Paderborn

Like Externsteine, the Ahnenerbe considered Paderborn to be of cultic significance. In a letter from Von Motz to Wolfram Sievers on 29 January 1937, Motz refers to a recent issue of the official SS magazine, *Das Schwarze Korps*:

> I am sending to you now … six photographs with explanatory text. Maybe these can appear in one of the next issues of *Schwarze Korps* in order to show that it is to some extent a favoured practice of the church on images of its saints and forth to illustrate the defeat of adversaries by [having them] step on them.
>
> The referenced essay also mentioned that there are depictions of the serpent's head, as the symbol of original sin, being stepped on [by the saints].
>
> These depictions are quite uncommonly prevalent. It is always Mary who treads on original sin.
>
> Now these pictures appear to me particularly interesting because the serpent refers to an ancient symbol of Germanic belief. At the Battle of Hastings the flag of the Saxons shows a golden serpent on a blue field …
>
> The Mary Statue at Paderborn was erected in the middle of the past century in the courtyard of the former Jesuit College. As professor Alois Fuchs related several times before in lectures concerning the Paderborn art monuments, the artist that created the Mary Statue must have been a Protestant. This is for me completely proven because the face in the moon-sickle in every case represents Luther.
>
> It is well known that Rome and Judah, preferring thus to take advantage of their own victims, created victory monuments for them.

These same motifs are found throughout Nazi literature. Representing Satan to Christians, the snake (or serpent) was sacred to Aryans. Himmler had a passionate interest in witchcraft and the Holy Inquisition, reading *The Witch Cult in Western Europe* (1921) and *The God of the Witches* (1933) by the British anthropologist Margaret Murray.[10] Himmler was of one mind with Murray in believing that the witches burned at the stake in medieval Europe were pagans. For Himmler, what was troubling was that in killing these women, 'much good German blood' had been 'stupidly destroyed' by the Church. Himmler was no supporter of the Catholic Church, but he did take time to admire their ritual and organisational strengths. Indeed, he used the principles of the Order of the Jesuits as a template for the organisation of the SS, with absolute obedience the overriding rule; each and every order had to be accepted without question.

As ever, Himmler saw the potential of archaeology as a political tool to provide a Germanic identity for the population and for the SS in particular, and also as a tool that would help in the creation of a new religion. He believed that by drawing on the power of prehistory, one would achieve success in the present day. He therefore continued to support archaeological excavations throughout Germany, notably in the Murg Valley, at Hedeby (Haithabu) and at the Mauern Caves (see Chapter 8).

The Murg Valley

Two important excavations were undertaken in the Murg Valley in the Black Forest during the Third Reich. The better recorded of the two was led by Gustav Riek and undertaken in 1937 and 1938. This excavation was of an ancient fortress, the *Grosse Heuneberg*, and the nearby burial mounds. A second, private expedition was undertaken by Richard Anders, Günther Kirchhoff, and Wiligut in 1936 and had nothing to do with the Ahnenerbe. This expedition was less well conducted—as one might expect with the involvement of the eccentric Wiligut—and undertook a study of a settlement consisting of old half-timbered houses, architectural ornaments, crosses, inscriptions, and natural and man-made rock formations, which they theorised showed it to be an ancient *Krist* settlement.

Haithabu

The excavations at the ninth century Viking Age settlement of Haithabu (Hedeby) in southern Jutland was much more significant. Excavations by Danish archaeologists were taken over by the Germans in the early 1900s. Herbert Jankuhn had worked at Haithabu since 1930; he shared Himmler's obsession with the 'Nordic spirit' and the war-like Vikings, and the two men became good friends, leading to his appointment as site supervisor in 1937.

Bayeux Tapestry

Der Normannenteppich—the Nazi name for the Bayeux Tapestry—also formed part of Himmler's interest in the Vikings. He considered it to be further evidence of Germanic hegemony rather than French national pride.[11] The Normans were the forerunners to the British and Nazi German empires, according to Himmler and the Ahnenerbe. His reasoning was that the Norman Conquest of England had injected an energy into the Anglo-Saxon people, without which the British Empire could never have happened. This view was widely accepted in England in the 1930s. Furthermore, the depictions in the tapestry (better described as an embroidery) reveal that the Viking tradition had survived into the culture of the Normans. To Himmler's satisfaction, the Normans were still Viking, therefore legitimising the inclusion of Norman history in the study of the Germanic people.

The Ahnenerbe turned to Peter Paulsen, professor of archaeology at the University of Berlin and an expert on the Vikings. He willingly worked for the Ahnenerbe, having joined the NSDAP in 1927, when he was just twenty-five years old. It was he who suggested an analysis of the images in the tapestry in order to confirm the link between the Normans and the Vikings. Thus began, in June 1941, the Bayeux Tapestry Project. Jankuhn, Himmler's most trusted archaeologist, led a team of four to study the 68-m-long (225 feet) treasure in Paris. The team consisted of Karl Schalbow (a textile expert), Herbert Jeschke (a specialist illustrator), and Rolf Alber (a photographer). During the last two days of the project, they were joined by a man named Loeb, who filmed the team for two propaganda films. The study lasted for just one month, beginning on 23 June and ending on 31 July 1941.

Jankhun was much-valued for his skills, and as soon as the project was completed in August 1941, Himmler put him in command of another team of archaeologists. This team was sent to Crimea to establish that the region was the homeland of the Goths. Dr Hermann Bunjes was left to study the images of the tapestry that had been created by Jankuhn's team, producing a glossy, four-volume book of their findings. The Nazi propaganda machine quickly leapt into action, with Lord Haw-Haw using the tapestry as an example of English vulnerability to invasion. For Himmler, the tapestry bore witness to the superiority of the German people, with the cultures of England, Normandy, and Scandinavia all falling within its cultural sphere—what he called 'Germania'.

Crimea

Meanwhile, Himmler had deployed his trusted friend Jankuhn, along with Karl Kersten (1909–1992) and Baron Wolf von Seefeld, to Crimea, which had been secured by the German Army in early July 1942. Their mission was to search out Gothic artefacts denoting German ancestry that could then be exhibited in Berlin, following the earlier success of the display of the Kerch 'Gothic crown of the Crimea'.

On arrival in Crimea, Einsatzgruppe D. Commander Otto Ohlendorf provided Jankuhn with a list of all the museums in the region that Jankuhn and his team might have liked to visit. Working from this information, Jankuhn made his way to Maykop. The journey was difficult because the Red Army were busy looting any valuables that they came across, and Jankuhn's party only managed to progress because they had the support of the Fifth SS Panzer. On arrival, they received a message from Sievers that informed them of Himmler's order to investigate the ancient fortress of Mangup Kal as a matter of urgency. Jankuhn decided to split his team, sending Kersten to Mangup Kale while the rest of the team continued to collect as many ancient artefacts as they could. Although the Red Army had already removed much that was of value, due to the active intervention of Einsatzkommando 11b's commander, Werner Braune, the team were able to recover some items. However, these items were not what the archaeologists had hoped for; ultimately, Jankuhn was unable to find any Gothic artefacts at all. The team had received intelligence about a shipment of seventy-two crates containing archaeological artefacts, but when they arrived at the medical warehouse where they were supposed to be hidden, they found that it had already been raided by the Red Army. All that remained of the secret consignment were twenty crates containing prehistoric and Greek artefacts. There was nothing of the country's Gothic past that would denote their German ancestry.

Poland

Following the 1939 invasion of Poland, Wolfram Sievers urged Himmler to order the forced removal of cultural treasures to Germany. Acting on this advice, Franz Six, the Reich Main Security Administration's Standartenführer, appointed Peter Paulsen, the SS-Untersturmführer who had helped in the analysis of the Bayeux Tapestry, as the head of a team. The team's mission was to enter Kraków and steal the Veit Stoss Altar. The fifteenth-century treasure had been secretly broken into thirty-two pieces by the Poles, each piece being hidden in a different hideaway. Although the poles had taken care to hamper the Nazis, Paulsen was still able to recover all the pieces by 14 October 1939, when they were shipped to Berlin in three trucks. Hitler was delighted to hear the treasure was in his possession and ordered it to be taken to a subterranean vault in Nurenberg for safe-keeping.

The head of the RuSHA, Reinhard Heydrich, decided to build on Paulsen's success by sending him back to Kraków to steal even more treasures. Paulsen was not the only one in the country seeking out rich pickings; Göring wished to form a collection of artworks, and he ordered SS-Sturmbannführer Kajetan Mühlmann to loot the museums for him. The two men met and established an uneasy agreement that Paulsen would collect scholarly works for the Ahnenerbe and Mühlmann would collect artworks for Göring. The head of the German General Government in occupied Poland, Hans Frank, then intervened. On 22 November 1939, he stopped the 'unapproved export' of all Polish property. Paulsen decided to obey the command, but his colleague Hans Schleif managed to organise the removal of five railway carriages of loot from the Archaeological Museum in Warsaw. The Ahnenerbe prompted Schleif for his audacity, while Paulsen was reassigned. Like many Nazis, Paulsen downplayed his role after the war; in 1981, he was able to secure a prestigious position as a medievalist in Würtemburg.

Biskupin

Poland also had a rich prehistoric past. In 1933, Polish archaeologists had discovered the remains of a later prehistoric fortified settlement on an island at Lake Biskupin *c.* 90 km northeast of Poznań, 8 km south of the small town of Żnin in Wielkopolska, north-central Poland. From 1934 onwards, a team of archaeologists from Poznań University excavated the site, led by Józef Kostrzewski (1885–1969) and Zdzisław Rajewski (1907–1974). Their first report was published in 1936, when an open-air reconstruction of the site was opened, making the site famous as the 'Polish Pompeii'. The reconstruction and many well-preserved remains attracted numerous distinguished guests, including officials of the Piłsudski government, members of the military, and churchmen such as the Primate of Poland. The site quickly became a symbol of Poland's proud Slavonic past, featuring in paintings and popular novels. Against a background of German nationalism and military threats, the site, which is located only 70 km from the German border, was used to show that the prehistoric 'Poles' had held their own against foreign invaders.

By the beginning of 1939, 2,500 square metres (26,909.78 sq. feet) had been excavated. These excavations revealed the existence of two different periods of settlement at Biskupin—the first was dated 800–650 BC, the second 650–475 BC. Both settlements were laid out on a rectangular grid with eleven streets each 3 metres wide. The older settlement dates to the early Iron Age and was established on an island more than 2 hectares in area.

The settlement consisted of approximately 100 houses built from oak and pine logs. Each dwelling had two rooms and measured 8 × 10 metres, capable of housing a family of up to a dozen. An open hearth was located in the centre of the biggest room. The settlement was surrounded by a tall wooden wall or palisade set on a 450-metre-long rampart constructed from wood and earth.

History records that whatever the strengths of their prehistoric cousins, the Poles of the twentieth century were no match for the overwhelming military might of the Nazis when they chose to invade in the autumn of 1939. Biskupin fell within the *Warthegau*, the area that German nationalists claimed to have been 'Germanic' since at least the Iron Age (Gustaf Kossinna, *Das Weichselland, ein uralter Heimatboden der Germanen*, Leipzig, Kabitzsch 1919). The Nazis were thus keen to claim Biskupin for themselves. Having renamed the site '*Urstädt*', the Ahnenerbe recommenced excavations at the site in 1940, directed by Hauptsturmführer Hans Schleiff, who published two popular short accounts of how Germanic tribes overran the 'small Lusatian settlement'.

Nazi-led excavation in the Czech village of Dolni Věstonice (Unterwisternitz), and the Ukrainian village of Solone (Soljonoje) were also interpreted as evidence for the supremacy of an ancient German empire. The Dutch prehistorians Assien Bohmers and Frans Bursch, both members of the SS-Ahnenerbe, undertook the archaeological excavations. These excavations illustrate the particular approach to the past developed by the Ahnenerbe; this 'Greater Germanic' scientific practice was directly linked to the ideology of National Socialism. Thus Dolni Věstonice was taken as evidence for the 'origin' of the Nordic people, and Solone symbolized their 'propagation', or expansion.

Whilst the Ahnenerbe's interpretations pleased their political masters in the SS (and particularly Himmler), Bohmers and Bursch's activities had little impact outside Germany. Their interpretations were considered too biased and obviously politically motivated to be taken seriously by those outside the closed circle of SS members. As a result, the two excavations were soon forgotten after 1945, along with the fact that SS archaeologists had ever been involved on site. The same can be said of the other German archaeological expeditions that took place in Bulgaria, Croatia, Romania, occupied Russia, and northern Africa.

South Tyrol

Beside the numerous archaeological excavations, the Ahnenerbe's Kulturkommission also undertook what was arguably the largest field investigation of folklore and linguistics in history. Between 1939 and 1942, the Kulturkommission exhaustively documented the material, linguistic, folk, and musical customs of the Alpine people of South Tyrol. In the words of Wolfram Sievers, head of the Ahnenerbe, its primary assignment was 'the investigation and processing of the entire material and intellectual goods of ... ethnic Germans'.[14]

The impetus for the study was the imminent division of the local population between fascist Italy and the Third Reich, which resulted from *Die Option* (The Option), a 1939 agreement between the Axis powers. Historically, South Tyrol had been politically unstable. The German-speaking region of South Tyrol had been annexed by Italy after the First World War, which had caused tensions between Germany and Italy. In a break with National Socialist ideology, the cultural and ethnic German population was given a choice between '*Blut oder Boden*' ('blood or soil')—a choice between relocating and retaining their Germanic culture and identity or becoming entirely Italianised. For those who chose to remain German, the Ahnenerbe were to preserve their culture, which would be made available to them after relocation to the Tatra Mountains, Burgundy, or the Crimea.

This work of 'rescue ethnography' was led by Richard Wolfram, head of the Ahnenerbe Kulturkommission studying South Tyrol, supported by the ethnomusicologist Alfred Quellmalz and the photographer Arthur Scheler. Together, they worked to preserve the folklore, cultural customs, music, dialect, and folk costumes of the South Tyrol region's German-speaking alpine population. The work was at times difficult as the German population was in the process of being relocated, and on occasions the Ahnenerbe had to bring people back to the region to stage and film their traditions and costumes.

During their three years of fieldwork, the researchers amassed a vast amount of photographs and film documenting the Tyrolean people; this material is now held in archives in Innsbruck, Vienna, and Bolzano. Together, it represents a valuable historical and anthropological document of the work of the largest study of its kind. Size, however, is no measure of quality, and the research of Wolfram and his colleagues was severely criticised by one of the foremost anthropologists of the twentieth century, Bronislaw Malinowski. Malinowski used to holiday in the South Tyrol and so knew the area from first-hand experience. As a Pole, he had no love for the Nazis, and he was an ardent opponent of the kind of *völkisch* approach represented by the Ahnenerbe. In particular, he was sharply critical of Europeans conducting anthropological studies on other Europeans, something he saw as irrevocably compromised.

The Quest for the Holy Grail

For as long as I am alive I will dream of Sabarthés, of Montségur, of the Grail castle, and of the Grail itself: the treasure the heretics spoke of in the Records of the Inquisition.[1]

Of all the stories about the Nazi interest in the occult, the one that resonates most is that of their quests for the Ark of the Covenant and the Holy Grail. These stories gained widespread publicity through their fictionalised retelling in Steven Spielberg's Indiana Jones films. Behind these action-packed adventures is a true story of secret SS-led operations to search for and capture these legendary lost relics.

The real-life operations were ordered by Himmler and undertaken by a young historian-turned-SS-officer, Otto Rahn (1904–1939). Rahn was responsible for igniting interest in the Grail amongst the Nazi hierarchy, and particularly Himmler. The traditional understanding of the Grail described it as a Christian relic of particular reverence to the Roman Catholic Church.[2] As such, it would have no particular interest to Himmler, whose focus was on establishing a Germanic faith in opposition to Christianity. Rahn stood this notion on its head. According to his thinking, the Grail was a symbol of Luciferian opposition to the established Church. This idea strongly appealed to the Nazis as it provided an intellectual justification (based in a historical relic) for their opposition to Christianity.[3]

The Cathars and the Grail

Himmler first became interested in the Grail after hearing about Rahn's book *Kreuzzug gegen den Graal* (*Crusade Against the Grail*).[4] This was a historical study of the Albigensian Crusade, the thirteenth century war between the Roman Catholic Church and the Cathars.[5] The Cathars ('the Pure') can be thought of as a fundamentalist Christian sect opposed to the Catholic Church's corruption of Christ's teachings. The Cathars believed that the spirit is pure but the body is impure and evil; this is ultimately a Gnostic belief. The idea of a 'god of evil' and a 'god of good' seem closer to those of the Gnostics and Manichaeans than to Roman Catholic doctrine, suggesting that the Cathars derived from the Middle Eastern Gnostics or Manichaeans, and that they were possessed of secrets concerning the life and death of Christ.[6] Whatever the truth of that, it is a fact that their beliefs were attractive to the large number of people (particularly in France) who converted to the order.

The Cathar association of the human body with evil led them to believe that death was not to be feared and that corpses should be treated with particular respect. They also attached importance to ritual suicide—the *endura*—where one brought about one's death through starvation, poison, strangulation, or suffocation. Contrary to Roman Catholic teaching, they believed that Christ had never taken human form because that would require him having a physical body, which the Cathars considered Satanic. Instead, they believed that Christ had existed as a spirit and was therefore pure. This meant they rejected many Roman Catholic traditions, including the taking of the holy sacrament, considering them to be nothing more than superstition. The Cathars also held that the Bible, and especially the Old Testament, was full of secret references to an 'Evil God'—Jehovah. This all placed them well beyond the pale as far as the Roman Catholic Church was concerned.

The established Church violently rejected the Cathars, branding them heretics and requiring them to recant. When they failed to comply, Pope Innocent III ordered Catholic armies to destroy the Cathars in 1209. When the Cathars took refuge in a French Catholic town, his army surrounded them, and the commander told his soldiers, 'Kill them all. God will recognise his own.'[7]

In his memoirs, Foreign Intelligence Chief Walter Schellenberg recalls a meeting with Himmler in the summer of 1942. The two were in Ukraine when the Reichsführer-SS began to reflect on Indian philosophy and set forth his views on early Christianity, Calvanism, the Spanish Inquisition, and the witch trials of the Middle Ages:

> At dinner ... he spoke of India and Indian philosophy. This led him to speak of a subject, which was a hobbyhorse of his: in a lively manner he described to me the result of researches in German witchcraft trials. He said it was monstrous that thousands had been burned during the

Middle Ages. So much good German blood had been stupidly destroyed. From this he began an attack on the Catholic Church, and at the same time on Calvin; before I had caught up with all this he was discussing the Spanish Inquisition and the essential nature of primitive Christianity.[8]

The word 'Cathar' means 'purity' (especially of blood), and thus the sect combined well with Nazi ideas of Aryan racial purity. Furthermore, the Cathars' opposition to the Roman Catholic Church (which they described as corrupt and materialistic) resonated with the Nazis' theoretical socialist and anti-capitalist manifesto. Hitler nominally opposed capitalism, although more in words than deed; he associated it with Jewish financiers and plutocrats whom he blamed for bringing the German nation to its knees during the depression that followed Germany's defeat in the First World War.

The Cathars' beliefs also appealed to the anti-Semitic narrative of the NSDAP. In undermining the teaching of the Old Testament, and in particular through their attacks on Jehovah, which portrayed him as Satan, the Cathar teachings seemed to support the views of the Nazis. Furthermore, the Cathars embodied a fanatical zeal that the Nazi leadership wished to inculcate within the SS. In their willingness to die in opposing the established Church, the Cathars seemed a good role model for the Third Reich. The part of Himmler that was entranced by historical romanticism seemed drawn to stories of Cathars professing their faith and hatred of Catholicism even as they died painfully, burned at the stake. Little did he and the other Nazi leaders realise how their own fanatical project would end only a matter of years later. Himmler killed himself following his capture by the Allies and Hitler and his mistress died by their own hands in their Berlin bunker, echoing the Cathar tradition of honourable *endura* deaths, which offered them the consolation of freedom for their pure spirit.

The tradition that the Cathars were possessed of secrets concerning the life and death of Christ runs very strongly and often places the Cathars in possession of either the Holy Grail, the Ark of the Covenant, or both. The story of how these sacred objects came into their possession has been the subject of much speculation and study by, in the main, French historians.[9] They explain how the treasure was in the possession of the Knights Templar, an Order created by St Bernard of Clairvaux, a Cistercian abbot. Different authors vary in whether it was the Grail or the Ark of the Covenant (or both) that the Knights Templar discovered at the site of King Solomon's Temple in the Holy Land.

Whether it was the Grail or the Ark, legend has it that the sacred object was imbued with powerful supernatural forces, which were harnessed by the Templars to bring about the financing, design, and construction of an unparalleled number of religious buildings across France. Between 1170 and 1270, the Church built eighty cathedrals in France and hundreds of other 'cathedral-class' churches.[10] Studies of the Templar cathedrals have been undertaken in support of this far-fetched claim, with Chartres being a favourite. These investigators searched for coded messages that would confirm that the Templars brought back a sacred object of great value from the Holy Land. The core of this belief in a secret Templar tradition was first promoted by Fulcanelli, the pseudonym of an anonymous French author whose *Le Mystère des Cathédrales* was first published in 1925 and later translated into English.[11]

Exactly how the Grail, Ark, or both objects came to pass from the hands of the Templars to the Cathars is left something of a mystery. There is, however, an entire body of literature given over to stories about the Holy Grail itself. These 'Grail Romances' attempt to identify the vessel, variously describing it as the *lapis exilis* or *lapis ex coelis*, a sacred stone that fell from the sky, or alternatively as the cup from which Jesus and his disciples drank at the Last Supper and subsequently used during the crucifixion to catch the last drops of his blood as he died on the cross. The romance of Chrétien de Troyes presents the Grail as a cup, a depiction continued by Malory in *Le Morte d'Arthur*.[12] In contrast, Wolfram von Eschenbach's *Parzival* depicts the Grail not as a cup but as a stone; at Chartres Cathedral, a carving of the High Priest Melchisedek has him holding a cup from which the stone arises.[13]

Of all the traditions concerning the Grail, the one that attracted the interests of the Nazis the most was that which tells how the Cathars, having inherited the Grail from the Templars, held it securely at their stronghold, the fortress of Montségur, in the south of France. This, their last redoubt, was besieged by Roman Catholic forces in 1244.[14] Shortly before it fell to the enemy on 14 March that year, a detachment of Cathars managed to make good their escape from the citadel, taking the sacred Grail to safety. The question of what became of the Grail intrigued historians and Nazis alike.

A number of artefacts make claim to being the Holy Grail, with varying degrees of persuasiveness. Some, such as the Emerald Chalice of Genoa, may be dismissed. The Chalice was first brought to Europe during the Crusades, when it had been captured at Caesarea Maritima at great cost. Its claim as the Grail was nullified when the cup was accidentally damage, revealing that its eponymous emerald was in fact green glass.[15]

In *Los Reyes del Grial* (*The Kings of the Grail*), the authors claim that the Chalice of Doña Urraca at the Basilica of San Isidoro, Leon, is the Grail.[16] They base this claim on the story that the Spanish Arabist and historian Gustavo Turienzo found two medieval Egyptian documents in al Azhar,

Cairo, which suggested that the Holy Grail was taken to the city of Leon in the eleventh century. Other claimants state that it was hidden by the Templars in the 'Money Pit' on Oak Island, Nova Scotia, while local folklore in Accokeek, Maryland, says that it was brought to the town by a closeted priest aboard Captain John Smith's ship.[17, 18] Nineteenth century accounts state that a member of the Irish Clan Dhuir (O'Dwyer or Dwyer) transported the Grail to the United States, and that it was kept by their descendants in secrecy in a small abbey in the upper-northwest US (believed to be southern Minnesota).[19] None of these claims seems particularly strong, only being able to trace their ancestry as far as the turn of the first millennium at best.

The legendary locations for the Grail fare no better. According to Wolfram von Eschenbach, the Grail was kept safe at the castle of Munsalvaesche (*mons salvationis*), where it was entrusted to Titurel, the first Grail King.[20] The Benedictine monks of Montserrat identify the legendary Munsalvaesche as the real castle of Montserrat in Catalonia, Spain; however, they have not been able to locate the Grail itself.[21] Other stories claim that the Grail is buried beneath Rosslyn Chapel in Scotland or lies deep in the spring at Glastonbury Tor, England.[22, 23]

The case of the Valencia Chalice is worthy of more serious consideration. Housed at the Cathedral of Saint Mary of Valencia, the Valencia Chalice has a longer biography.[24] Tradition has it that it was taken by Saint Peter to Rome in the first century. Examination of the stone cup by Antonio Beltrán confirms that the artefact does date to the first century and that it is of Middle Eastern origin, possibly from Antioch in Syria (now Turkey). This makes it unique among the various vessels that claim to be the Grail, as it is the only one that actually dates from the time of Christ. The cup was taken from Rome to Spain by St Lawrence in the third century; it passed through a number of monasteries in Rome, being hidden from Islamic invaders. During the Medieval period, the cup was mounted on an ornate gold and alabaster base decorated with gemstones. It now resides in an ornate reliquary within the cathedral at Valencia and has been acknowledged *de facto* as a Christian relic by the Catholic Church; it has been used by two different popes as a chalice, most recently by Pope Benedict XVI on 9 July 2006. However, that is no guarantee of its authenticity. The only established fact is that it dates to the days of Christ, which is by no means the same as saying that it was ever used by Christ or any of his disciples.

Rahn

One of the most influential Grail romances is Wolfram von Eschenbach's *Parzival*, inspiring both Otto Rahn in his research and Richard Wagner in the composition of his opera.[25] Rahn was a historian, and as a young man he spent five years travelling across Europe and researching records, legends, and myths relating to the Grail and the heretical Cathar cult. He passionately believed that this study would reveal the existence of a pagan, Gnostic religion native to Europe. At the end of his search, he concluded that he had evidence to prove that the established Church had actively suppressed the existence of an ancient Germanic religion.[26]

In 1931, Rahn visited the private Cathar museum of Antonin Gadal in the French town of Ussat-les-Bains. This small spa town in the Pyrenees reportedly had a long Cathar connection. Gadal was a member of 'The Friends of Montségur and the Grail', a society that believed that a connection existed between the Cathar sect and the Grail romances. This idea had been proposed by Joséphin Péladin in *Les Secret des Troubadours* (1906).[27] The book would no doubt have formed part of Gadal's large Grail and Cathar library, which Rahn accessed as part of his research. This allowed him to put pen to paper in 1932, resulting in his book on the subject, *Kreuzzug gegen den Graal* (*Cathars and Grail*), which was published in 1933.[28] It was translated into French by the noted French historian René Nelli, who was also a member of 'The Friends of Montségur and the Grail', in 1944 as *Croisade contre le Graal* (*Crusade Against the Grail*).[29] Rahn identified Parzival as a pure Cathar knight in the tradition of the Grail romances, from which starting point he rewrote the history of the Cathar rebellion. This work was grounded in his legitimate studies of the records of the Spanish Inquisition, medieval Grail legends, and the oral tradition of the troubadours, although his own interpretation of this primary data was heavily skewed by his personal beliefs.

Rahn's book came to the attention of Himmler, who was greatly impressed by the scholarly approach adopted by Rahn to one of Himmler's pet subjects. As a consequence, Rahn was invited to meet Himmler in person. By the end of the meeting Rahn had been taken under Himmler's wing, leaving with a commission in the SS and almost unlimited resources to enable him to focus on his further studies of the Aryan race through the Grail legends and the Cathar sect.

Rahn struck up an unusual friendship with Karl Maria Wiligut, also known as Weisthor. Wiligut was a mercurial figure claiming to be of aristocratic origin and able to recall the entire ancient history of the Teuton people going back over 200,000 years. Himmler held him in high regard and would consult him as an authority on matters of racial history. Wiligut claimed that his own family had kept their bloodline pure through the millennia. He was also a scholar of runic inscriptions, a clairvoyant, and a mystic who would hold forth in his salon—at which both Himmler and Rahn were frequent guests.[30]

Wiligut's views of religion were even more outlandish than Himmler's. According to Wiligut, Christianity was a German invention and Christ was the ancient Teutonic god Baldur, who was crucified by a schimatic group of Wotan-worshipping thugs. However, Wiligut claimed, Baldur managed to escape death, fleeing to the Middle East, where the story is taken up by the New Testament. Meanwhile, Baldur's Germanic followers built a cult centre at the ancient site of Externsteine, which became a site of specific interest to the Nazi Ahnenerbe as a result.[31]

As with all the best mystery stories, Wiligut's occult theory is built on elements taken from verifiable historical texts in order to give it the veneer of truth. In Wiligut's, case he drew from Scandinavian texts, particularly the *Eddas*, which predate the Christian conversion of the northern people. Baldur is attested in texts as an agricultural deity who was slain and then resurrected. In this respect, the Norse creation story has much in common with that of Sumaria, where the known universe was created out of the body of another slain god. Christianity in turn co-opted many pagan ceremonies, cult centres, holidays, and myths into its own tradition; that much is uncontroversial. However, what Wiligut did was to blend, combine, and coin historical stories into his own fantastic mythology, which had little relation to historical fact.

Curiously, Wiligut's powers of storytelling were such that he was able to talk himself into the role of head of the Department of Prehistory at the Race and Settlement Office (RuSHA) of the SS, eventually attaining the rank of SS-Brigadeführer (Brigadier) on Himmler's Personal Staff. Wiligut designed the *Schutzstaffel's* special Death's Head (*totenkopf*) ring, replete with runic symbols, swastika, and Wiligut's personal armorial design. This design suggested that Wiligut was the last and sole physical repository of pure Teutonic blood.

Wiligut and Rahn were in communication from their frist meeting onwards. Rahn wrote letters to Wiligut as he travelled through France, Germany, and Iceland, searching for the Cathar Grail. Wiligut in turn shared the contents of these letters with Himmler.[32] The surviving letters hint at the reverence with which these communications were treated, as they are all classified 'extremely confidential'. The contents refer to the linguistic evidence of pagan sites contained within modern German names. Rahn was clearly an intimate of the highest-ranking SS aristocracy. Paul Ladome, a confidante of Rahn, stressed that Rahn had no interest in Nazi politics or ideology, and that when the two met in Berlin in July 1936, Ladome asked how Rahn came to be in full SS uniform, his reply was simply, 'My dear Paul, a man has to eat!'[33] Reading Rahn's books, a different picture emerges. In his writing, he reveals a belief that the religion of ancient Germany had been destroyed by the Catholic Church. This had begun in the thirteenth century, when the Cathars were hunted, and ended with the destruction of the Templar Order 100 years later.

According to Rahn, we see the remnants of the German religion in elements preserved by the Church, such as the Grail, the knightly orders, and the struggle between light and dark. In the pagan religion, light represented the spirit of the 'Light-Bearer'—the highest good—rather than Jesus.

Himmler had a particular, personal agenda—to prove the superiority of the Germans as the descendants of the Aryan race. Following from this, he believed that in the past, the Germans owned all the lands of Europe, thus legitimising Hitler's drive to the east. He was therefore keen to find evidence (archaeological, historical, cultural, and ritual) for an unknown ancient German religion. An advantage in re-establishing this religion, a 'blood-religion', was the potential to unite the Aryan diaspora of a Nazi empire.

Himmler met opposition from two directions. On one side were scientists who found it hard to stomach the Nazi claims of a pan-European-Asian Aryan history and the possibility of a racially pure people. Himmler's response to these opponents was to provide concrete scientific evidence that the Aryan (and thus Germanic) people had established communities ranging from Minsk, in Russia, to northern India and Tibet. The '*Deutsche Akademie*' and later the Ahnenerbe were both engaged in archaeological excavations to find this evidence.

The second direction from which opposition came was the established Church. Himmler's personal ambition for Germany was to establish a new religion based on an earlier, pre-Christian, Ur-Ayran religion of ancient India and Europe. However, he was hampered in this by the many devout Catholic Germans. Hitler was more at ease in dealing with the Church than Himmler; he saw the necessity for a pragmatic approach to what remained a popular movement. Himmler, however, took a harder line, wanting to undermine and ultimately destroy Christianity and replace it with a more 'German' faith. Working with Wiligut and others, Himmler had ceremonies and a new religious calendar drawn up to replace their Christian equivalents. It was in this context that Himmler considered the appropriation of the Holy Grail as a purely Aryan symbol of their pagan religion.

Rahn's thesis repudiated any claims the Christian Church had to the Grail, and it was therefore attractive to Himmler and the Nazis in general. Based on his research in the Languedoc region of southern France and at Montségur itself, the site of the Cathars' last stand, Rahn believed he had plentiful evidence to support his thesis. The Grail of von Eschenbach and Richard Wagner was transfigured into the ultimate Aryan symbol, around which Himmler would build his pagan temple at Wewelsburg castle. The castle was to be the heart of a new SS metropolis, inside which a chamber would house a 'Round Table' for the meetings of the inner circle of the SS. This Aryan Camelot would have its own King Arthur at its head—Himmler himself. All that was missing to recreate this medieval fantasy was the Holy Grail itself.

The extent to which Rahn was a 'true believer' in the Nazi ideology he worked to establish is debateable. According to Paul Ladame, he at first thought the Nazis 'faintly ridiculous', and his primary motive in joining the SS was material. The offer of employment was a lucrative one and appealing to an impoverished young researcher. There may also have been a fear in the back of his mind, as no one refused Himmler without facing repercussions.[34]

Rahn's time as Himmler's 'blue-eyed boy' was short-lived. As time passed, Himmler grew increasingly frustrated by Rahn's lack of progress in finding evidence to support the Aryan ideology that was so important to the SS. Finally, through frustration, Himmler set Rahn a deadline to finish his study and produce a book outlining his findings for the pagan celebrations of Samhain on 31 October 1936, or else face the consequences. Rahn somehow managed to complete the work, but his fate had already been sealed. In 1937, he was posted to Dachau for compulsory training, following which he resigned his commission at the earliest opportunity. By 1939, he was dead; he was just thirty-five years old. [35]

Rahn's Nazi-funded research resulted in his book *Luzifers Hofgesind* or '*Lucifer's Servants*', sometimes translated as '*Lucifer's Court*'.[36] It is quite different to his first book, which had his historical research at its core. In this case, the book is an overt work of Nazi propaganda. Several passages make the disturbing case for the worship of Lucifer, drawing on *Parzival* and the texts of the troubadours and Cathars. For example:

> It was necessary, in effect, to be faithful to God until death, 'and God will give up to his servant the crown of eternal life,' as it is written in the Bible. Having established that, for the Church of Rome, the sole repository of 'Truth' in the eyes of the faithful, the troubadours were members of the servants of the Devil; having also established that they were faithful to the God of Love; and finally having established that they celebrated, as numerous examples have proved, the marvels of the crown of Lucifer, it is permitted to believe that they had faith in the existence of a *Luciferian crown of eternal life* (to speak Biblically). And if we follow this thought to its logical conclusion, we will say that, for them, *the God of Love was none other than Lucifer in person.*
>
> This hypothesis will become certain if we allow our thought to range more widely: the god *Amor* is the god of Spring, as is Apollon

... Apollon brought back the light of the Sun: he is a light-bearer, or 'Lucifer'. According to the *Apocalypse* of John, Apollyo-Apollon was equated with the Devil, and according to the belief of the Roman Church ... Lucifer is Satan. Consequently, the god of Spring *Apollon-Amor* is, according to the doctrine of the Church, *the Devil and Satan.*[37]

In a further comment on the subject of Lucifer, Rahn writes:

There is much more [Light] than in the houses of God—cathedrals and churches—where Lucifer neither is able nor wishes to enter due to all the sombre, stained glass windows wherein are painted the Jewish prophets and apostles, the Roman gods and saints. The forest, that, that was free![39]

These two passages show how Rah used Biblical language to support his thesis that the Cathars and the troubadours were, in a sense, Devil-worshippers, but only so far as they worshipped pagan gods demonised by the Church.

In another passage, Rahn declares that the famous Cathar saint, Esclarmonde, was 'one of the noblest women of the Middle Ages' and a heretic of the highest order. She believed that Jehovah, the Old Testament God of the Jews, was none other than Satan himself, that Christ had not been crucified to death, and that, as a consequence, the Church was wrongly teaching that his suffering and death would redeem the souls of Christians. The Cathar doctrine that Jesus did not die on the cross may explain why Templars are recorded trampling a crucifix underfoot as part of their initiation into the order, and it may also explain why there were no crucifixes at Chartres Cathedral. Esclarmonde was 'cursed by the Pope, detested by the King of France, she thought, until her dying breath, of nothing other than the religious and political independence of her country'. The aforementioned views and the notion that falsehoods were inherent in the Gospel's accounts of the life of Jesus all found a receptive audience amongst the scholars of the Ahnenerbe and within the SS in general, as did the idea that dying for the religious and political independence of the state was glorious.

The Cathars represented a pure form of Christianity that denied a large part of the Bible as we have come to know it and posed a real threat to the established Catholic Church. These ideas were particularly attractive to Himmler, combining as they did the notion of a pagan Grail and the Cathars as 'guardians of the Grail'. The representation of Jehovah as an evil demon fit nicely with the persecution and mass murder of his Jewish followers, justifying the extermination of the 'race of Jehovah' as a spiritual necessity. Himmler no longer considered the Jews to be simply members of an inferior race that also conspired to rob the honest German of his money, pride, and birth right; now, the Jews were also the children of Satan.

By extension, this line of reasoning (if we can call it such) led Himmler to conclude that if the Jews of the Old Testament were worshippers of Satan, then Christ could not possibly have been Jewish. By removing the Jewish content from the New Testament and replacing it with the 'revisionist' scholarship of German academics who cast doubt on the accuracy of the Gospels, one is able to reinterpret the text in line with the works of Wiligut—recasting Christ as Baldur, a Teutonic Sun God.

Rahn's thesis was inherently anti-Catholic. To Rahn, the Catholic Church had been the enemy since the persecution of the Cathars in the thirteenth century. In support of this thesis, he cited the brutal murder of hundreds of thousands of Cathars by the Church. Furthermore, he stressed that the Church was the enemy of all that the Grail stood for—purity, nobility, and all that was good in the world—as represented in Wagner's *Parzival*, the *Morte d'Arthur*, and the romance of Camelot. Nothing was more appealing to the romantic Rahn than the idea of a virgin knight crossing Europe on his quest for the sacred cup. The idea was equally appealing to Himmler, who referred to his SS men as the knights of a new order. One must wonder if Rahn felt, in his heart of hearts, somehow at home in his elegant black Hugo Boss uniform, decorated with silver runic insignia. He must have seen himself as a new Teutonic Knight on his own sacred quest for the Holy Grail.[40]

In his introduction to the French translation of *Luzifers Hofgesind* (*La Cour de Lucifer*), Paul Ladame insists that Rahn joined the SS because there was no option—Himmler offered him a salary, perks, and the freedom to conduct his own academic research unhindered. To refuse would have seemed like madness, and perhaps it would have resulted in Rahn's eventual imprisonment. A different perspective, from the Nazi side, depicts him as an enthusiastic Nazi, a believer in the Grail and an admirer of Wiligut. Wiligut claimed that the Bible was a Germanic creation, a view that no serious scholar could accept, and was an enthusiastic member of the SS. There is support for placing Rahn in this category; for example, he wrote in *Lucifer's Servants* that his 'ancestors were pagans ... [his] forebears were heretics'. On the other side of the coin, how do we explain his sudden resignation from the SS in February 1939, a year after completing service at Dachau, or his death within a month of said resignation, on 13 March 1939?

There is evidence that Rahn lectured on his research in *Luzifers Hofgesind* to the Dietrich Eckhart Society in Dortmund, Westphalia, in January 1938, just one year before his death. A flavour of his lecture can be garnered from a newspaper report:

The Albigensians were exterminated. 205 leading followers of Lucifer were burnt on a huge pyre by Dominicans in the South of France after a large-scale priestly Crusade in the name of Christian clemency. With fire and sword, the Lucifer doctrine of the Light-Bearer was persecuted along with its followers. The Albigensians are dead, but their spirit lives on and has an effect today through new devotion and rejuvenated enthusiasm. The Vicar of Christ could truly burn men; but he was mistaken if he believed that he burned along with them their spirit, devotion and longing. This spirit became alive again before many men yesterday, powerfully and visibly, in Otto Rahn, a descendant of the old Troubadors.[41]

In this and in Rahn's writings, one finds an intelligent man struggling to develop his line of reasoning through analysis of primary historical texts. Much as we may disagree with his interpretation, he was too intelligent a man to be taken in by the ideas of Wiligut. It was Wiligut who argued that the Teutonic tribes had a verifiable history dating to the year 228,000 BC, a time, he argued, when the earth had three suns. It is hard to see how Rahn could have reacted with anything but disdain to these unscientific and unsupported claims. Instead he had to bite his tongue for fear of dismissal from his well-paid post; perhaps after witnessing the true horror of the Reich first-hand at Dachau, he felt he had no alternative but to resign his commission in quiet disgust. Perhaps he mentioned his misgivings, being secretly murdered in retribution a month later, on the orders of Himmler. One might like to think so, but further facts rather complicate this story; Wiligut also chose to retire from the SS during the same month as Rahn, pointing to some shared motive.

There has been much speculation about this in the past, with wild claims that Rahn's research had finally led to the discovery of the Grail and that he had confided this to Wiligut. This line of argument says that both men 'knew too much' for their own good, and had to be murdered to silence them and protect the secret discovery. Rahn was murdered, whilst Wiligut was kept locked away until he died in 1946. This is a rather far-fetched explanation, and the truth may be rather more prosaic, if equally brutal. In his study of Wewelsberg Castle, Hüser comments in a note that Rahn was dismissed from the SS due to his homosexual inclinations. This is much more believable as it is well known that Himmler had no time for homosexuals, considering them to be degenerates. The best such a person could hope for was a period of treatment by psychiatrists; the worst was a shorter stay at a concentration camp. It would be too personally embarrassing to Himmler to have Rahn publicly identified as a homosexual; instead, an 'accidental' death was staged in order to be rid of him. Wiligut, meanwhile, had suffered periods of mental illness for which he had been confined to hospital in the past, and it is likely that Himmler had him locked away following the onset of another bout of illness.[42]

Holy Blood, Holy Grail

Rahn's research and its implications for the Nazis (and specifically the SS) may be summarised as follows. The Cathars and troubadours were heirs of a European Gnostic tradition most likely brought from the Middle East by the Knights Templar. Within their distinctly pagan rites, the Holy Grail held a special place, clearly identifying it as a pagan rather than Christian symbol. Having established that the Grail was a pagan rather than a Christian relic, the Nazis, as overt pagans, identified in the Grail a sacred artefact of divine power that they could use for their own ends. Seeing themselves as the inheritors of the European pagan tradition, the Nazis confidently believed that it was their rightful property. It was, they believed, they who were the spiritual descendants of the Teutonic Knights, a chivalric order that pressed Germany on in a drive to the east centuries before Hitler's invasion of Russia. They claimed to be the people of pure blood—the people of the Runes.

Conclusion:
A Warning from the Past

We have learnt nothing.[1]

Introduction

We have travelled a long way from the adventures of Indiana Jones, where we began. It has been a tale of dark deeds, espionage camouflaged by archaeology, myth taken for historical record, and bizarre occultism raised to the level of the sacred. This has been a story that leaves one cold. For every participant that might be forgiven their misguided interpretation of the past, there were others who actively promoted the idea of an Aryan master race, who took pride in their membership of the SS-Ahnenerbe, and who looked forward to a Greater Germanic Empire, caring little for the lives they destroyed in the process.

Sixty years after the fall of the Third Reich, we may be forgiven for assigning the Nazi fascination with the prehistoric origins of the German people as an interesting footnote to their nasty reign. Alas, nationalism, racism, and anti-Semitism are ideas too persistent for that to happen. As we have seen, these concepts existed prior to the emergence of National Socialism, and they continue in one form or another to the present and, sad to say, will no doubt continue in the future. What we have learnt from the preceding chapters is how appealing these simplistic notions can be, not least to intellectuals, who, we might think, are least susceptible to the idea that the world's problems can be resolved by recourse to scapegoating the most vulnerable in society. Democratic societies need to be ever vigilant and ready to combat the pernicious ideas of hatred while also holding the right to speak freely sacred. Rather than foolishly attempting to curtail freedom of speech through misguided 'bans', we should actively challenge those who promote ideologies of nationalism and hatred. The role of archaeologists and historians should be obvious given the Third Reich's misuse of their disciplines in the past.

Occult Science

The Nazis tapped into a strand of pre-existing thought connected to the occult and esoteric that extended across Europe, where it had gone largely unchallenged by the scientific community. For mainstream science, these fringe ideas were considered bizarre but harmless, and their proponents were eccentrics not worthy of debating. Supporters of this approach may well point to the alternative World Ice science of the Nazis. Beyond serving to provide an alternative to orthodox 'Semitic' science, World Ice Theory was also supposed to provide more accurate weather forecasting, a belief that was taken very seriously by some German scientists. For example, Dr E. Dinies wrote a reference book on the subject, *Zur Welteismeteorologie* (*On World Ice Meteorology*), which was published in 1938.[2] In his book, Dinies, after quoting from Hörbiger's 'epic work' *Glazialkosmogonie* (*Glacial Cosmology*), provided tables of meteorological data comparing ice and air temperature for relative humidity values.[3] The details are confusing, but the Nazi student newspaper *Rhein-Mainische Studentenzeitung* helpfully provided a more accessible introduction to the science behind the theory in a series of articles. Their introduction to the series, dated 1 June 1938, reads:

> Our time is rich in theories about the formation and structure of the world. Frequently these days such matters are dealt with by laymen. In our opinion only scientists and experts can successfully answer these kinds of questions. For instance, there has been a great deal of talk in recent years about the World Ice Theory. We have asked therefore a variety of scientists to tell us their position on the questions piling up concerning the World Ice Theory and we offer them now to the public.[4]

The paper places the theories of Hörbiger and his co-author Fauth on a par with Galileo, indicating the importance of World Ice Theory to the Nazis. In a report written by an anonymous SS-Obersturmführer, the 'scientific' framework underlying the theory was further emphasised:

The Need and Format of a New Implementation of the World Ice Theory

As the Reichsführer-SS himself first spoke out in support of the Viennese engineer Hans Hörbiger's World Ice Theory, he offered, by way of substantiation, the following: 'Hans Hörbiger's monument doesn't need to wait a hundred years before it is built; one can employ these ideas even today.' Of course, the implementation of the World Ice Theory ordered by the Reichsführer-SS must be planned in accord with scientific methodology. Thus is the manner of working in the Administration for Scientific Research in the Ahnenerbe unambiguously set forth. At the same time, however, a change from the usual method of implementing the World Ice Theory has been decided upon as well:

A scientifically thorough study of the World Ice Theory, together with a proof of its veracity, should be preserved from false teachers. This is only what official science attempts to do itself.[5]

This document offers an unusual insight into the internal machinations within the Ahnenerbe. It reveals rivalry between factions within the World Ice Department, with those who considered themselves 'scientists' seeking to displace the occultists and non-scientists. The scientific faction was led by Dr Hans Robert Scultetus, who wanted a department of scientists so that he could focus on scientific experiments to prove the theory's validity.[6] It was Scultetus who eventually persuaded Himmler to put the theory to the test as part of Schäfer's expedition to the Himalayas, where variations in altitude, humidity, and temperature could be recorded scientifically. Schäfer again stood out against pseudoscience when he decided not to include the archaeologist Dr Erwin Schirmer in the expedition team.[7] Schirmer was recommended to him for his work at the Ahnenerbe's Kyffhauser Castle dig, which had searched for evidence of '*Indogermanische Volksgruppen*' and the sacred remains of the German ruler who provided the code name for Hitler's invasion of Russia, Barbarossa. However, when Schäfer found out Schirmer's work was considered '*durftig*' ('miserable' or 'wretched') he rejected him.

The reliance on World Ice Theory, which we now know has no serious scientific support, to generate weather predictions was ultimately to prove nothing less than disastrous for the Nazis. The Third Reich's invasion of the Soviet Union went well at first, from the point of view of the Nazi generals. In less than a month of the offensive beginning, they had been able to push the Soviet forces back to just 200 miles short of Moscow. The Allied forces watched in horror at the Germans' rapid advance, which seemed to be taking them inevitably forward to outright victory. However, inexplicably, Hitler then ordered the advancing forces to halt. The German Army's offensive paused for two long months, giving the beleaguered Soviet forces time to regroup. Just as significantly, as time passed, the seasons slowly changed, bringing the harsh Russian winter ever closer. The first snow began to fall in October, and as the bleak winter set in, the poorly equipped German Army began to lose men to the cold. Within a matter of six months, they lost over 1 million men to the freezing temperatures. Wearing only their light summer uniforms and without any winter clothing, the Germans lost more men to the cold than they did to Soviet bullets, losing all but eight of the 162 divisions set against the Red Army.

To understand why Hitler deliberately ordered his army to pause outside Moscow, we need look no further than to the Ahnenerbe's meteorological division. Working within the framework of Hörbiger's World Ice Theory, they confidently predicted that the winter of 1941 would be mild. Listening to this advice, the Nazis failed to take the proper steps to equip their army for the notoriously brutal Russian winter.[8]

For some, this example proves that physics will always ultimately trump ideology without the need for active rebuttal on the part of the scientific community. Just as the Catholic Church had ultimately been forced to accept that the world was round, so the Third Reich had been unable to bend nature to its meteorological theories. Comforting as this may be, scientific truth only came about after the brutal deaths of millions of infantry conscripts. Worse still, many of the occult ideas that supported the Nazi ideology have proved remarkably persistent.

The Nazis had tapped into an existing tradition of ideas that had usually developed in parallel with intellectual thought, rather than forming the mainstream. These ideas included Nordicism, World Ice Theory, and, most controversially, eugenics. Eugenics policies were probably most highly developed in the United States, and it was to these that the Nazis looked for confirmation of their own eugenics programmes. The wholesale slaughter of the Native American population in the United States was a practical model for the Nazi *Lebensraum* programme and particularly for the genocide of Jews, gypsies, and other indigenous populations of Eastern Europe. The Nazis even had support from the United States, most notably from businessmen—including Henry Ford, who wholeheartedly supported the Nazi Party (with cash donations) from its infancy.[9] This inconvenient history proved embarrassing as the atrocities of the Nazis became publicly known at the end of hostilities, and it coloured the manner in which the Americans led the de-Nazification of Germany.

As we have seen, belief in the occult ran through the Third Reich, but at the end of the war it was considered one of their more harmless eccentricities when compared to the violence of their racist and anti-Semitic ideologies. The occultists' ideas of lost civilisations were famously embodied in the fictional Shangri-La described by British author James Hilton in his 1933 novel *Lost Horizon*.[10] Hilton's Shangri-La has become synonymous with any earthly paradise, and particularly a mythical

Himalayan utopia, a permanently happy land isolated from the outside world. Some scholars, following the tradition of Madame Blavatsky, believe that the Shangri-La story owes a literary debt to Shambhala, which was sought by Eastern and Western explorers.[11] Whatever the truth of this, the occult undercurrent, which had never disappeared from European thought, was rekindled in the early 1960s when the French authors Louis Pauwels and Jacques Bergier published *The Morning of the Magicians*.[12] They presented fantasy as fact, describing how the Nazis had secret extra-terrestrial technologies in their possession.

Holocaust denier Ernst Zündel developed the theme of Nazi secret weapons, this time hiding them in Antarctic bases colonised by the surviving members of the Third Reich.[13] His 'evidence'—a combination of pro-Nazi propaganda and anti-Semitism—has attracted a 'cult' following of individuals intrigued by the notion of ancient civilisations, extra-terrestrials, and Aryan supremacy. This combination of beliefs found wider currency when presented by the prolific Austrian author Erich von Däniken.[14] His recipe for success depended on the idea that ancient civilisations came about through the mating of humans with intellectually superior aliens, a theme reminiscent of Nazi Aryan mythology. Däniken's work is ignored by the scientific community and ridiculed by archaeologists, who pigeonhole him as a successful novelist in the same category as Dan Brown. This lack of rebuttal leaves Däniken free to fill the void. Däniken's writing is always supported by carefully constructed argument underpinned by evidence. He frequently references the site of Tiwanaku in Bolivia, familiar to us from the work of the SS archaeologist Edmund Kiss. Däniken had first encountered the site after reading the books of Arthur Posnansky, with whom Kiss had collaborated (see Chapter 3).

Däniken might be considered a pioneer of the 'alternative history' that became popular in the 1990s. This genre awoke interest in ancient cultures and lost civilisations, exemplified by books like Graham Hancock's *Fingerprints of the Gods*.[15] The language of these books was tailored to a contemporary audience and carefully avoids the direct mention of Aryans, but the core narrative harks back to the writing of the 1930s. The basic message is that at the end of the last ice age, approximately 10,000 years ago, there was a superior people with godlike powers. A great flood destroyed their advanced culture, forcing them to flee their homeland. As these people scattered across the globe, they settled in new lands where they attempted to recreate their culture. In the process, they created the great civilisations of Egypt, Mesopotamia, and South America. This mythology is remarkably reminiscent of the writings of the nineteenth century occultists.

These ideas have persisted today in blockbuster films such as *Avengers Assemble* (2012), which combines superheroes (read Aryans) equipped with advanced scientific technologies, extra-terrestrials, and the Norse gods Thor and Loki.[16] Similar as these contemporary accounts are to the themes found in nineteenth century writing, this is not to say that the authors are Nazis, Nazis sympathisers, or even racists, but then neither were all of the originators of these ideas, many of whom had died before the emergence of the Third Reich. In the same way, these ideas remain dangerous when they go unchallenged; they fill a vacuum left vacant by orthodox archaeology and science and give succour to those disillusioned with the modern world, providing spiritual values and a feeling of ethnic superiority. In this way, the persistence of these ideas is pernicious. The danger lies in leaving them unchallenged to grow into something more substantial, as they did in the 1930s.

What makes matters worse is that during the Cold War, which followed the end of the Second World War, NATO governments actually encouraged belief in the occult, using the cover of UFOs to protect various secret testing of developmental aircraft and missiles, and also to explain away embarrassing Soviet spy craft seen over Europe.[17] Newspaper reports of UFOs were incorporated by conspiracy theorists into the occult repertoire to create an alternative creation narrative that explained ancient archaeological remains, the lost continent of Atlantis, and Norse mythology. This thinking has left an indelible mark on the public's consciousness, as demonstrated by a recent press report.

'Russian aggression in the Ukraine [*sic.*] is being caused by extra-terrestrial reptiles,' Whitby town councillor Simon Parkes told a meeting in Wallsend, 'who are advising Vladimir Putin to resist American influence, and supply him with technology. These alien reptiles are called "The Nordics", and know that Putin is a strong character with an independent mind. That's why they are advising him. It's not really a big deal, this sort of thing happens all the time.'

Parkes, a fifty-five-year-old father of three who represents Stakesby, added that 'I don't think we have anything to fear from extraterrestrials. They've been around for a long time, and if they were going to attack earth or wanted to do us any harm, they would have done so by now. Those in the higher echelons of power are aware of the truth about aliens, but keep it hidden from ordinary people. Aliens are not the problem, it's greedy power-mad humans in positions of great influence that people need to be worrying about.'

Parkes also claimed that his mother was a nine-foot-tall green extra-terrestrial, and that he lost his virginity to an alien at the age of five.[18]

A Warning from History

In the immediate aftermath of the war, racism and anti-Semitism declined, remaining beyond the pale of mainstream political thought in Europe and North America. As time has passed, however, we have seen a resurgence of these ideas. In the 1990s, an upsurge in nationalism following the unfolding of the Soviet Union was actually led by archaeologists, philologists, and ancient historians, illustrating the intimate link between past perceptions and present realitities.[19] There has been an increase in anti-Semitism in Europe, with attacks on Jewish communities in Britain, France, and Germany influenced by the rise of Islamic fundamentalism. The Muslim Brotherhood, with whom the Nazis cooperated, have grown in strength and influence in the post-war period. Indeed, Islamic fascism has to an extent replaced the racial ideology of Nazism with a religious ideology that is equally dangerous, justifying the destruction of pre-Islamic monuments and the murder of innocent people who do not 'fit in'.

Those living in liberal democracies seem to have made a mistake in not taking the rise of these groups seriously; instead, they have adopted a culturally relativistic perspective that fears challenging the cultures and beliefs of other peoples. Even now, we seem ill-equipped to tackle the challenge of extremism in our own countries, let alone in the Middle East. As with the pre-war engagement with Nazi Germany, we see short-term advantages in not taking action, ignoring the potential for a wider conflagration down the line.

Politics of the Past

The preceding chapters have outlined some of the ways in which the relationship between politics and archaeology, history, and anthropology was abused during the Third Reich. The historical narratives that were created by experts were used to promote the cultural and racial superiority of Nazi Germany and to justify the invasions of neighbouring countries by 'proving' the German ownership of land held 'from time immemorial'. The writing of history, as first Hobsbawn and Ranger (1983) and then Silberman (1989) pointed out, therefore carries with it a heavy responsibility that has the potential to shape the future.[20]

The manipulation of archaeological data for political ends has not been confined to Germany, nor did it end with the conclusion of the Second World War. The politicisation of archaeology occurred during the Cultural Revolution in Communist China (Tong), but it was most marked in the Soviet Union during the 1930s (Shnirelman).[21, 22] In the years following the communist revolution, archaeology underwent a transition, becoming an internationalist, anti-imperialist, and anti-racist-inspired discipline. Adopting a position that sounds fashionably post-processual:

> Consciously or unconsciously, a historian performs a political task expressing his political interests and inclinations in his choice of a particular topic, in his methodological tools, and in his representation of historical data.[23]

The anti-racist and anti-imperialist agenda was short-lived and easily subverted when state policies changed, and Soviet internationalist archaeology was replaced by Russian chauvinist archaeology.[24] One reason for this was the willingness of archaeologists to act, as they had in Nazi Germany, 'in the service of the state', which led them to abandon evidentiary standards.

The lesson drawn from archaeology in Mao's China, Stalin's Soviet Union, and also Salazar's Portugal, Franco's Spain, and Milosevic's Yugoslavia is that when archaeology is too closely identified with the state's policy, it all too readily becomes distorted, bending the rules of evidence to promote the glories of the ethnic group in command.[25] Those engaged in historical research have to determine the point at which legitimate interpretation becomes unacceptable political propaganda. This boundary is mediated through the adoption of evidentiary standards by which archaeological reconstructions can be evaluated.[26] The ability to distinguish between plausible and unbelievable reconstructions of the archaeological data is an essential safeguard against the widespread adoption of occult and fantastical narratives, but runs contrary to the fashionable relativism of post-processual archaeology. The difficulty is that while most archaeological tales are innocuous, others fan the passions of ethnic pride and fuel racial conflict.[27] In Saddam Hussein's Iraq, for example, ancient history was deliberately manipulated to justify the attempted annexation of Kuwait.[28] This graphically illustrates the limits of archaeological relativism when it comes to reconstructions of ancient origins:

> Nationalist or racist agendas are only encouraged in an intellectual environment where the 'real' world is visualised as a web of competing ideologies, all of which are equally true and all of which are equally false.[29]

The relativism of post-processualism is no guide for deciding when we should actively encourage feelings of patriotism and national pride, nor when we should discourage such feelings as overtly nationalistic.

If we abandon our standards for choosing between alternate explanations, we abdicate any right to exclude explanations that promote bigotry, nationalism and chicanery.[30]

The solution to this philosophical conundrum is to adopt an anthropological approach to investigations of the past. Adopting this mind-set, the task of archaeologists, historians, linguists, and folklorists is to document the rich diversity of the human past.[31] Focusing on cultural diversity located within specific social, economic, and historical contexts, the lives of past people may be traced from the emergence of the first societies. Importantly, historical studies provide a depth through which the transformation of peoples' lives over time may be studied.[32]

When interpreting these temporal data, each case must be examined in terms of its specific historical circumstances and judged according to a standard. That standard necessitates that the past of one group is not constructed at the expense of another, and that all cultures are respected.[33] Sensitivity and awareness are key to developing interpretations of the archaeological past that recognise the limits of the data when it comes to postulating the nature and extent of ethnic groups and territories.[34] This approach provides objective criteria that limit what can and what cannot be reconstructed from archaeological data. This allows archaeologists to distance themselves from myths and legends that resort to extraterrestrial beings or long-lost continents to explain the past.[35]

Endnotes

Chapter 1

1. *Indiana Jones and the Kingdom of the Crystal Skull* (2008, Lucasfilm Ltd).
2. *Raiders of the Lost Ark* (1981, Lucasfilm Ltd); *Indiana Jones and the Temple of Doom* (1984, Lucasfilm Ltd); *Indiana Jones and the Last Crusade* (1989, Lucasfilm Ltd); *Indiana Jones and the Kingdom of the Crystal Skull* (2008, Lucasfilm Ltd).
3. *The Young Indiana Jones Chronicles* (1992–1996, Amblin Entertainment, Lucasfilm, and Paramount Network Television)
4. *Indiana Jones and the Fate of Atlantis* (1992, LucasArts); *Indiana Jones and the Infernal Machine* (1999, LucasArts); *Indiana Jones and the Emperor's Tomb* (2003, LucasArts); *Indiana Jones and the Staff of Kings* (2009, LucasArts).
5. https://en.wikipedia.org/wiki/Empire_(film_magazine).
6. Muscutt, *Warriors of the Clouds* (1998); Schjellerup. *Incas and Spaniards in the Conquest of the Chachapoyas* (1997).
7. Exodus 25.
8. Joshua 3:15–16; Joshua 4:7–18; Joshua 6:4–20.
9. Gibson and Jacobson, *Below the Temple Mount in Jerusalem* (1996).
10. 1 Kings 8:9
11. Ritmeyer, *The Ark of the Covenant* (1998) pp. 91–110; Rohl, *Pharaohs and Kings* (1995).
12. Fisher, *The Ark of the Covenant* (1995) pp. 65–72; Munro-Hay, *The Quest For The Ark of The Covenant* (2006); Carew, *Tara and the Ark of the Covenant* (2003); Haran, *The Disappearance of the Ark* (1963) pp. 46–58; Hertz, *The Pentateuch and Haftoras* (1936).
13. Loth, *Tanis: 'Thebes of the North'* (2014); Montet, *La nécropole royale de Tanis* (1947); Montet, *La nécropole royale de Tanis* (1951); Flinders Petrie, *Seventy Years in Archaeology* (1932); Pfeiffer, *Das Dekret von Kanopos* (2004); Peck, *Lepsius, Karl Richard* (2001), pp. 289–290.
14. Loth, *Tanis: 'Thebes of the North'* (2014); Yoyotte, *The Treasures of Tanis* (1999), pp. 302–333.
15. Tyldesley, *Nefertiti* (1998); Perre, Van der, *Nefertiti's Last Documented Reference (For Now)* (2012), pp. 195–197; Schneider, *Ägyptologen im Dritten Reich* (Reprinted 2013); Schneider, *Egyptology Under National Socialism* (2014).

16. Gensicke, *Der Mufti von Jerusalem und die Nationalsozialisten* (2007);
    Lia, *The Society of the Muslim Brothers in Egypt* (1998); Mallmann and
    Cüppers, *Halbmond und Hakenkreuz* (2006); Soage, *Hasan al-Banna or the
    Politicisation of Islam* (2008), pp. 21–42.

17. Peterson, *The Cambridge History of China, the Ch'ing dynasty to 1800*
    (2002).

18. Hale, *Himmler's Crusade* (2003); Pringle, *The Master Plan* (2006), p. 221.

19. Debnath, *The Meanings of Hindu Gods, Goddesses and Myths* (2009); Flood,
    The Śaiva Traditions (2003).

20. Harding, *Kali* (1993).

21. Dash, *Thug* (2005); Paton, *Collections on Thuggee and Dacoitee* (n.d.);
    Woerkens, *The Strangled Traveller* (2002).

22. Bolton, *Coronado* (1949); Day, *Coronado's Quest* (1981); Hammond and
    Goad, *The Adventure of Don Francisco Vásquez de Coronado* (1938); Deni,
    *Evaluating Eyewitness Accounts of Native Peoples Along the Coronado Trail
    From the International Border to Cibola* (2009), pp. 399–435.

23. Andrea, *Encyclopedia of the Crusades* (2003); Phillips, *Holy Warriors* (2010).

24. Butler and Dafoe, *The Warriors and the Bankers* (1998); Ralls, *The Templars
    and the Grail* (2003); Barber, *The New Knighthood* (1994).

25. Stevenson, *The Origins of Freemasonry* (1988).

26. Frappier, *Chrétien de Troyes* (1982).

27. Frappier, *Chrétien de Troyes in Arthurian Literature in the Middle Ages*
    (1959); Foster, 'Gereint, Owein and Peredur' *in Arthurian Literature in the
    Middle Ages* (1959).

28. Brown, *The Da Vinci Code* (2003); Baigent, Leigh, and Lincoln, *The Holy
    Blood and the Holy Grail* (1982).

29. *Indiana Jones and the Last Crusade* (1989).

30. Graves, *Lawrence and the Arabs* (1927); Scott, *Lawrence in Arabia* (2013).

31. Hemming, *Red Gold* (1978); Bandelier, *The Gilded Man* (1893); Gonzalo,
    Historia General y Natural de las India, islas y Tierra-Firme del Mar Oceano
    (1851); Freyle, *El Carnero* (1961); Hagen, *The Gold of El Dorado* (1968).
    The British hero of the First World War, Col. Percy Fawcett, is also often
    considered a template for the character of Indiana Jones, see Grann, *The Lost
    City of Z* (2009).

32. Reinhard, *The Nazca Lines* (1996); Lambers, *The Geoglyphs of Palpa, Peru*
    (2006).

33. Sax, Walsh, Freestone, Rankin, and Meeks, *The Origins of Two Purportedly
    Pre-Columbian Mexican Crystal Skulls* (2008), pp. 2751–2760.

34. Joint Hearing before the Select Committee on Intelligence and the
    Subcommittee on Health and Scientific Research of the Committee on Human
    Resources, *Project MKUltra, the Central Intelligence Agency's Program of
    Research into Behavioral Modification* (1977); Marks, *The Search for the
    Manchurian Candidate* (1999); Stevens, *Storming Heaven* (1987); Lee and
    Shlain, *Acid Dreams* (1985); Ronson, *The Men Who Stare At Goats* (2012).

35. Kirchweger, *Die Geschichte der Heiligen Lanze vom späteren Mittelalter bis
    zum Ende des Heiligen Römischen Reiches* (1806); Kunsthistorisches Museum,
    Die Heilige Lanze in Wien (2005), pp. 71–110; Crowley, *The Legend of the
    Wanderings of the Spear Of Longinus* (1972).

36. Ravenscroft, *Spear of Destiny* (1973).

37. *Ibid.*

38. Pringle, *The Master Plan* (2006), p. 221; Kleinschmidt, *People on the Move*
    (2003), p. 262; Hodder, *Archaeological Theory in Europe* (1991), pp.

190–191; Olender, *Race and Erudition* (2009), p. 63; Arnold, *The Past as Propaganda* (1992), 30–37; Hale, *Himmler's Crusade* (2003), p. 200; Kater, *Das 'Ahnenerbe' der SS 1935–1945* (1997); Heim, *Archaeology, Ideology, and Society* (2002); Härke, *Archaeology, Ideology, and Society* (2002); Kohl and Fawcett, *Archaeology in the Service of the State* (1995), pp. 3–18; Arnold and Hassmann, *Archaeology in Nazi Germany* (1995), 70–81; Härke, *Archaeology, Nationalism, Nazism* (2013).

39. Kiss, *La Puerta del Sol and the Doctrine of Tiahuanacu Ice Universal Hörbiger* (1937); Rubio, *Nazi Archaeology in the Canary Islands* (2009); Pringle, *The Master Plan* (2006).
40. Hale, *Himmler's Crusade* (2003).
41. Pringle, *The Master Plan* (2006).
42. Rahn, *Kreuzzug gegen den Graal* (1933).
43. Brown, *Decoding Operation Matilda* (2011); Bower, *On the Nazis and the Bayeux Tapestry* (2011); 'The Strange Tale of the Bayeux Tapestry, Archaeology and the Nazi party', *British Archaeology* (2012).
44. Pringle, *The Master Race* (2006).
45. Gobineau, *Essay on the Inequality of the Human Races* (1855); Chamberlain, *The Foundations of the Nineteenth Century* (1911); Stoddart, *The Rising Tide of Color* (1919) and *Racial Realities in Europe* (1925).
46. Kossinna, *Die deutsche Vorgeschichte: eine hervorragend nationale Wissenschaft* (1921).
47. Arnold, *Race and Archaeology in Nazi Germany* (2006).
48. Hale, *Himmler's Crusade* (2003); Pringle, *The Master Race* (2006); Goodrick-Clarke, *The Occult Roots of Nazism* (1985).
49. Hale, *Himmler's Crusade* (2003); Pringle, *The Master Race* (2006); Goodrick-Clarke, *The Occult Roots of Nazism* (1985).
50. Gilbhard, *Die Thule-Gesellschaft* (1994); Phelps, *Before Hitler Came* (1963), pp. 245–261; Sklar, *The Nazis and the Occult* (1977); Lavenda, *Unholy Alliance* (2007); Goodrick-Clarke, *The Occult Roots of Nazism* (1985).
51. Johnson, *The Masters Revealed* (1994); Goodrick-Clarke, *Black Sun* (2003); Balzli, *Guido v. List* (1917).
52. Kossinna, *The German Ostmark* (1919); Arnold, *The Past as Propaganda* (1992), pp. 30–37.
53. Bollmus, *Amt Rosenberg* (2007), pp. 400–402; Kater, *Das Ahnenerbe der SS, 1933–1945* (2005); Pringle, *The Master Race* (2006).
54. Arnold, *The Past as Propaganda* (1992), pp. 30–37.
55. Bollmus, *Das Amt Rosenberg und seine Gegner* (1970).
56. Cecil, *The Myth of the Master Race* (1972); Chandler, *Rosenberg's Nazi Myth* (1945).
57. Rosenberg, *Der Mythus des 20. Jahrhunderts* (1930).
58. Kater, *Das Ahnenerbe der SS, 1933–1945* (2005); Pringle, *The Master Race* (2006).
59. Darré, *Neuadel aus Blut und Boden* (1935); Bramwell, *Blood and Soil* (1985); Poliakov, *The Aryan Myth* (1974).
60. Hale, *Himmler's Crusade* (2006) p. 74.
61. Kater, *Das 'Ahnenerbe' der SS 1935–1945* (2001); Epstein, *War-Time Activities of the SS-Ahnenerbe* (1971), pp. 79–81; Shirer, *The Rise and Fall of the Third Reich* (1960), p. 981.
62. Hale, *Himmler's Crusade* (2006), pp. 321, 323–4; Pringle, *The Master Race* (2006).
63. Wirth, *The Rise of Mankind* (1928); Pringle, *The Master Race* (2006).

64. Hedin, *Mein Leben als Entdecker* (1926); Wennerholm, *Sven Hedin 1865–1952* (1978); Levenda, *A History of Nazi Involvement with the Occult* (2010), pp. 173.
65. Bowen, *Universal Ice* (1993), pp. 146–150; Levenda, *Unholy Alliance* (2002), p. 198; Pringle, *The Master Race* (2006).
66. Goodrick-Clarke, *The Occult Roots of Nazism* (1985), p. 159; Sturluson, *The Prose Edda* (1964).
67. Bowen, *Universal Ice* (1993), pp. 146–150; Levenda, *Unholy Alliance* (2002), p. 198; Pringle, *The Master Race* (2006).
68. Blavatsky, *Isis unveiled* (1877); Blavatsky, *The Secret Doctrine* (1999, originally published 1888).
69. Pringle, *The Master Plan* (2006); Sievers, *Tagebuch* (1941).
70. Pringle, *The Master Plan* (2006); Letter from Rascher to Himmler, *Trials of War Criminals before the Nurenberg Military Tribunals* (1943), pp. 249–251; Moreno, *Undue Risk* (2000), pp. 7–17.

Chapter 2

1. McDougall, *The Group Mind* (1920, reprinted 1973).
2. Browning, *The Origins of the Final Solution* (2004); Burleigh and Wippermann, *The Racial State: Germany 1933–1945* (1991); Weindling, *Health, Race and German Politics between National Unification and Nazism, 1870–1945* (1989).
3. Hitler, *Mein Kampf* (1925).
4. *Ibid.*
5. Poliakov, *The Aryan Myth* (1974).
6. *Ibid.*
7. Nietzsche, *The Birth of Tragedy* (1871)
8. Sieg, *Deutschlands Prophet* (2007); Snyder, *Encyclopedia of the Third Reich* (1998), p. 203.
9. Poliakov, *The Aryan Myth* (1996); Arvidsson, *Aryan Idols* (2006); Lapouge, *Old and New Aspects of the Aryan Question* (1899), pp. 329–346.
10. Gobineau, *Essay on the Inequality of the Human Races* (1855).
11. Tacitus, *Agricola and Germany* (2009); Krebs, *A Most Dangerous Book* (2011).
12. Poesche, *Die Arier, ein Beitrag zur historischen Anthropologie* (1878).
13. Penka, *Origines Ariacae* (*Origins of the Aryans*) (1883).
14. Huxley, *Life and Letters* (1890); Huxley, *On the Geographical Distribution of the Chief Modifications of Mankind* (1870).
15. Morris, *The Aryan Race* (1888).
16. Agustus, Quiggin and Haddon, *Man, Past and Present* (1899).
17. Lapouge, *L'Aryen: son Rôle Social* (The Aryan: His Social Role) (1899).
18. Nietzsche, *On the Genealogy of Morals* (1887).
19. Arnold, *The Past as Propaganda* (1992), pp. 30–37; Klein, *Gustaf Kossinna: 1858–1931* (1999), pp. 233–246; Kossinna, *Die deutsche Vorgeschichte: eine hervorragend nationale Wissenschaft* (1921).
20. Coon, *The Races of Europe* (1939); Dobzhansky and Montagu, *Two Views of Coon's Origin of Races with Comments by Coon and Replies* (1963), pp. 360–367.
21. Williamson, *Houston Stewart Chamberlain* (1973); Snyder, *Houston Stewart Chamberlain and Teutonic Nordicism* (1939); Redesdale, *Houston Stewart Chamberlain* (1914); Biddiss, *History as Destiny* (1998).

22. Chamberlain. *The Foundations of the Nineteenth Century* (1911).
23. *Ibid.*
24. Chamberlain, 'Letter of William II 31 December 1901' in *Briefe* II (1928), pp. 141–4.
25. McDougall, *The Group Mind* (1920, reprinted 1973).
26. Ripley (revised by Coon), *The Races of Europe* (1899, revised 1939, reprinted 1975).
27. Georges Vacher de Lapouge had called this race '*Homo Europaeus*'.
28. Grant, *The Passing of the Great Race* (1916).
29. Baur, Fischer and Lenz, *Human Heredity* (1921).
30. Hale, *Himmler's Crusade* (2003); Klee, *Das Personenlexikon zum Dritten Reich* (2005); Ryback, *Hitler's Private Library* (2008).
31. Günther, *Short Ethnology of the German People* (1929).
32. Günther, *Rassenkunde des deutschen Volkes* (1922).
33. Gauch, *Vaterspuren* (1979), p. 92; Gauch, *New Foundations of Racial Science* (1934), p. 281.
34. Galton, *Hereditary Genius* (1869), pp. 336–62.
35. Bendersky, *A History of Nazi Germany* (2000); Fest, *Hitler* (1973, reprinted 1974); Hitler, *Mein Kampf* (1925, reprinted 1999); Speer, *Inside the Third Reich* (1969, reprinted 1971); Hitler, *Hitler's Table-Talk* (1953, reprinted 1988).
36. Broca, *On the Phenomena of Hybridity in the Genus Homo* (1864); Pineau, *Paul Broca and Anthropology* (1980), pp. 557–62; Androutsos and Diamantis, *Paul Broca (1824–1880)* (2007), pp. 557–64.
37. Leroy, *Chavée (Honoré-Joseph)* (1985), pp. 197–206; Pottelberge, van, *Chavée, Honoré (1815–1877)* (2006).
38. Gobineau, '*Essai sur l'inégalité des races humaines*' (1853–1855).
39. Pictet, '*Essai de paléontology linguistique*' (1859).
40. Tylor, *Primitive Culture* (1871); Tylor, *Anthropology an Introduction to the Study of Man and Civilization* (1881); Leopold, *Culture in Comparative and Evolutionary Perspective* (1980); Hodgen, *The Doctrine of Survivals* (1931), pp. 307–324.
41. Topinard, *l'Anthropologie* (1876).
42. Ackerknecht, *Rudolf Virchow* (1953); Boak, *Rudolf Virchow: Anthropologist and Archeologist* (1921), pp. 40–45.
43. Rowley-Conwy, *From Genesis to Prehistory* (2007), p. 120.
44. Ruse, *The Darwinian Revolution* (1999); Darwin, *On the Origin of Species* (1859).
45. Tylor, *Professor Adolf Bastian* (1905), pp. 138–143.
46. Beckett, *Richard Wagner* (1981); Potter, *Wagner and the Third Reich* (2008); Grey, *The Cambridge Companion to Wagner* (2008).
47. Prof. Leopold von Schröder of Vienna University (1851–1920) was a German academic and Indologist. He notably translated the Bhagavadgita from Sanskrit to German, and he also engaged in scientific studies of legends and myths. His publications included: *Die Wurzeln der Sage vom Heiligen Gral* (*Bohmeier Verlag*); *Bhagavadgita, Diederichs* (1952); *Bhagavadgita–Aschtavakragita–Indiens heilige Gesänge* (with Heinrich Zimmer, Diederichs Gelbe Reihe, 2004),
48. de Lagarde, P., *Deutsche Schriften* (1903).

1. Hitler, *Mein Kampf* (1939), pp. 243–8.
2. Rahn, *Luzifers Hofgesind* (1937, reprinted 2008)
3. Wirth, *Der Aufgang der Menschheit* (1934), pp. 55–63, 126–127.
4. Bowen, *Universal Ice* (1993), pp. 140–150; Brugg, *Die Welteislehre nach Hanns Hörbiger* (1940); Rosenberg, *Der Mythus des 20. Jahrhunderts* (1930).
5. Wiwjorra, *Herman Wirth* (1995), pp. 97–99.
6. Wirth, *Der Aufgang der Menschheit* (1934), pp. 105–109.
7. *Ibid.*
8. *Ibid.*
9. *Ibid.*
10. Huth, *Fragebogen für Mitglieder (*1933); Huth, *R.u.S—Fragebogen* (1939).
11. Conrado, *The Guanche Mummies* (1998), p. 283.
12. Huth, *Die Gesittung der Kanarier als Schlussel zum Ur-Indogermanentum* (1937), p. 50.
13. Hooton, *The Ancient Inhabitants of the Canary Islands* (1925), p. 44.
14. Huth, *Die Gesittung der Kanarier als Schlüssel zum Ur-Indogermanentum* (1937), p. 54.
15. This is one of the expeditions shown on the Ahnenerbe map in *Das Ahnenerbe* (Offenbach am Main: Gebrüder Klingspor, n.d., p, 13)
16. Huth to Wüst (1939).
17. *Ibid.*
18. Huth to Wüst (1939); Alonso, *La arqueología durante el primer franquismo (1939–1956)* (2009), p. 551.
19. Bowen, *Universal Ice* (1993), p. 76.
20. *Abschrift Pyrmonter Protokoll* (NARA, RG242, T580/194/465, 19.07.1936); Bowen, *Universal Ice* (1993), pp. 146–150.
21. Hitler, *Hitler's Table Talk 1941–1944* (2000), p. 249.
22. Breton. *Proceedings of Americanists' Congress* (1910).
23. Vranich, *Tiwanaku Q&A* (n.d.)
24. Kiss, *Das Sonnentor von Tihuanaku* (1937), pp. 130–132.
25. Kiss, *Die Kordillerenkolonien der Atlantiden* (1931), p. 259.
26. Kiss, *Die Kordillerenkolonien der Atlantiden* (1931), p. 261; Pringle, *A Chilling Fantasy at Tiwanaku* (2009).
27. Kiss, *Nordische Baukunst in Bolivien?* (1933), p. 144.
28. Kiss, *Das Sonnentor von Tihuanaku* (1937), pp. 144–145.
29. *Ibid.*, pp. 106–107.
30. von Elmayer-Vestenbrugg, *Versunkene Reiche* (1937).
31. Sievers to Koehler and Amelang (1937).
32. Wüst to Himmler (1938).
33. Kiss, *Personalangaben* (1944); Kiss, *Abschrift* (n.d.).
34. Kiss, *Dienstlaufbahn* (n.d.).
35. Riepe, *Leumundszeugnis* (1948); Bury, *Eidesstattliche Erklärung* (1948).
36. Kiss, *SS-Stammrollenauszug* (1939).
37. For further information on this research trip, see: Kiss, *Programm der Forschungsreise des SS-Hauptsturmführers Kiss* (1939); Sievers, *Abrechnung fur die Tripolis-Reise von* (1939); Kiss to Sievers (1939); Kiss, *Niederschrift betreffend Vortrag des SS-Hauptsturmführers Kiss beim Reichsführer SS* (1939); and Kiss, *Ergebnisbericht der Forschungsreise des SS-Hauptsturmführers Kiss each Tripolis* (1939).
38. Sievers to Himmler (1939).

39. Kiss, *Vorläufiges Programm* (1939).
40. Sievers to Himmler (1939).
41. Gousseva, M. (transl.), *Nastoyashchy Saratov* (n.d.).

Chapter 4

1. Schellenberg, *The Schellenberg Memoirs* (1956), p. 347.
2. Hörbiger and Fauth, *Glac(z)ial-Kosmogonie* (1912).
3. Levenda, *Unholy Alliance* (2010), pp. 192–4.
4. Schäfer, *Berge, Buddhas und Bären* (1933); *Unbekanntes Tibet* (1938); *Dach der Erde* (1938); *Four New Birds from Tibet* in the *Proceedings of the Academy of Natural Sciences, Philadelphia* (1937).
5. Levenda, *Unholy Alliance* (2010), 194.
6. Hale, *Himmler's Crusade* (2006), pp. 111–114.
7. *Ibid*. p. 114.
8. *Ibid*. p. 115.
9. Reportedly told the British Himalayan Club in 1938, when visiting London.
10. Cecil, *The Myth of the Master Race* (1972); Chandler, *Rosenberg's Nazi Myth* (1945); Graves, *The Truth about the Protocols* (1921).
11. Schäfer, *Berge, Buddhas und Baren* (1933).
12. Schäfer, *Dach der Erde* (1938); *Unbekanntes Tibet* (1938).
13. Hörbiger and Fauth, *Glac(z)ial-Kosmogonie* (1912); Levenda, *Unholy Alliance* (2010), pp. 197–200.
14. Hitler, *Table Talk* (2000).
15. Hale, *Himmler's Crusade* (2006), pp. 120–121.
16. *Ibid*.
17. Levenda, *Unholy Alliance* (2010), p. 196; Hale, *Himmler's Crusade* (2006).
18. Schäfer, *Geheimnis Tibet* (1943).
19. Gould, *The Mismeasure of Man* (1996); Fabian, *The Skull Collectors* (2010); Barkan, *The Retreat of Scientific Racism* (1992); Dain, *A Hideous Monster of the Mind* (2002).
20. Brookes, *Extreme Measures* (2004); Gillham, *A Life of Sir Francis Galton* (2001); Ewen and Ewen, *Nordic Nightmares* (2006, 2008), pp. 257–325.
21. Knoll, von Luschan, *Ergänzungen und Beiträge zu biographischen Daten eines Pioniers der Ethnologie* (2004); Stelzig, *Felix von Luschan* (2005).
22. Chisholm, H. (ed.), 'Schlagintweit', *Encyclopædia Britannica* (11th ed.) (1911). For a contemporary comment on this, see the death masks collection at 'The Loggia of Death' by the artist Mark Dion's *The Academy of Things* at HFBK, Dresden, Oct 2014–Feb 2015
23. Günther, *The Racial Elements of European History* (1927).
24. *Ibid*.
25. *Ibid*.
26. Günther, *Die Nordische Rasse bei den Indogermanene Aliens* (1933).
27. Beger, *Goals and Plans of the Tibet Expedition of the Society 'Das Anenerbe'* (1938).
28. Hale, *Himmler's Crusade* (2006), p. 123.
29. Tauxe, *Paleomagnetic Principles and Practice* (1998); Merrill, *Our Magnetic Earth* (2010).
30. Hale, *Himmler's Crusade* (2006), p. 177.
31. *Ibid*. p. 166.
32. *Ibid*. p. 171.

33. Schäfer, *Fest der weissen Schleier; eine Forscherfahrt durch Tibet nach Llahsa, der heiligen Stadt des Gottkönigtums* (1943).
34. NA, CDS, T580, R202, Ord. 637 file Tibetexpedition.
35. *Ibid.*
36. Sykes, *Wassmuss 'The German Lawrence'* (1936).
37. Buchan, *Greenmantle* (1916).
38. Sykes, *Wassmuss 'The German Lawrence'* (1936).
39. *Ibid.*
40. Hale, *Himmler's Crusade* (2006), pp. 307–315.
41. Hale, *Himmler's Crusade* (2006); Orwell, *As I Please* (1944).
42. Hale, *Himmler's Crusade* (2006).

Chapter 5

1. Tylor, *Anthropology* (1881).
2. Levenda, *Unholy Alliance* (2010), pp. 182–3.
3. Virgil, *Georgic I,* Line 30 (2009); Burton, *Ultima Thule or, A Summer in Iceland* (1875); Frye, *North to Thule* (1985); Strabo, *The Geography of Strabo I.4.2.* (2014); Whitaker, *The Problem of Pytheas' Thule* (December 1981–January 1982), pp. 148–164.
4. von Sebottendorff, R., *Bevor Hitler kam: Urkundlich aus der Frühzeit der Nationalsozialistischen Bewegung* (1933).
5. Poliakov, *The Aryan Myth* (1974), Chapter 11.
6. Levenda, *Unholy Alliance* (2010), pp. 184–5.
7. Sturluson, *The Prose Edda* (1964); Byock, J. (transl.), *The Prose Edda* (2006); Anderson, *Norse Mythology* (1876).
8. Goodrick-Clarke, *The Occult Roots of Nazism* (1992), pp. 154–163.
9. *Ibid.* p 159.
10. Hitler, *Hitler's Table Talk, 1941–1944* (2000), p. 249.
11. Himmler, *Heinrich Himmler's Reading List* (n.d.).
12. Das Ahnenerbe, *Offenbach am Main: Gebrüder Klingspor* (n.d.), p. 13.
13. Himmler to Wüst (1940). See also Himmler to Wüst (1938).
14. Himmler to Wüst (1940).
15. Aspendorf, *Die Edda als Welteislehre* (1933).
16. Byock, J. (transl.), *The Prose Edda* (2006)
17. Hollander, *The Skalds* (1968).
18. Sverdlov, *Kenning Morphology* (2006).
19. Sturluson, *The Prose Edda* (1964).
20. Anderson, *Norse Mythology* (1876).
21. Tolkien, *The Battle of the Goths and the Huns* (1955–6).
22. Davidson, *Introduction to Saxo Grammaticus: The History of the Danes, Book I–IX. Volume II: Commentary* (1980).
23. Haymes, *The Saga of Thidrek of Bern* (1988).
24. Donnelly, *Ragnarok* (1887).
25. Jakobsson, *A Contest of Cosmic Fathers* (2008).
26. Rosenberg, *Tagebuch* (1934), p. 26.
27. Lutzhöft. *Der Nordische Gedanke in Deutschland 1920–1940* (1971).
28. Bowen, *Universal Ice* (1993), pp. 140–150; Brugg, *Die Welteislehre nach Hanns Hörbiger* (1940).
29. Bowen, *Universal Ice* (1993), pp. 148–9.
30. Byock, *Medieval Iceland* (1988).

31. MacCulloch, *The Mythology of all Races Vol. II, Eddic* (1964).
32. Greger and Geisler, *Myt och Propaganda* (2007); *Statens Offentliga Utredningar, 1946:86. Den tyska propagandan i Sverige under krigsåren 1939–1945* (1946).
33. *Volkischer Beobachter* (NA, CDS, T580, R202, 22.8.38).
34. Weindling, *Health, Race, and German Politics Between National Unification and Nazism, 1870–1945* (1993).
35. Rahn, *Luzifers Hofgesind* (1937).
36. *Das Anenerbe Forschungsstatte fur Germanenkunde, Detmold* (NA, CDS, T580, R202, Ord 627, Sommer 1938).
37. Bittner, *The Lion and the White Falcon* (1983).
38. Guðmundsson, *A Nazi's Disappointment With Iceland* (2014)
39. *Ibid.*
40. *Ibid.*
41. *Ibid.*
42. *Ibid.*
43. Kress, *Icelandic Grammar* (1955), see also Kress, *Die Laute des modernen Isländischen* (1937).

Chapter 6

1. Åberg, *Herman Wirth* (1933), pp. 247–249.
2. Findell, *Runes* (2014).
3. Goodrick-Clarke, *The Occult Roots of Nazism* (2004).
4. *Ibid.* pp. 155–160.
5. *Nordland Und Unser Deutsches Ahnenerbe* (NA, CDS, T580, R202, Ord. 62) (n.d.).
6. Steigmann-Gall, *The Holy Reich* (2003), pp. 86–114.
7. *Ibid.* pp. 106–108.
8. *Völkischer Beobachter* 1 July 1935, quoted in Steigmann-Gall, *The Holy Reich* (2003), p. 129.
9. Kersten, *The Memoirs of Doctor Felix Kersten* (1947), p. 61.
10. Wirth, *Lebenslauf* (n.d.).
11. Wirth, *Der Aufgang der Menschheit* (1928), p. 14.
12. Baumann, *Verzeichnis der Schriften* (1995), p. 357.
13. Wirth, *Der Aufgang der Menschheit* (1928), pp. 15–17.
14. *Ibid.* pp. 622–626.
15. 'Inscriptions', *Encyclopaedia Britannica 14th Edition* (1938).
16. 'Runes', *Encyclopaedia Britannica 14th Edition* (1938).
17. Wirth, *Der Aufgang der Menschheit* (1928), p. 22.
18. Huxley and Haddon, *We Europeans* (1935), p. 94.
19. Wirth, *Der Aufgang der Menschheit* (1928), pp. 55–63, 126–7.
20. Wiwjorra, *Herman Wirth* (1995), pp. 97–99.
21. Plassmann to Galke (1937).
22. *Gedächtnisprotokoll. Unterredung Prof. Dr Herman Wirth und Michael H. Kater* (1963).
23. Wirth, *Der Aufgang der Menschheit* (1928), pp. 105–109.
24. Leers to Mack, *Die Meinung anderer Leute über Herman Wirth* (1933).
25. Strohmeyer, *Der gebaute Mythos: Das Haus Atlantis in der Bremer Böttcherstrasse* (1993).

26. Hans Müller-Brauel described the collection during a walking tour of *Haus Atlantis* in 1932, see *Haus Atlantis* (2001).
27. Merhart, *Zu dem Buche Herman Wirth, 'Der Aufgang der Menschheit'* BDQ REM: Wirth, Herman (06.05.1885).
28. Köfler to Archivrat (1935).
29. Åberg, *Herman Wirth* (1933), pp. 247–249.
30. Sievers to Himmler (1936).
31. *Uddevalla: Bohusläns museum och Bohusläns hembygdsförbund* (1990), p. 14.
32. Hygen and Bengtsson, *Rock Carvings in the Borderlands* (2000), pp. 172–184.
33. Coles (w. Bengtsson), *Images of the Past* (1990).
34. *Ibid.*
35. Hygen and Bengtsson, *Rock Carvings in the Borderlands* (2000), p. 186.
36. *Ibid.* pp. 210–211. In 1994, UNESCO classified the rock-art sites in Bohuslän as a World Heritage Site, noting: 'The rock carvings of Tanum region constitute an outstanding example of Bronze Age art of the highest quality'.
37. Wirth, *Bericht über die Hällristninagr-Expedition des 'Deutschen Ahnenerbe' vom* (1935).
38. *Ibid.*
39. *Gedächtnisprotokoll. Unterredung Prof. Dr Walther Wüst und Michael H. Kater* (1963).
40. Speer, 'Inside the Third Reich', in Arnold, *The Past as Propaganda: Totalitarian Archaeology in Nazi Germany* (1990), pp. 469.
41. *Gedächtnisprotokoll Unterredung Prof. Dr Walther Wüst und Michael H. Kater* (1963).
42. Sievers to Kotte (1937).
43. Tresidder, *Dictionary of Symbols* (1998).
44. Biedermann, *Dictionary of Symbolism: 'Swastika'* (1992).
45. Wirth to Schindler (1929); Roselius to Wirth (1933).
46. Roselius to Mack, C. W., *Die Meinung anderer Leute über Herman Wirth* (BA (ehem. BDC) Ahnenerbe: Wirth, Herman Felix (06.05.1885), 27.07.1932)
47. Himmler to Galke (1936).
48. Bericht (1935).
49. Sievers to Bousset (1936).
50. Sievers to Bousset (1936).
51. Galke to Reichsführer-SS (1936).
52. Bousset, *Stammrollenauszug* (BA (ehem.BDC)), SSO: Bousset, Helmut (08.12. 1902).
53. Ahnenerbe to Landesfinanzamt (1936).
54. Löw, *Herman Wirth and die Suche nach der Germanischen Geistesurgeschichte in Skandinavien* (n.d.).
55. Wirth to Reichsantiquar Stockholm (1936).
56. Wirth, *Bericht uber die erste Hällristninagr-Expedition des 'Deutschen Ahnenerbes'* (1935).
57. Galke to Sievers. *Betr. Forschungsreise nach Skandinavien* (1936).
58. Sievers, *Bericht über die Forschungsfahrt* (1936).
59. Wirth, *Bericht* (1935).
60. Hygen and Bengtson, *Rock Carvings in the Borderlands* (2000), pp. 150–151.
61. Wirth once told a Swedish antiquity official that he intended to expand on Almgren's work. Wirth to Curman (1939).
62. Wirth dates the Swedish engravings to both the Neolithic and Bronze Age. Wirth to Reichsantiquar Stockholm (1936); Wirth, *Der Aufgang der Menschheit* (1928), p. 57.

63. Wirth, *Die Heilige Urschrift der Menschheit* (1936), pp. 84–93.
64. Wirth, *Der Aufgang der Menschheit* (1934), p. 90.
65. Wirth, *Die Heiligen Zeichen der Weihenacht unserer Ahnen* (1934); Wirth, *Die Heilige Urschrift der Menschheit* (1936), p. 518.
66. Wirth to Himmler, *Bericht fiber die Arbeiten der 2. Expedition des Deutschen Ahnenerbes* (1936).
67. *Tysk professor avgjuter Tanums manga hallristningar* (1935).
68. Wirth to Reichsantiquar Stockholm, *Bericht fiber die zweite Hällristningar Expedition des Ahnenerbes* (1936).
69. Wirth to Reichsantiquar Stockholm. *Bericht fiber die zweite Hällristningar Expedition des Ahnenerbes* (1936).
70. Pringle, 'Ms. Camilla Olsson' in *The Master Plan* (2006), p. 39.
71. *Tysk nazistungdom till Halland* (1934).
72. Wirth to Reichsantiquar Stockholm, *Bericht fiber die zweite Hällristningar Expedition des Ahnenerbes* (1936).
73. Wirth to Himmler, *Bericht uber die Arbeiten der 2.Expedition des Deutschen Ahnenerbes* (1936).
74. Pringle, 'Dr Jan Brøgger' in *The Master Plan* (2006), p. 74.
75. Brøgger, *Arkeologien og samfundenes åndelige balanse* (1936).
76. Brøgger, *Viking: tidskrift for norrøn arkeologi* (1937).
77. Wirth to Brøgger (1936).
78. *Ibid.*
79. *Ibid.* Wirth refers to the island as 'Røddy', but it is clear from the letter that he means 'Rødøya' in Alstadhaug County, Norway. It is on Rødøya that the engraving of the skier is found.
80. The Rødøya skier is so famous in Norway that organisers of the 1994 winter Olympics in Lillehammer chose it for their logo.

Chapter 7

1. Kessler, *Walther Rathenau* (1933), pp. 31–2.
2. Bose, *Typen der Volksmusik in Karelien* (1938), pp. 20–21.
3. Lebenslauf, *Reichskulturkammer Fragebogen* (1942); Grönhagen, *Einige Angaben uber das Geschlecht Grönhagen* (n.d.)
4. Grönhagen, *Karelien* (1942).
5. Pringle, 'Juhani von Grönhagen' in *The Master Plan* (2006), p. 89. 6. Grönhagen, *Journal* (n.d.).
7. Grönhagen, *Zum Geleit* (1941).
8. Grönhagen, *Journal* (n.d.).
9. Crawford, *Preface, The Kalevala: The Epic Poem of Finland* (1891), p. xxxvii.
10. Pentikäinen, *Kalevala Mythology* (1989), pp. 22–26.
11. Crawford, *Preface, The Kalevala* (1891), pp. xliii.
12. Grönhagen, unpublished journal (1935).
13. Pentikäinen, *Finland as a Cultural Area* (1995), pp. 11–12.
14. *Bericht über die Arbeitssitzung der Mitarbeiter des Ahnenerbes* (1937).
15 Crawford, *Preface, The Kalevala* (1891), pp. vi–vii.
16. *Bericht über die Arbeitssitzung der Mitarbeiter des Ahnenerbes* (1937).
17. Pentikäinen, *Finland as a Cultural Area* (1995), pp. 12–13.
18. *Ibid.* pp. 12–13.
19. Grönhagen, *Das Antlitz Finnlands* (1942), p. 20.
20. *Ibid.* p. 22.

21. *Ibid.* p. 30.
22. Grönhagen, *Karelische Zauberbeschwörungen* (1937), pp. 54–57.
23. *Ibid.* p. 54.
24. Sünner, *Schwarze Sonne* (1999), p. 234, footnote 152.
25. Moynihan, and Flowers, *The Secret King* (2007); Goodrick-Clarke, N., *The Occult Roots of Nazism* (2004); Lange, H-J., *Weisthor—Karl-Maria Wiligut— Himmlers Rasputin und seine Erben* (1999).
26. Grönhagen, *Himmlerin salaseura* (1948).
27. Wüst, *Zeugnis* (1939).
28. Pentikäinen, *Kalevala Mythology* (1989).
29. Padfield, *Himmler* (2001), pp. 172–174.
30. *Ibid.* pp. 172.
31. Himmler to Grönhagen (1936).
32. *Ibid.*
33. Juhani von Grönhagen.
34. Himmler to Grönhagen (1936).
35. Potter, *Most German of the Arts* (1998), p. 133.
36. Bose, *Racial Aspects in Music* (1934); Eggebrecht and Potter, 'Fritz Bose', in *Grove Music Online Edition* (2001).
37. Behrendt, *Bericht: Dr Fritz Bose* (1937).
38. Potter, *Most German of the Arts* (1998) pp. 106, 132.
39. Ritter, *An Introduction into Storage Media and Computer Technology* (1988), pp. 10–12.
40. Sievers to Himmler (1937).
41. Bose, *Law and Freedom in the Interpretation of European Folk Epics* (1958), p. 31.
42. Grönhagen, *Finnische Gespräche* (1941), pp. 81–88; Bose, *Typen der Volksmusik in Karelien: Ein Reisebericht* (1938), pp. 96–118. We know that Grönhagen went to see Timo Lipitsä during this field trip in 1936 because he presented a photograph he had taken of Lipitsä to Himmler in the autumn of 1936.
43. Grönhagen, *Finnische Gespräche* (1941), p. 82.
44. *Ibid.* p. 84.
45. Hyvärinen to Haavio (1936).
46. Grönhagen, *Finnische Gespräche* (1941), p. 84.
47. *Ibid.* p. 86.
48. It is possible that this is the version of *The Kalevala* creation story that is preserved in a collection of Bose's recordings at the *Lautarchiv der Humboldt Universität zu Berlin*. See LHUB, LA1512-LA1514, which is described as *Runengesang Karelisch*.
49. Fritz Bose, *Typen der Volksmusik in Karelien* (1938), p. 100.
50. *Ibid.*
51. *Abbildung* 4, p. 107.
52. *Ibid.*
53. Pringle, 'Lawergren, B. and Victor Mair, V.' in *The Master Plan* (2006), p. 87.
54. Grönhagen, *Finnische Gespräche* (1941), p. 54.
55. *Ibid.* p. 55.
56. Bose, *Zauber Spruch. Karelisch* (n.d.).
57. Bose, *Folk Music Research and the Cultivation of Folk Music* (1957), pp. 20–21.
58. Grönhagen, *Finnische Gespräche* (1941), p. 41.
59. *Musik-ges* (LHUB, LA 1504-1505).

60. Bose, *Typen der Volksmusik in Karelien* (1938), p. 102.
61. *Ibid.* p. 117.
62. Kater, *Das Ahnenerbe der SS 1935–1945* (1974), p. 105.
63. Grönhagen, *Karelische Zauberbeschwörungen* (1937), pp. 54–57.
64. Hyvärinen to Haavio (1936).
65. Pringle, 'Dr Juba Pentikäinen' in *The Master Plan* (2006), p. 89.
66. Hyvärinen to Haavio (1936)
67. Grönhagen *Himmlerin salaseura* (1948).
68. Pringle, 'Dr Juhani von Grönhagen' in *The Master Plan* (2006), p. 89.
69. Weisthor to Wolff (1937); Bose (1906); Sievers to Galke. (1938); Sievers to Reichsführer-SS (1941).
70. Reichsführer-SS (ed.), *Deutsche Geschichte. Lichtbildvortrag: Erster Tel: Germanische Frühzeit 'Das Licht aus dem Norden'* (IfZ, DC 25.10, n.d.).
71. Potter, *Most German of the Arts* (1998), p. 134.
72. Himmler to Grönhagen (1937).
73. Kater, *Das Ahnenerbe* (2005), p. 134.
74. Grönhagen, *Ungefährer Plan für die Arbeit der Abteilung Pflegestätte für indogermanische-finnische Kulturbeziehungen* (1937).
75. Sievers to Wüst (1937). The letter includes a copy of Grönhagen's report, *Arbeitsplan der Abteilung 'Pflegestätte für indogermanisch-finnische Kulturbeziehungen.*
76. Sievers to Grönhagen (1937).

Chapter 8

1. Lapouge, *L'Aryen* (1899), p. vii.
2. *Vorgeschichte (Felsbilder): Val Camonica, Italien* (1936); Altheim, *Forschungsbericht zur riimischen* (1936); *Geschichte 2*, (1936), pp. 68–94; Pringle, *The Master Plan* (2006), pp. 126–7.
3. Bohmers, *Stellungnahme zum Vorbericht* (n.d.); Bohmers, *Die Mauerner Höhlen and ihre Bedeutung für die Einteilung der Altsteinzeit* (1944), p. 65; Pringle, *The Master Plan* (2006), pp. 123–5.
4. Günther, *Rassenkunde des deutschen Volkes* (1924), pp. 257–258.); Pringle, *The Master Plan* (2006), pp. 128; Trinkhaus, and Shipman, *The Neandertals* (1993), pp. 109–110.
5. Bohmers to *Abteilung Ausgrabungen des Ahnenerbes*, (BA, NS 21/60, 27.10.1938); Pringle, *The Master Race* (2006), p. 131.
6. *Vorgeschichte I (Felsbilder) Juli-August 1934: Südfrankreich und Ostspanien* (FIA, LF 514. n.d.)
7. *Ibid.*
8. Nehring, *Die Schwestern Eva und Erika Nehring* (1975), p. 77.
9. Nehring, *Erika und Eva Nehring aus Osterwieck* (1973).
10. Tuchel and Schattenfroh, *Zentrale des Terrors* (1987), pp. 29–30.
11. *Frobenius Institut*, 'Forschungsreisen des Frobenius-Institute' in *Das Frobenius–Institut an der Johann Wolfgang Goethe–Universität 1898-1998* (1998), pp. 36–40.
12 *Fotos: Expedition XIV Süd-Frankreich/Ost-Spanien* (1934), p. 108.
13. Elmayer-Vestenbrugg, *Rätsel des Weltgeschehens* (1937).
14. Altheim, *Forschungsbericht zur riimischen Geschichte* (1936), pp. 68–94.
15. Anati, *Camonica Valley* (1961); *Evolution and Style in Camunian Rock Art* (1976); *I Camuni* (1982); *Valcamonica Rock Art* (1994).

16. Altheim, Trautmann, *Nordische und italische Felsbildkunst* (1937), pp. 1–82.
17. *Ibid.*
18. Marretta, *Una breve storia delle ricerche in Valcamonica (Parte 1)*
19. Gehl, *The Roman Empire as a Nordic Creation* (1940), pp. 72–122.
20. Himmler to Wüst (1937).
21. Himmler to Höhne (1937).
22. Trautmann, *Deutsches Reich Reisepass* (undated); Himmler to Höhne (1937); Höhne to Trautmann (1937); Altheim to Höhne (1937); Altheim, *Personalnachweis* (1937); Trautmann to RFSS (1937); Höhne to Ullmann (1937).
23. Sievers to Trautmann (1937).
24. Altheim and Trautmann to Ahnenerbe (1938).
25. *Ibid.*
26. *Ibid.*
27. *Ibid.*
28. *Ibid.*
29. Trautmann, *Anmerkung* (1938).
30. *The Petroleum Almanac* (1946).
31. *Pravda* (1938) quoted in Nagy-Talavera, *The Green Shirts and Others* (1970), p. 300.
32. Price, *Cloak and Trowel* (2003), pp. 30–35.
33. Pringle, 'Dr. Bernhard Caemmerer' in *The Master Plan* (2006).
34. Altheim and Trautmann, *(Vertraulicher) Bericht: Rumanien* (undated).
35. *Ibid.*
36. *Ibid.*
37. Holmes, *The Spell of Romania* (1934), pp. 399–450.
38. Altheim and Trautmann, *(Vertraulicher) Bericht: Rumanien* (undated).
39. Nagy-Talavera, *The Greenshirts and the Others* (1970), pp. 251–254.
40. *Ibid.* p. 247.
41. Altheim and Trautmann, *(Vertraulicher) Bericht: Rumänien* (undated)
42. *Ibid.*
43. *Ibid.*
44. *Ibid.*
45. *Ibid.*
46. Hirszowicz, *The Third Reich and the Arab East* (1966), p. 18.
47. Altheim and Trautmann, *(Vertraulicher) Bericht: Irak* (undated); Jordan, *Personalnachweis* (1877).
48. Günther, *Die Nordische Rasse bei den Indogermanen Asiens* (1934), pp. 124–125.
49. Altheim and Trautmann, *(Vertrauhcher) Bericht: Irak* (undated).
50. *Ibid.*
51. Altheim and Trautmann, *(Vertraulicher) Bericht: Unsere Vorschläge sind* (undated).
52. Sievers to Himmler (1939).
53. Sievers to Altheim (1939).
54. Altheim to Ahnenerbe (1939).

Chapter 9

1. Feist, *Archäologie und Indogermanentum* (1916), p. 68.
2. *Das Ahnenerbe in Greece* (undated).
3. Kokkinidou, and Nikolaidou, *Archaeology under Metaxas* (2000–2007).

4. Mackenzie, *Half-Finished People: Thomas Meaney, Review of The Tyranny of Greece over Germany by E. M. Butler, Cambridge, 2012* (2012), pp. 14–16.
5. *Das Ahnenerbe in Greece* (undated).
6. Hörbiger, Fauth, *Glac(z)ial-Kosmogonie* (1912).
7. Schöbel, *Hans Reinerth: Forscher, NS-Funktionär, Museumsleiter* (2002), pp. 321–396.
8. *Das Ahnenerbe in Greece* (undated)
9. *Ibid.*
10. Paschalidis, *The Buried Statues of War: The Hiding of the Ancient Treasures of the National Archaeological Museum on the Eve of the German occupation of Athens, 1941* (2013).
11. Petrakos, *The Antiquities of Greece during the War 1940–1944* (1994).
12. Vernardou, *A Hiding Different from all Others. Operation 'Hidden Treasures'* (2013); Nikolakea, *The Protection of Antiquities during World War II* (2008), pp. 57–59; Paschalidis, *The Founding, History and Adventures of the National Archaeological Museum: 130 Years of Service in One Lecture*; Salta, *National Archaeological Museum* (2002), pp. 116–119; Flessa, *At the Edge* (2012).

Chapter 10

1. Schellenberg, *The Schellenberg Memoirs* (1956), p.32.
2. Hüser, *Wewelsburg 1933–1945* (1982), p. 384.
3. Levenda, *Unholy Alliance* (2010), pp. 175–177.
4. Schellenberg, *The Schellenberg Memoirs* (1956), p. 32.
5. Chadwick, *The Mycenaean World* (1976); Papadimitriou, *Built Chamber Tombs of Middle and Late Bronze Age Date in Mainland Greece and the Islands* (2001).
6. http://www.oxforddictionaries.com/definition/english/swastika
7. Heller, *The Swastika: Symbol Beyond Redemption?* (2008).
8. Oldenberg, *Hymnen des Rigveda* (1888, reprinted 1982); Lal, *The Homeland of the Aryans* (2005).
9. Liebenfelds, *Ostara* (1927).
10. Griffith, *The Rig Veda* (2008).
11. Gardner, *Multiple Meanings: The Swastika Symbol* (2006), pp. 35–37; Heller, *The Swastika* (2008), pp. 156–7.
12. Freed, *Origin of the Swastika* (1980), pp. 68–75; Gardner, *Multiple Meanings* (2006), pp. 35–37; 'The Swastika', *Annual Report of the Board of Regents of the Smithsonian Institution* (undated).
13. Bibikova, *On the Origin of Mezin Paleolithic Ornamenta* (1965), pp. 3–8.
14. Bachrach, *Restructuring the Eastern Frontier: Henry I of Germany, 924–936* (2014), pp 9–36; Gwatkin and Whitney (eds), *The Cambridge Medieval History: Volume III* (1926); Levenda, *Unholy Alliance* (2010), pp. 175–177.
15. Hüser, *Wewelsburg 1933–1945: Kult- und Terrorstatte der SS. Eine Dokumentation* (1982). All this was the subject of James Herbert's novel *The Spear* (1979), in which Himmler returns as a kind of odd Nazi zombie, planning to take possession of the Heilige Lance and reinstate the Satanic Reich.
16. Hüser, *Wewelsburg 1933–1945: Kult- und Terrorstatte der SS. Eine Dokumentation* (1982), p. 384.
17. Levenda. *Unholy Alliance* (2010), pp. 176–181.
18. Jensen, *Manden i kisten* (1998).
19. Birley (transl.), Tacitus, *Agricola and Germany* (2009).

20. Birley, 'Introduction' in *Tacitus Agricola and Germany* (1956, reprinted 1999), p. *xxxviii*.
21. Birley (transl.), Tacitus, *Agricola and Germany* (2009).
22. *Ibid.*
23. Lund, *De etnografiske kilder til Nordens tidlige historie* (1993).
24. Birley (transl.), Tacitus, *Agricola and Germany* (2009).
25. Sanden, van der, *Through Nature to Eternity* (1996), p. 167.
26. Glob, *The Bog People* (1971), pp. 113–14.
27. Sanden, van der, *Through Nature to Eternity*, (1996), p. 167; United States Holocaust Memorial Museum, *Homosexuals: Victims of the Nazi Era 1933–1945* (2003), p.6.
28. United States Holocaust Memorial Museum, *Homosexuals: Victims of the Nazi Era 1933–1945* (2003), p.6.
29. Cooper and Leeuwen, van, *Alan Turing: His Work and Impact* (2013).
30. United States Holocaust Memorial Museum, *Homosexuals: Victims of the Nazi Era 1933–1945* (2003).
31. Lautmann, *The Pink Triangle* (1980–81), p. 7.
32. Gudeman, *The Sources of the Germania of Tacitus* (1900), pp. 93–111.
33. Fleck, *Der Codex Hersfeldensis des Tacitus: eine abenteuerliche Geschichte aus der Zeit der Renaissance* (2006), pp. 98–113.
34. Krebs, *A Most Dangerous Book* (2012), p. 22.
35. Krebs, *A Most Dangerous Book* (2012).
36. *Ibid.*

Chapter 11

1. Topinard, *L'Anthropologie*, IV (1893), p. 505.
2. Schmidt, *Externstein-Führer* (1973).
3. Matthes, *Corvey und die Externsteine* (1982), p. 172; Matthes and Speckner, *Das Relief an den Externsteinen* (1997); Halle, *Die Externsteine sind bis auf weiteres germanisch!* (2002); Dirk, *Schwarmgeister und Phantasten* (2013), pp. 50–56; Halle, *Wichtige Ausgrabungen der NS-Zeit* (2013), pp. 65–73; Runge, *Westfälische Bibliographie* (1973); Becher, *Charlemagne* (2003).
4. Bünte (ed.), *Die Geschichte der Externsteine* (1940), pp. 65–78; Dirk, *Schwarmgeister und Phantasten* (2013), pp. 50–56.
5. Pryor, *The Externsteine* (2011).
6. Schlosser and Cierny, *Sterne und Steine* (1996), pp. 93–95.
7. Pryor, *The Externsteine* (2011).
8. Matthes, *Corvey und die Externsteine* (1982), p. 172.
9. Müller, *Lower Saxony* (1903–04); Levenda, *Unholy Alliance* (2010), pp. 178–179.
10. Murray, *The Witch Cult in Western Europe* (1921); Murray, *The God of the Witches* (1933); Levenda, *Unholy Alliance* (2010), p. 180.
11. Brown, *Decoding Operation Matilda* (2011).
12. Bower, *Sarah Bower on the Nazis and the Bayeux Tapestry* (Historical Novel Society, 2011).
13. British Archaeology, *The Strange Tale of the Bayeux Tapestry, Archaeology and the Nazi Party* (2012).
14. Dow and Bockhorn, *The Study of European Ethnology in Austria* (2004).

Chapter 12

1. Rahn, *La Cour de Lucifer* (1974), p. 86.
2. Barber, *The Holy Grail* (2004).
3. Rahn, *Kreuzzug gegen den Graal* (*Crusade Against the Grail*) (1933); Levenda, *Unholy Alliance* (2010), p. 204.
4. Rahn, *Kreuzzug gegen den Graal* (1933).
5. Lambert, *The Cathars* (1998); Pegg, *A Most Holy War* (2008).
6. Runciman, *The Medieval Manichee* (1947); Filoramo, *A History of Gnosticism* (1990).
7. *Caedite eos. Novit enim Dominus qui sunt eius* (*Kill Them All, God will Recognize his Own*) attributed to the Abbot of Citeaux, Arnaud Amalric. Strange, *Cæsarii Heisterbacensis Dialogus Miraculorum* (1851); Gregory, *Just Baptize Them All and Let God Sort Them Out* (2014).
8. Schellenberg, *The Schellenberg Memoirs* (1956), p. 347.
9. The French historian Deodat Roche (1877–1978) was the founder of the journal *Cahiers d'Etudes Cathares*, whilst Jean Duvernoy edited and translated medieval sources, studying their beliefs from an historical point of view in the 1960s and 1970s.
10. Adams, *Mont-Saint-Michel and Chartres* (1933), p. 92.
11. Fulcanelli, *Le Mystère des Cathédrales* (1925, transl. 1971).
12. Frappier, *Chrétien de Troyes* (1982).
13. von Eschenbach, *Parzival* (1980).
14. Lebédel, *Understanding the Tragedy of the Cathars* (2011).
15. Tafur, *Andanças e viajes* (1436).
16. del Rio, and Sevilla-Quiñones de León, *Los Reyes del Grial* (*The Kings of the Grail*) (2014).
17. O'Connor, *The Secret Treasure of Oak Island* (2004).
18. Wagner, *Romance and Epics of Our Northern Ancestors, Norse, Celt and Teuton* (1906).
19. *Ibid.*
20. von Eschenbach, *Parzival* (1980).
21. Hall, 'The Real Last Crusade' in the *Daily Mail* (2013).
22. Forbes, *An Account of the Chapel of Roslin* (2000); Oxbrow and Robertson, *Rosslyn and The Grail* (2005).
23. Hodapp and Kannon, *The Templar Code for Dummies* (2007).
24. Eisen, *The Great Chalice of Antioch, on which are depicted in sculpture the earliest known portraits of Christ, apostles and evangelists* (1923); Salvador, *Truth and Symbolism of Holy Grail* (1999); Glatz, 'At Mass in Valencia, Pope uses what tradition says is Holy Grail' (2006).
25. Green, *The Art of Recognition in Wolfram's Parzival* (1982); Groos, *Romancing the Grail* (1995).
26. Sabeheddin, *Otto Rahn and the Quest for the Holy Grail* (1997); Preston, *The original Indiana Jones* (2008).
27. Péladin, *Les Secret des Troubadours* (1906).
28. Rahn, *Kreuzzug gegen den Graal* (1933).
29. Rahn (transl. Nelli), *Croisade contre le Graal* (1944).
30. Levenda, *Unholy Alliance* (2010), p. 211.
31. *Ibid.*
32. *Ibid.* p. 213.
33. Rahn, 'Ladame', in *La Cour de Lucifer* (1974), p. 13.
34. Levenda, *Unholy Alliance* (2010), p. 216.

35. Goodrick-Clarke, *The Occult Roots of Nazism* (1992), p. 189.
36. Rahn, *Luzifers Hofgesind* (1937).
37. Rahn, *La Cour de Lucifer* (1974), p. 93.
38. *Ibid.* p. 94-5.
39. Timm, *Hugo Ferdinand Boss (1885–1948) und die Firma Hugo Boss* (1999).
40. Levenda, *Unholy Alliance* (2010), p. 219.
41. Hüser, *Wewelsburg 1933–1945* (1982), p. 208.
42. Levenda, *Unholy Alliance* (2010), pp. 221–222.

Chapter 13

1. Pablo Picasso quoted in Spivey, *How Art Made the World* (2005), p. 24.
2. Dinies, *Zur Welteismeteorologie* (1938).
3. Hörbiger and Fauth, *Glac(z)ial-Kosmogonie* (1912).
4. *Rhein-Mainische Studentenzeitung* NA, CDS, T580, R195, Ord. 469, *Welteislehre* (1 June 1938).
5. Anon. SS-Obersturmführer NA, CDS, T580, R195, Ord. 469, *Welteislehre* typescript entitled '*Die Welteislehre und Ihr Erster Bearbeiter Philipp Fauth*' (9 December 1937).
6. Gratzer, *The Undergrowth of Science* (2001), pp. 235–236.
7. Hale, *Himmler's Crusade* (2006), p. 123.
8. Levenda, *Unholy Alliance* (2010), pp. 199–200.
9. Higham, *Trading with the Enemy* (1983); Reich, 'The Ford Motor Company and the Third Reich' in *Dimensions* (1999), 13(2), pp. 15–17; Silverstein, 'Ford and the Führer' in *The Nation* (2000), 270 (3), pp. 11–16.
11. LePage, *Shambhala* (1996); Allen, *The Search for Shangri-La* (1999–2000).
12. Pauwels and Bergier, *The Morning of the Magicians* (initially published as *Le Matin des Magiciens*, 1960, transl. 1963).
13. Zundel's publications include *Secret Nazi Polar Expeditions* (1978) and *Hitler at the South Pole* (1979). For a critique of Zundel, see Connolly, 'Holocaust denial writer jailed for five years' in *The Guardian* (February 16 2007).
14. Krassa, *Disciple of the Gods* (1976).
15. Hancock, *Fingerprints of the Gods* (2001).
16. *Avengers Assemble* (2012)
17. Graham, and Alford, 'A History of Government Management of UFO Perceptions through Film and Television' in *49th Parallel*: 25 (Spring 2011).
18. Reported by *The Whitby Gazette* (27 March 2015), reproduced in *Private Eye* No. 1391, 1–14 May 2015, p. 18.
19. Chernykh, 'Postscript: Russian archaeology after the collapse of the USSR—infrastructural crisis and the resurgence of old and new nationalism' in Kohl and Fawcett, *Nationalism, Politics and the Practice of Archaeology* (1995), pp. 139–148.
20. Hobsbawn and Ranger, *The Invention of Tradition* (1983); Silberman, *Between Past and Present* (1989).
21. Tong, 'Thirty Years of Chinese Archaeology (1949–1979)' in Kohl and Fawcett, *Nationalism, Politics and the Practice of Archaeology* (1995), pp. 177–197.
22. Shnirelman, 'From Internationalism to Nationalism: Forgotten Pages of Soviet Archaeology in the 1930s and 1940s' in Kohl and Fawcett, *Nationalism, Politics and the Practice of Archaeology* (1995), pp. 120–138.
23. Bykovski is cited in Shnirelman, 'From Internationalism to Nationalism:

Forgotten Pages of Soviet Archaeology in the 1930s and 1940s' in Kohl and Fawcett, *Nationalism, Politics and the Practice of Archaeology* (1995), pp. 120–138.

24. Kohl and Fawcett (eds), 'Archaeology in the Service of the State: Theoretical Considerations' in *Nationalism, Politics and the Practice of Archaeology* (1995), p. 6.

25. *Ibid.*

26. *Ibid.* p. 5; Silberman, 'Promised Lands and Chosen Peoples: the Politics and Poetics of Archaeological Narrative' in Kohl and Fawcett, *Nationalism, Politics and the Practice of Archaeology* (1995), p. 250.

27. Kohl and Fawcett (eds), 'Archaeology in the Service of the State: Theoretical Considerations' in Kohl and Fawcett, *Nationalism, Politics and the Practice of Archaeology* (1995), p. 6.

28. *Ibid.* p. 5

29. Anthony, 'Nazi and Eco-Feminist Prehistories: Ideology and Empiricism in Indo-European Archaeology' in Kohl and Fawcett, *Nationalism, Politics and the Practice of Archaeology* (1995), p. 85.

30. *Ibid.* p. 88.

31. Kohl and Fawcett (eds), 'Archaeology in the Service of the State: Theoretical Considerations' in Kohl and Fawcett, *Nationalism, Politics and the Practice of Archaeology* (1995), p. 18.

32. For an example of this approach, see Barrowclough, *Prehistoric Lancashire* (2008).

33. Kohl and Fawcett (eds), 'Archaeology in the Service of the State: Theoretical Considerations' in Kohl and Fawcett, *Nationalism, Politics and the Practice of Archaeology* (1995), p. 8.

34. *Ibid.* p. 9

35. *Ibid.* p. 8

Bibliography

Key to Abbreviations

BA	Federal Archives, Berlin-Lichterfelde
BK	Federal Archives, Koblenz
CUP	Cambridge University Press
IZ	*Institut für Zeitgeschichte*, Munich
NARA	National Archives, Washington DC
OIOC	Oriental and India Office Collections, British Library
OUP	Oxford University Press
PAS	Academy of Natural Sciences, Philadelphia
PRO	Public Record Office, Kew

Microfiche Records at the National Archives, Washington DC

Roll	Number	Topic
121		Sievers Diary 1944
128		Sievers Diary 1943
144	170	Wüst on the Rigveda
	171	Wüst on Indo-Germanic beliefs
147	199	Hörbiger's World Ice Theory
148	199	Hörbiger's World Ice Theory (cont.)
	200	Hörbiger's World Ice Theory: Weather Science
193	434	Kafiristan Expedition Records
195	469	Hörbiger's World Ice Theory
202	627	Externsteine: Icelandic, Runic, and Teutonic Research
	633	Celtic Studies
	637	Tibet Expedition
210	97a	Bayeux Tapestry
211		Bayeux Tapestry
999		Ahnenerbe Personnel Files

Abbildung 4, p. 107.

Åberg, N., 'Herman Wirth: En Germansk Kulturprofet' in *Fornvännen* 28, 1933

Abschrift Pyrmonter Protokoll (NARA, RG242, T580/194/465, 19.07.1936)

Ackerknecht, E. H., *Rudolf Virchow: Doctor, Statesman, Anthropologist* (New York: Madison, 1953)

Adams, H., *Mont-Saint-Michel and Chartres* (New York: Houghton Mifflin Company, 1933)

Ahnenerbe to Landesfinanzamt (BA, NS 21/556, 22.07.1936)

Allen, C., *The Search for Shangri-La* (London: Little, Brown and Co, 1999)

Alonso, F. G., *La arqueología durante el primer franquismo (1939-1956)* (Barcelona, 2009)

Altheim, F. and Trautmann, E. to Ahnenerbe (NARA, RG242, A3345 DS G112, Altheim, F. (06.10.1898, 30.06.1938); *Nordische und italische Felsbildkunst* (Die Welt als Geschichte 3, 1937: 1–82); *(Vertraulicher) Bericht: Irak* (BA (ehem. BDC) Ahnenerbe: Altheim, F. (06.10.1898, n.d.); *(Vertraulicher) Bericht: Rumänien* (BA (ehem. BDC) Ahnenerbe: Altheim, Franz (06.10.1898), n.d.); *(Vertraulicher) Bericht: Syrien* (BA (ehem. BDC) Ahnenerbe: Altheim, F. (06.10.1898, n.d.); *(Vertraulicher) Bericht: Unsere Vorschläge sind,* (BA (ehem. BDC) Ahnenerbe: Altheim, F. (06.10.1898, n.d.)

Altheim, F. to Ahnenerbe (BA, NS 21/ 166, 21.06.1939); *Forschungsbericht zur riimischen* (Die Welt, 1936); to Höhne (BA, NS 21/687, 24.08.1937); to Höhne (BA, NS 21/687, 01.09.1937); to Hohne (BA, NS 21/687, 09.09.1937); to Höhne (BA, NS 21/687, 01.10.1937); *Personalnachweis* (BA (ehem. BDC) RFR: Altheim, F. (06.10.1898, 31.08.1937)

Anati, E., *Camonica Valley* (New York: A.A. Knopf, 1961); *Evolution and Style in Camunian Rock Art (Luine: Collina Sacra: Archivi di Arte Preistorica* 8. Capo di Ponte, 1982); *Valcamonica Rock Art (Capo di Ponte Edizioni del Centro,* 1994)

Anderson, R. B., *Norse Mythology* (Honolulu: University Press of the Pacific, 1876)

Anderson, S., *Lawrence in Arabia* (London: Doubleday, 2013)

Andrea, A. J., *Encyclopedia of the Crusades* (Westport: Greenwood, 2003)

Androutsos G. and Diamantis A., 'Paul Broca (1824-1880)' in *Journal of the Balkan Union of Oncology* 12 (4), 2007, pp. 557-564

Anon. SS-Obersturmführer, *Welteislehre* typescript entitled '*Die Welteislehre und Ihr Erster Bearbeiter Philipp Fauth*', NA, CDS, T580, R195, Ord 469 (9.12.1937)

Anthony, D. W., 'Nazi and eco-feminist prehistories' in Kohl, P. L. and Fawcett, C. *Nationalism, Politics and the Practice of Archaeology* pp. 82-98 (Cambridge: CUP, 1995)

Arnold, B. and Hassmann, H., 'Archaeology in Nazi Germany' in Kohl and Fawcett, *Nationalism, Politics and the Practice of Archaeology* pp. 70-81 (Cambridge: CUP, 1995)

Arnold, B., 'The Past as Propaganda' in *Archaeology*, July/Aug 1992 pp. 30-37); '*Arierdammerung:* Race and Archaeology in Nazi Germany' in *World Archaeology* 38 (1), 2006, pp. 8–31

Arvidsson, S., *Aryan Idols: The Indo–European Mythology as Science and Ideology* (Chicago: University of Chicago Press, 2006)

Aspendorf, W., *Die Edda als Welteislehre* (Hohns: Krefeld, 1933)

Bachrach, D. S., 'Restructuring the Eastern Frontier: Henry I of Germany, 924–936' in *Journal of Military History* 78.1, Jan 2014, pp. 9-36

Baigent, M., Leigh, R., and Lincoln, H., *The Holy Blood and the Holy Grail* (London: Jonathan Cape, 1982)

Balzli, J., *Guido v. List: Der Wiederentdecker Uralter Arischer Weisheit—Sein Leben und sein Schaffen* (Leipzig and Vienna: Guido-von-List-Gesellschaft, 1917)

Bandelier, A. F. A., *The Gilded Man, El Dorado* (New York, 1893)

Barber, M., *The New Knighthood* (Cambridge: CUP, 1994)

Barber, R., *The Holy Grail* (Cambridge, Mass.: Harvard University Press, 2004)

Barkan, E., *The Retreat of Scientific Racism* (New York: CUP, 1992)

Barrowclough, D., *Prehistoric Lancashire* (Stroud: History Press, 2008)

Baumann, E. (ed.), *Verzeichnis der Schriften* (Toppenstedt: Uwe Berg, 1995)

Baur, E., Fischer, E., and Lenz, F., *Human Heredity and Racial Hygiene* (1936)

Becher, M., *Charlemagne* (New Haven: Yale University Press, 2003)

Beckett, L., *Richard Wagner* (Cambridge: CUP, 1981)

Beger, B., *Goals and Plans of the Tibet Expedition of the Society 'Das Anenerbe'* (R73/12198(BA), 1938)

Behrendt, *Bericht: Dr. Fritz Bose* (NARA, RG242, A3345 DS G113: Bose, Fritz: 28.07.1906, 01.03.1937)

Bendersky, J. W., *A History of Nazi Germany: 1919-1945* (New York: Rowman and Littlefield, 2000)

Bericht (BA, NS 21/693, 13.12.1935)

Bericht über die Arbeitssitzung der Mitarbeiter des 'Ahnenerbes' (25.10.1937, NARA, RG242, T580/128/47)

Bibikova V., *On the Origin of Mezin Paleolithic Ornamenta* (CA, 1965, X 1)

Biddiss, M., 'History as Destiny: Gobineau, H. S. Chamberlain and Spengler' in *Transactions of the Royal Historical Society* Vol. VII, Sixth Series, 1998

Biedermann, H., *'Swastika' Dictionary of Symbolism* (New York: Facts on File, 1992)

Birley, A., 'Introduction' in Tacitus, *Agricola and Germany* (Oxford: OUP, 1999)

Bittner, D. F., *The Lion and the White Falcon* (Hamden: Archon Books, 1983)

Blavatsky, H. P., *Isis Unveiled* (New York: J. W. Bouton, 1877); *The Secret Doctrine: The Synthesis of Science, Religion, and Philosophy* (London: The Theosophical Publishing Company, 1999)

Boak, A., 'Rudolf Virchow: Anthropologist and Archeologist' in *The Scientific Monthly* 13 (1), 1921, pp. 40–45

Bohmers, A., to *Abteilung Ausgrabungen des Ahnenerbes*, (BA, NS 21/60, 27.10.1938); 'Die Mauerner Höhlen and ihre Bedeutung für die Einteilung der Altsteinzeit', in *Ahnenerbe Jahrestagungen. Bericht über die Kieffer Tagung 1939*, Jankuhn, H. (ed) (Neumunster: Karl Wachholtz, 1944); *Stellungnahme zum Vorbericht* (BA, NS 21/ 60, n.d.)

Bolton, H. E., *Coronado* (New York: Whittlesey, 1949)

Bose, F., 'Folk Music Research and the Cultivation of Folk Music' in *Journal of the International Folk Music Council* 9, 1957, pp. 20-21; 'Law and Freedom in the Interpretation of European Folk Epics' in *Journal of the International Folk Music Council* 10, 1958, p. 31; *Racial Aspects in Music* (1934); 'Typen der Volksmusik in Karelien: Ein Reisebericht' in *Archiv für Müsikforschung* 3, 1938, pp. 96-118; *Zauber Spruch. Karelisch* (Lautarchiv der Humboldt-Universität zu Berlin LA 1519, n.d.)

Bowen, R., *Universal Ice* (London: Belhaven Press, 1993)

Bower, S., 'Sarah Bower on the Nazis and the Bayeux Tapestry' in *Historical Novel Society*, 2011

Bramwell, A., *Blood and Soil* (Bourne End: Kensal Press, 1985)

Breton, A., 'Proceedings of Americanists' Congress' in *Man* 84, 1910

Broca, P., *On the Phenomena of Hybridity in the Genus Homo* (London: Anthropological Society, 1864)

Brøgger, A. W., *Arkeologien og Samfundenes åndelige Balanse* (Morgenbladet KHM, 29.07.1936); editor's comment, *Viking: tidskrift for norrøn arkeologi* (November 1937)

Brookes, M., *Extreme Measures* (London: Bloomsbury, 2004)

Brown, S. A., 'Decoding Operation Matilida: the Bayeux Tapestry, the Nazis and German Pan-nationalism' in Lewis, M. J. (ed.), Owen-Crocker, and Terkla, D., *The Bayeux Tapestry: New Approaches* (Oxford: Oxbow Books, 2011); 'The Strange Tale of the Bayeux Tapestry, Archaeology, and the Nazi Party' in *British Archaeology* 122, Jan/Feb 2012

Browning, C., *The Origins of the Final Solution* (Lincoln: University of Nebraska Press, 2004)

Brugg, E., *Die Welteislehre nach Hanns Hörbiger* (Leipzig: Hase und Koehler, 1940)

Brynjar, L., *The Society of the Muslim Brothers in Egypt* (Reading: Garnet, 1998)

Buchan, J., *Greenmantle* (London: Hodder and Stoughton, 1916)

Bünte, R., 'Die Geschichte der Externsteine' in *Wilhelm Teudt im Kampf um Germanenehre: Eine Auswahl von Teudts Schriften* (Bielefeld: Delhagen and Klasing, 1940)

Burleigh, M. and Wippermann, W., *The Racial State: Germany 1933–1945* (Cambridge: CUP, 1991)

Burton, R. F., *Ultima Thule* (London and Edinburgh: William P. Nimmo, 1875)

Bury, R., *Eidesstattliche Erklärung* (HHA, Abt.520 KS-HL Nr.88, Spruchkammer Kassel, 06.07.1948)

Butler, A., and Dafoe, S., *The Warriors and the Bankers* (Belleville: Templar Books, 1998)

Byock, J., *Medieval Iceland* (Oakland: University of California Press, 1988); (transl.), *The Prose Edda* (London: Penguin Classics, 2006)

Carew, M., *Tara and the Ark of the Covenant* (Dublin: Royal Irish Academy, 2003)

Cecil, R., *The Myth of the Master Race* (New York: Dodd Mead and Co., 1972)

Chadwick, J., *The Mycenaean World* (Cambridge: CUP, 1976)

Chamberlain, H. S., *The Foundations of the Nineteenth Century* (London: John Lane, the Bodley Head, 1911); 'Letter of William II 31 December 1901' in *Briefe* II (Munich, 1928)

Chandler, A. R., *Rosenberg's Nazi Myth* (Westport, Conn: Greenwood Press, 1945)

Chef des Sicherheitshauptamtes, Der Leiter der Zentralabteilung II 112 to Sievers (NARA, RG242, T580, R124/35; Sievers to Altheim, 23.05.1939); (NARA, RG242, T580, R124/35, 23.05.1939)

Chernykh, E., 'Postscript' in Kohl, P. L., and Fawcett, C., *Nationalism, Politics and the Practice of Archaeology* (Cambridge: CUP, 1995)

Chisholm, H. (ed.), *'Schlagintweit'* in *Encyclopaedia Britannica* (11th ed.) (Cambridge: CUP, 1911)

Coles, J., with Bengtsson, L., *Images of the Past* (Uddevalla: *Bohusläns museum och Bohusläns hembygdsförbund*, 1990)

Connolly, K., 'Holocaust Denial Writer Jailed for Five Years' in *The Guardian*, 16 February 2007

Conrado, R. M., 'The Guanche Mummies' in Cockburn, A., Cockburn, E., and Reyman, T. A., *Mummies, Disease and Ancient Cultures, 2nd ed.* (Cambridge: CUP, 1998)

Coon, C. S., *The Races of Europe* (Westport, Conn: Greenwood Press, 1975)

Cooper, S. B., and van Leeuwen, J., *Alan Turing* (New York: Elsevier, 2013)

Crawford, J. M., 'Preface' in *The Kalevala* (New York: The Columbian Publishing Co., 1891)

Crowley, C. J., *The Legend of the Wanderings of the Spear Of Longinus* (Winnipeg: Heartland Book, 1972)

Dain, B. R., *A Hideous Monster of the Mind* (Cambridge, Mass.: Harvard University Press, 2002)

Darré, W., *Neuadel aus Blut und Boden* [*A New Nobility Based on Blood and Soil*] (Munich: J. F. Lehmanns Verlag, 1935)

Darwin, C., *On the Origin of Species* (London: John Murray, 1859)

Das Ahnenerbe (Offenbach am Main: *Gebrüder Klingspor*, n.d.)

Das Anenerbe Forschungsstatte fur Germanenkunde, Detmold. Plan Einer Island–Forschungsfahrt (NA, CDS, T580, R202, Ord 627, Sommer 1938)

Dash, M., *Thug* (London: Granta Books, 2005)

Davidson, H. E., *Introduction to Saxo Grammaticus: The History of the Danes, Book I-IX. Volume II: Commentary* (Cambridge: D. S. Brewer, 1980)

Day, A. G., *Coronado's Quest* (Westport, Connecticut: Greenwood Press, 1981)

Debnath, S., *The Meanings of Hindu Gods, Goddesses and Myths* (New Delhi: Rupa and Co., 2009)

Deni J., 'Evaluating Eyewitness Accounts of Native Peoples Along the Coronado Trail From the International Border to Cibola' in *New Mexico Historical Review* 84(3), 2008, pp. 339-435

Dinies, E., *Zur Welteismeteorologie* [*On World Ice Meteorology*] (Reichs Office for Weather Service, 1938)

Dirk, M., '*Schwarmgeister und Phantasten—die völkische Laienforschung*' in Focke, *Museum, Bremen, Graben für Germanien—Archäologie unterm Hakenkreuz* (Wissenschaftliche Buchgesellschaft, 2013)

Dobzhansky, T., Montagu, A., and Coon, C. S., 'Two Views of Coon's Origin of Races with Comments by Coon and Replies' in *Current Anthropology* Vol. 4, No. 4., Oct. 1963, pp. 360-367

Donnelly, I., *Ragnarok: The Age of Fire and Gravel* (Chicago: Peale & Co, 1887)

Dow, J. R., and Bockhorn, O., *The Study of European Ethnology in Austria* (Aldershot: Ashgate, 2004)

Eggebrecht, H. H., and Potter, P. M., 'Fritz Bose' in *Grove Music* (Oxford: OUP, 2001)

Eisen, G. A., *The Great Chalice of Antioch* (New York: Kouchakji Frères, 1923)

Elmayer-Vestenbrugg von, R., *Rätsel des Weltgeschehens. Kampf-schriften der Obersten SA–Führung: Band 4* (München: Zentralverlag der NSDAP, Franz Eher Nachf, 1937

Elmayer-Vestenbrugg von, R., *Versunkene Reiche* (Die H.J., BA, NS 21/714, 24.04.1937)

Epstein, F. T., 'War-Time Activities of the SS-Ahnenerbe' in *On the Track of Tyranny* (North Stratford: Ayer Publishing, 1971)

Eschenbach, von, W., *Parzival* (London: Penguin Classics, 1980)

Ewen, S., and Ewen, E., 'Nordic Nightmares' in *Typecasting* (New York: Seven Stories Press, 2008)

Fabian, A., *The Skull Collectors* (Chicago, Ill.: University of Chicago Press, 2010)

Feist, S., '*Archäologie und Indogermanentum*' in *Correspondenzblatt der deutschen Gesellschaft fur Anthropologie*, 1916, p. 68

Fest, J. C., *Hitler* (London: Weidenfeld and Nicolson, 1974)

Filoramo, G., *A History of Gnosticism* (Oxford: Basil Blackwell, 1990)

Findell, M., *Runes* (London: The British Museum, 2014)

Fisher, M. C., 'The Ark of the Covenant' in *Bible and Spade* 8/3, 1995, pp. 65-72

Fleck, M., '*Der Codex Hersfeldensis des Tacitus: eine abenteuerliche Geschichte aus der Zeit der Renaissance*' in *Hersfelder Geschichtsblätter* Bd. 1, 2006, pp. 98-113

Flessa, V., *At The Edge* (Athens: New Greek Television, 26 October 2012)

Flinders Petrie, W. M., *Seventy Years in Archaeology* (London: H. Holt and Company, 1932)

Flood, G., 'The Śaiva Traditions' in *The Blackwell Companion to Hinduism* (Malden, MA: Blackwell Publishing, 2003)

Forbes, R., *An Account of the Chapel of Roslin* (Grand Lodge of Scotland, 2000)

Foster, I. L., 'Gereint, Owein, and Peredur' in *Arthurian Literature in the Middle Ages* (Oxford: Clarendon Press/Oxford University, 1959)

Fotos: Expedition XIV Süd-Frankreich/Ost-Spanien (FIA, *Fotoarchiv*. 44, 1934)

Frappier, J., *Chrétien de Troyes* (Athens: Ohio University Press, 1982); *'Chrétien de Troyes' in Arthurian Literature in the Middle Ages* (Oxford: Clarendon Press/ Oxford University, 1959)

Freed, S. A., and Freed, R. S., 'Origin of the Swastika' in *Natural History*, January 1980, pp. 68-75

Freyle, J. R., *El Carnero* (transl. Atkinson, W. C.) (London: Folio Society 1961)

Frobenius Institute, 'Forschungsreisen des Frobenius-Institute' in *Das Frobenius–Institut an der Johann Wolfgang Goethe–Universität 1898-1998* (Frankfurt a. M.: Frobenius Institute, 1998)

Frye, J., and Frye, H., *North to Thule* (Chapel Hill, NC: Algonquin Books, 1985)

Fulcanelli, *Le Mystère des Cathédrales* [*The Mystery of the Cathedrals*] (Paris: Jean Schemit, 1925)

Galke, H. to Reichsführer–SS (NARA, RG242, T580/203/686, 09.05.1936); to Sievers, *Betr. Forschungsreise nach Skandinavien* (NARA, RG242, T580/203/686, 30.07.1936)

Galton, F., *Hereditary Genius* (London, 1869)

Gardner, N., 'Multiple Meanings' in *Hidden Europe* 11, 2006, Berlin

Gauch, H., 'New Foundations of Racial Science' in *Encyclopedia of the Third Reich* p. 281 (USA, 1934)

Gauch, S., (transl. Radice, Wilhem), *Vaterspuren* [*Traces of My Father*] (Chicago: Northwestern University Press, 1979)

Gedächtnisprotokoll. Unterredung Prof Dr. Herman Wirth und Michael H. Kater (IfZ. ZS/A-25, vol. 2, 22.06.1963); (IfZ, ZS/A-25, vol. 3, 04.04.1963)

Gehl, W., *The Roman Empire as a Nordic Creation* (Breslau: Ferdinand Hirt, 1940)

Gensicke, K., *Der Mufti von Jerusalem und die Nationalsozialisten* (Darmstadt: Wissenschaftliche Buchgesellschaft, 2007)

Gilbhard, H., *Die Thule–Gesellschaft* (Kiessling Verlag, 1994)

Gillham, N. W., *A Life of Sir Francis Galton* (Oxford: OUP, 2001)

Glatz, C., 'At Mass in Valencia, Pope Uses What Tradition Says is Holy Grail' in *Catholic News*, 10 July 2006

Glob, P. V., *The Bog People* (London: Paladin, 1971)

Gobineau de, J. A., *Essai sur l'inégalité des races humaines* [*Essay on the Inequality of the Human Races*] (London: William Heinemann, 1855)

Gonzalo, F. de O., *Historia General y Natural de las India, islas y Tierra–Firme del Mar Oceano* (Madrid: *Real Academia de la Historia*, 1851)

Goodrick-Clarke, N., *Black Sun* (New York: New York University Press, 2003); *The Occult Roots of Nazism* (London: Tauris Parke, 2004)

Gould, S. J., *The Mismeasure of Man* (New York: Norton, 1996)

Gousseva, M., (transl.), *Nastoyashchy Saratov* (n.d.)

Graham, R., and Alford, M., 'A History of Government Management of UFO Perceptions through Film and Television' in *49th Parallel 25*, Spring 2011

Grann, D., *The Lost City of Z* (London: Simon and Schuster, 2009)

Grant, M., *The Passing of the Great Race* (New York: Scribner, 1916)

Gratzer, W. B., *The Undergrowth of Science* (Oxford: OUP, 2001)

Graves, P., 'The Truth About the Protocols: A Literary Forgery' in *The Times*, 16-18 August 1921

Graves, R., *Lawrence and the Arabs* (London: Jonathan Cape, 1927)

Green, D. H., *The Art of Recognition in Wolfram's Parzival* (Cambridge and New York: CUP, 1982)

Greger, A., and Geisler, U., *Myt och propaganda* (*Forum för Levande Historia*, 2007)

Gregory, R. L., *Just Baptize Them All and Let God Sort Them Out* (Nashville, TN: Cross Books, 2014)

Grey, T. S. (ed.), *The Cambridge Companion to Wagner* (Cambridge: CUP, 2008)

Griffith, R. T. H. (transl.), *The Rig Veda* (London: Forgotten Books, 2008)

Grönhagen von, G., *Karelische Zauberbeschwörungen* (Germanien, February 1937)

Grönhagen von, H., and von Grönhagen, Y., *Das Antlitz Finnlands* (Berlin: Wiking Verlag, 1942)

Grönhagen von, Y., *Einige Angaben uber das Geschlecht Grönhagen* (unpublished document, n.d., see also ARK, A 3860, 13.10.1935); *Finnische Gespräche* (Berlin: Nordland Verlag, 1941); *Himmlerin salaseura* (Helsinki: Kansankirja, 1948); *Karelien: Finnlands Bollwerk gegen den Osten* (Dresden: Franz Müller Verlag, 1942); *Ungefährer Plan für die Arbeit der Abteilung Pflegestätte für indogermanische-finnische Kulturbeziehungen* (NARA, RG242, T580/206/716, 25.02.1937); *'Zum Geleit'* in *Finnische Gespräche* (Berlin: Nordland Verlag, 1941)

Groos, A., *Romancing the Grail* (Ithaca: Cornell University Press, 1995)

Gudeman, A., 'The Sources of the Germania of Tacitus' in *Transactions and Proceedings of the American Philological Association* pp. 31, 93-111 (Baltimore: The Johns Hopkins University Press, 1900)

Guðmundsson, H. H., *A Nazi's Disappointment With Iceland* (2014)

Günther, H. F. K., *Die Nordische Rasse bei den Indogermanen Asiens* (Munich: J. F. Lehmanns, 1934); (transl. Wheeler, G. C.) *The Racial Elements of European History* (London: Methuen and Co., 1927); *Rassenkunde des deutschen Volkes [Race-Lore of the German People]* (München: J. F. Lehmann, 1924); *Short Ethnology of the German People* (1929)

Gwatkin, H. M. and Whitney, J. P., *The Cambridge Medieval History: Volume III.* (Cambridge: CUP, 1926)

Hale, C., *Himmler's Crusade* (Hoboken, NJ: John Wiley and Sons, 2003)

Hall, A., 'The Real Last Crusade' in *The Daily Mail*, 25 March 2013

Halle, U., *'Die Externsteine sind bis auf weiteres germanisch!'* in *Prähistorische Archäologie im Dritten Reich* (Bielefeld: Verlag für Regionalgeschichte, 2002); *'Wichtige Ausgrabungen der NS-Zeit'* in *Focke-Museum, Bremen, Graben für Germanien —Archäologie unterm Hakenkreuz* (*Wissenschaftliche Buchgesellschaft*, 2013)

Hammond, G. P., and Goad, E. R., *The Adventure of Don Francisco Vásquez de Coronado* (Albuquerque: University of New Mexico Press, 1938)

Hancock, G., *Fingerprints of the Gods* (London: Century, 2001)

Haran, M., 'The Disappearance of the Ark' in *IEJ* 13, 1963

Harding, E. U., *Kali: The Black Goddess of Dakshineswar* (Lake Worth, Fl.: Nicolas-Hays, 1993)

Härke, H., *Archaeology, Ideology, and Society* (Frankfurt: Peter Lang, 2002); *Archaeology, Nationalism, Nazism* (Academia.edu, 2013)

Haymes, E. R. (transl.), *The Saga of Thidrek of Bern* (New York: Garland, 1988)

Hedin, S., *Mein Leben als Entdecker [My Life As An Explorer]* (Leipzig, 1926)

Heim, S., *Autarkie und Ostexpansion* (*Pflanzenzucht und Agrarforschung im Nationalsozialismus*, 2002)

Heller, S., *The Swastika* (New York: Allworth Press, 2008)

Hemming, J., *Red Gold* (Cambridge, Mass.: Harvard University Press, 1978)

Herbert, J., *The Spear* (London: Pan Books, 1979)

Hertz, J. H., *The Pentateuch and Haftoras. Deuteronomy* (Oxford: OUP, 1936)

Higham, C., *Trading with the Enemy* (Delacorte Press, 1983)

Hilton, J., *Lost Horizon* (Summersdale Publishers, March 2005)

Himmler, H., 'Heinrich Himmler's Reading List' (BAK, NL Himmler, N 1126/9. No. 180, n.d.); to Galke (BA (ehem. BDC) Ahnenerbe: Wirth, Herman Felix (06.05.1885, 28.10.1936); to Grönhagen (ARK: A3860, 19.04.1936); to Grönhagen (ARK, A3860, 28.04.1937); to Höhne (BA, NS 21/687, 03.07.1937); to Wüst (NARA, RG242, T580/207/725, 10.12.1937); to Wüst, 05.09.1938, in Heiber, H., *Reichsführer! Briefe an and von Himmler* (Stuttgart: *Deutsche Verlags-Anstalt*, 1968); to Wüst (BA, NS 21/227, 28.05.1940)

Hirszowicz, L., *The Third Reich and the Arab East* (London: Routledge and Kegan Paul, 1966)

Hitler, A., *Hitler's Table Talk 1941-1944* (Oxford: OUP, 1988); (transl. Murphy, J.), *Mein Kampf*, (London: James Murphy, 1939)

Hobsbawn, E., and Ranger, T. (eds), *The Invention of Tradition* (Cambridge: CUP, 1983)

Hodapp, C., and Von Kannon, A., *The Templar Code for Dummies* (London: John Wiley and Sons, 2007)

Hodder, I., *Archaeological Theory in Europe* (London: Routledge, 1991)

Hodgen, M. T., 'The Doctrine of Survivals' in *American Anthropologist* vol. 33. 1931, pp. 307-324

Höhne, H. to Trautmann (BA, NS 21/687, 15.07.1937); to Ullmann (BA, NS 21/687, 23.10.1937)

Hollander, L. M., *The Skalds* (Michigan: University of Michigan Press, 1968)

Holmes, H. A., 'The Spell of Romania' in *National Geographic*, April 1934, vol. LXV, pp. 399-450

Hooton, E., *The Ancient Inhabitants of the Canary Islands* (Cambridge, Mass.: Peabody Museum of Harvard University, 1925)

Hörbiger, H., and Fauth, J. P. H., *Glac(z)ial-Kosmogonie* (Kaiserlautern: *Hermann Kaysers Verlag*, 1912)

Hüser, K., *Wewelsburg 1933-1945: Kult- und Terrorstatte der SS* (Padderborn: *Verlag Bonifatius-Druckerei*, 1982)

Huth, O., '*Die Gesittung der Kanarier als Schlussel zum Ur-Indogermanentum*' in *Germanien* 2, February 1937, pp. 50-54; *Fragebogen für Mitglieder: Reichsverband Deutscher Schriftsteller* (BA (ehem BDC) RKK, 05.12.1933); *R.u.S—Fragebogen* (BA (ehem.BDC) RS: Huth, Otto Herbert (09.05.1906, 30.01.1939); to Wüst, (BA (ehem.BDC) Ahnenerbe: Huth, Otto. (09.05.1906, 14.02.1939)

Huxley, J., and Haddon, A. C., *We Europeans* (London: Jonathan Cape, 1935)

Huxley, T. H., *Life and Letters* (Collected Essays VII, 1890)

Huxley, T., 'On the Geographical Distribution of the Chief Modifications of Mankind' in *Journal of the Ethnological Society of London, Scientific Memoirs* III, 1870

Hygen, A. S., and Bengtsson, L., *Rock Carvings in the Borderlands* (Gothenburg, Sweden: *Warner Förlag*, 2000)

Hyvärinen, J., to Haavio (M. 16.10.1936; SKS, Folklore Archives: Correspondence, 1936); to Haavio (M. 29.10.1936. SKS, Folklore Archives: Correspondence, 1936); to Haavio (M. 12.11.1936. SKS, Folklore Archives: Correspondence, 1936)

Jakobsson, Á., 'A Contest of Cosmic Fathers' in *Neophilologus* 92/2, 2008

Johnson, K. P., *The Masters Revealed* (Albany: State University of New York Press, 1994)

Jordan, *Personalnachweis* (BA (ehem. BDC) REM: Jordan, J. (27.10.1877, n.d.)

Kater, M., *Das 'Ahnenerbe' der SS 1935-1945* (Stuttgart: Deutsche Verlags-Anstalt, 1974)

Keane, H., Quiggin, A. H., and Haddon, A. C., *Man, Past and Present* (Cambridge: CUP, 1899)

Kersten, F., *The Memoirs of Doctor Felix Kersten* (Garden City, NY: Doubleday, 1947)

Kessler, H., *Walther Rathenau* (Paris, 1933)

Kirchweger, F., *Die Geschichte der Heiligen Lanze vom späteren Mittelalter bis zum Ende des Heiligen Römischen Reiches* [*The History of the Holy Lance from the Later Middle Ages to the End of the Holy Roman Empire*] (1806)

Kiss, E., *Abschrift (Ärztlicher Untersuchungsbogen)* (BA (ehem.BDC) Ahnenerbe: Kiss, Edmund (10.12.1886), n.d.); *Das Sonnentor von Tihuanaku* (Leipzig: Verlegt bei Koehler & Amelang, 1937); '*Die Kordillerenkolonien der Atlantiden*' in *Schlüssel zum Welt geschehen* 8/9, 1931 pp. 259-261; *Dienstlaufbahn* (NARA, RG242, A3343, SSO Kiss, Edmund (10. 12.1886, n.d.); *Ergebnisbericht der Forschungsreise des SS-Hauptsturmführers Kiss each Tripolis* (BA, NS 21/415, 15.05.1939); *Niederschrift betreffend Vortrag des SS-Hauptsturmführers Kiss beim Reichsführer SS* (BA (ehem. BDC) Ahnenerbe: Kiss, Edmund (10.12.1886, 08.05.1939); '*Nordische Baukunst in Bolivien?*' in *Germanien* 5, May 1933, p. 144); *La Puerta del Sol and the Doctrine of Tiahuanacu Ice Universal Hörbiger* (1937); *Personalangaben* (NARA, RG242, A3343, SSO: Kiss, Edmund (10.12.1886, 04.04.1944); *Programm der Forschungsreise des SS-Hauptsturmführers Kiss* (BA, NS 21/415, 30.01.1939); *to Sievers* (BA NS, 21/415, 20.02.1939); *SS-Stammrollenauszug* (NARA, RG242, A3343, SSO: Kiss, Edmund (10.12.1886, 31.01.1939); Kiss, E., *Vorläufiges Programm* (BA, NS 21/171, 15.04.1939)

Klee, E., *Das Personenlexikon zum Dritten Reich* (Frankfurt: Fischer-Taschenbuch-Verlag, 2005).

Klein, L., 'Gustaf Kossinna: 1858-1931' in Murray, T., *Encyclopedia of Archaeology: The Great Archaeologists: Volume I* (ABC-CLIO, 1999)

Kleinschmidt, H., *People on the Move* (Greenwood Publishing Group, 2003)

Knoll, L., *Felix von Luschan. Ergänzungen und Beiträge zu biographischen Daten eines Pioniers der Ethnologie* (University of Vienna: Thesis, 2004)

Köfler to Archivrat, (BA (ehem. BDC) REM: Wirth, Herman (06.05.1885, 09.10.1935)

Kohl, P. L., and Fawcett, C., 'Archaeology in the Service of the State' in *Nationalism, Politics and the Practice of Archaeology* pp. 3-20 (Cambridge: CUP, 1995)

Kokkinidou, D., and Nikolaidou, M., *Archaeology under Metaxas* (Athens: Metaxas Project, 2000-2007)

Kossinna, G., *Die deutsche Ostmark* [*The German Ostmark*] (Berlin, 1919); *Die deutsche Vorgeschichte* [*German Prehistory*] (Hlannus-Bibliothek 9, 1921)

Krassa, P., *Disciple of the Gods* (London: W. H. Allen & Unwin, 1976)

Krebs, C. B., *A Most Dangerous Book* (New York: W. W. Norton, 2012)

Kress, B., *Die Laute des modernen Isländischen* (Diss. Schulze, Berlin: *Universität Berlin*, 1937); Kress, B., *Icelandic Grammar* (Berlin, 1955)

Kunsthistorisches Museum, *Die Heilige Lanze in Wien. Insignie—Reliquie—Schicksalsspeer* (Vienna: Kunsthistorisches Museum, 2005)

Lagarde de, P., *Deutsche Schriften* (Göttingen, 1903)

Lal, B. B., *The Homeland of the Aryans* (New Delhi: Aryan Books International, 2005)

Lambers, K., *The Geoglyphs of Palpa, Peru* (Aichwald: *Lindensoft Verlag*, 2006)

Lambert, M., *The Cathars* (Oxford: Blackwell, 1998)

Lange, H. J., *Weisthor—Karl-Maria Wiligut—Himmlers Rasputin und seine Erben* (Engerda: *Biografie und Quellen*, 1999)

Lapouge, de V., *L'Aryen* [*The Aryan*] (Paris: Albert Fontemoing, 1899); (transl. Clossen, C.), 'Old and New Aspects of the Aryan Question' in *The American Journal of Sociology* 5, 1997

Lautmann, R., 'The Pink Triangle' in *The Journal of Homosexuality* 6, no. 1/2, Fall/ Winter 1980, p. 81, p. 157

Lebédel, C., *Understanding the Tragedy of the Cathars* (France: Editions Ouest-France, 2011)

Lebenslauf, *Reichskulturkammer Fragebogen* (BA (ehem. BDC) RKK: Grönhagen, Yrjö von (03.10.1911, 06.05.1942)

Lee, M. and Shlain, B., *Acid Dreams* (New York: Grove Press, 1985)

Leers, von G., to Mack, C. W., *Die Meinung anderer Leute über Herman Wirth* (BA (ehem. BDC) Ahnenerbe: Wirth, Herman Felix 06.05.1885, 14.05.1933)

Leopold, J., *Culture in Comparative and Evolutionary Perspective* (Berlin: *Dietrich Reimer Verlag*, 1980)

LePage, V., *Shambhala* (1996)

Leroy, M., 'Chavée, Honoré-Joseph' in *Biographie nationale publiée par l'Académie royale des sciences, des lettres et des beaux-arts de Belgique* Vol. 44 (Brussels: Bruylant, 1985)

Levenda, P., *Unholy Alliance* (London: Continium Books, 2010)

Liebenfels von, L., *Ostara* (Wien, 1927)

Loth, M., 'Tanis: 'Thebes of the North' in Bakr, M. I., Brandl, H., and Kalloniatis, F. (eds), *Egyptian Antiquities from the Eastern Nile Delta, Museums in the Nile Delta*, Vol. 2 (Cairo/Berlin: Opaion, 2014)

Löw, L., *Herman Wirth and die Suche nach der germanischen Geistesurgeschichte in Skandinavien* (unpublished paper, n.d.)

Lund, A., *De etnografiske kilder til Nordens tidlige historie* (Aarhus: Aarhus University Press, 1993)

Lutzhöft, H-J., *Der Nordische Gedanke in Deutschland 1920–1940* (Stuttgart: *Ernst Klett Verlag*, 1971)

MacCulloch, J. A., *The Mythology of All Races. Volume II, Eddic* (New York: Copper Square Publishers Inc., 1964)

Mackenzie, 'Half-Finished People' in *London Review of Books* Vol. 34 No. 19-11, October 2012, pp. 14-16

Mallmann, K. M., and Cüppers, M., *Halbmond und Hakenkreuz* (Darmstadt: *Wissenschaftliche Buchgesellschaft*, 2006)

Malory, T., and Cooper, H., *Le Morte d'Arthur* (Oxford: OUP, 2008)

Marks, J., *The Search for the Manchurian Candidate* (London: W. W. Norton and Co., 1999)

Matthes, W., and Speckner, R., *Das Relief an den Externsteinen. Ein karolingisches Kunstwerk und sein spiritueller Hintergrund. edition tertium* (Stuttgart: Ostfildern vor, 1997)

Matthes, W., *Corvey und die Externsteine. Schicksal eines vorchristlichen Heiligtums in karolingischer Zeit* (Stuttgart: *Urachhaus*, 1982)

McDougall, W., *The Group Mind* (Cambridge: CUP, 1920)

Merhart von, G., *Zu dem Buche Herman Wirth, 'Der Aufgang der Menschheit'*, (BA, ehem. BDQ REM: Wirth, Herman (06.05.1885)

Merrill, R. T., *Our Magnetic Earth* (Chicago: University of Chicago Press, 2010)

Montet, J. P. M., *La nécropole royale de Tanis. Volume 1:* (Paris, 1947); *La nécropole royale de Tanis. Volume 2* (Paris, 1951); *La nécropole royale de Tanis. Volume 3* (Paris: Jean Pierre Marie Montet, 1960)

Mookerjee, A., *Kali* (Rochester: Destiny Books, 1993)

Moreno, J. D., *Undue Risk* pp. 7-17 (London: Routledge, 2000)

Morris, C., *The Aryan Race* (S. C. Griggs, 1888)

Moynihan, M., and Flowers, S., *The Secret King* (Port Townsend, WA: Feral House, 2007)

Müller, A. E., *Lower Saxony* (Lower Saxony, 1904)

Müller-Brauel, H., 'Haus Atlantis', *Die Böttcherstrasse in Bremen* (*Deutsches Rundfunkarchiv*/Radio Bremen, 2001)

Munro-Hay, S., *The Quest For The Ark of The Covenant* (London: L. B. Tauris and Co., 2006)

Murray, M., *The God of the Witches* (London: Sampson, Low, Marston and Co., 1933); *The Witch Cult in Western Europe* (Oxford: OUP, 1921)

Muscutt, K., *Warriors of the Clouds* (Albuquerque, NM: University of New Mexico Press, 1998)

Nagy-Talavera, N. M., *The Greenshirts and the Others* (Stanford: Hoover Institute Press, 1970)

Nehring, E., '*Die Schwestern Eva und Erika Nehring*' in *Familie Nehring 3*, September 1975, p. 77

Nehring, W. K., '*Erika und Eva Nehring aus Osterwieck*' in *Familie Nehring 2*, 1973

Nietzsche, F., *The Birth of Tragedy* (London: George Allen and W. Unwin, 1909); *Zur Genealogie der Moral* [*On the Genealogy of Morals*] (Leipzig: *Verlag von C. G. Neumann*, 1887)

Nikolakea, N., 'The Protection of Antiquities During World War II' in Tsitopolou, M. (ed.), *I Reported in Writing* (Athens: Treasures of the Historical Archive of the Archaeological Service, 2008)

Nordland Und Unser Deutsches Ahnenerbe (NA, CDS, T580, R202, Ord. 62, n.d.)

O'Connor, D., *The Secret Treasure of Oak Island* (Guilford, CT: Globe Pequot Press, 2004)

Oldenberg, H., *Hymnen des Rigveda. 1. Teil* (Wiesbaden: Nachdruck, 1982)

Olender, M., *Race and Erudition* (Cambridge, Mass.: Harvard University Press, 2009)

Orwell, G., 'As I Please' in *Tribune*, 13 October 1944

Oxbrow, M., and Robertson, I., *Rosslyn and The Grail* (Edinburgh: Mainstream Publishing, 2005)

Padfield, P., *Himmler* pp. 172-174 (London: Cassell, 2001)

Papadimitriou, N., *Built Chamber Tombs of Middle and Late Bronze Age Date in Mainland Greece and the Islands* (Oxford: BAR International Series 925, 2001)

Paschalidis, K., 'The Buried Statues of War: The hiding of the ancient treasures of the National Archaeological Museum on the eve of the German occupation of Athens, 1941' in *Lifo Magazine*, 31 March 2013, Athens; 'The founding, History and Adventures of the National Archaeological Museum: 130 Years of Service in one lecture'

Paton, J., *Collections on Thuggee and Dacoitee* (British Library Add. Mss. 41300, n.d.)

Pauwels, L. and Bergier, J., *The Morning of the Magicians* (Paris: Éditions Gallimard, 1960)

Peck, W. H., 'Lepsius, Karl Richard' in *The Oxford Encyclopaedia of Ancient Egypt*, Vol. 2 pp. 289-290 (Oxford, New York, and Cairo: OUP and The American University in Cairo Press, 2001)

Pegg, M., *A Most Holy War* (Oxford: OUP, 2008)

Péladin, J., *Les Secret des Troubadours* (1906)

Penka, K., *Origines Ariacae*. [*Origins of the Aryans*] (Vienna, 1883)

Pentikäinen, J. Y., *Kalevala Mythology* (Bloomington: Indiana University Press, 1989); 'Finland as a Cultural Area' in *Cultural Minorities in Finland* p. 11-13 (Helsinki: Finnish National Commission for UNESCO, 1995)

Perre, A., 'Nefertiti's last documented Reference (For Now)' in *In the light of Amarna* pp. 195-197 (Berlin: *Ägyptisches Museum und Papyrussammlung, Staatliche Museen zu Berlin*)

Peterson, W. J., *The Cambridge History of China, the Ch'ing Dynasty to 1800* (Cambridge: CUP, 2002)

Petrakos, V. X., 'The Antiquities in Greece During the War 1940-1944' in *O Mentor* 31, 1994, pp. 73-185

Pfeiffer, S., *Das Dekret von Kanopos* (Munich: K. G. Sauer, 2004)

Phelps, R. H., 'Before Hitler Came' in *Journal of Modern History* 35(3), 1963, pp. 245-261

Phillips, J., *Holy Warriors* (London: Vintage, 2010)

Pictet, A., *Essai de paléontology linguistique* (Paris, 1859)

Pineau, H., 'Paul Broca and Anthropology' in *Bulletin de l'Académie Nationale de Médecine* 164(6), 1980, pp. 557-62

Plassmann to Galke (BA (ehem.BDC) Ahnenerbe: Plassmann, Otto: 12.06.1895, 27.01.1937)

Poesche, T., *Die Arier, ein Beitrag zur historischen Anthropologie* [*The Aryans: A contribution to historical Anthropology*] (Jena, 1878)

Poliakov, L., *The Aryan Myth* (London: Heinemann, 1996)

Pott, A. F., *Inequality of Human Races, especially from the point of view of philological science, based on a consideration of the work of Count Gobineau which bears the same title* (Lemgo, 1856)

Pottelberge van, J., 'Chavée, Honoré (1815–1877)' in *Encyclopedia of Language and Linguistics* 2nd ed. (Boston: Elsevier, 2006)

Potter, P., *Most German of the Arts* (New Haven and London: Yale University Press, 1998); 'Wagner and the Third Reich' in *The Cambridge Companion to Wagner* (Cambridge: CUP, 2008)

Preston, J., 'The Original Indiana Jones' in *The Telegraph*, 22 May 2008

Price, D., 'Cloak and Trowel' in *Archaeology*, September/October 2003, pp. 30-35

Pringle, H., 'A Chilling Fantasy at Tiwanaku' in *Archaeology*, 5 June 2009; *The Master Plan* (New York: Hyperion, 2006)

Pryor, D., *The Externsteine* (New York: Threshold Publishing, 2011)

Rahn, O., *Kreuzzug gegen den Graal* [*Cathars and the Grail*] (1933); (transl. Nelli, R.) *La Cour de Lucifer* (Paris: Claude Tchou, 1974); *Luzifers Hofgesind* [*Lucifer's Court*] (Rochester: Inner Traditions International, 2008)

Ralls, K., *The Templars and the Grail* (Wheaton: Quest Books, 2003)

Rascher to Himmler, *Trials of War Criminals before the Nurenberg Military Tribunals, Vol. 1, Case 1: The Medical Case* pp. 249-251 (Washington, DC: US Government Printing Office, 1949–1950, 17 Feb 1943)

Ravenscroft, T., *The Spear of Destiny* (London: Neville Spearman, 1974)

Redesdale, Lord, 'Houston Stewart Chamberlain' in *The Edinburgh Review* No. 447, Vol. CCXIX, 1914

Reich, S., 'The Ford Motor Company and the Third Reich' in *Dimensions*, 13(2), 1999 pp. 15-17

Reichsführer-SS (ed.), *Deutsche Geschichte. Lichtbildvortrag: Erster Tel: Germanische Frühzeit 'Das Licht aus dem Norden'* (IfZ, DC 25.10, n.d.)

Reinhard, J., *The Nazca Lines* (Lima: Los Pinos, 1996)

Rhein-Mainische Studentenzeitung, NA, CDS, T580, R195, Ord 469, (*Welteislehre*, 1 June 1938)

Riepe, *Leumundszeugnis* (HHA, Abt.520 KS-HL Nr.88, Spruchkammer Kassel, 05.07.1948)

Rio, del, J. M. O., and Sevilla-Quiñones de León, M. C. T., *Los Reyes del Grial* [*The Kings of the Grail*] (Madrid: *Reino De Cordelia*, S.L., 2014)

Ripley, W. Z. (rev. Coon, C. S.), *The Races of Europe* (Westport, Conn.: Greenwood Press, 1975)

Ritmeyer, L., 'The Ark of the Covenant' in *Secrets of Jerusalem's Temple Mount* pp. 91-110 (Washington, DC: Biblical Archaeology Society, 1998)

Rohl, D. M., *Pharaohs and Kings* (New York: Crown Publishers, 1995)

Ronson, J., *The Men Who Stare At Goats* (London: Picador, 2012)

Roselius to Mack, C. W., *Die Meinung anderer Leute über Herman Wirth* (BA (ehem. BDC); Ahnenerbe: Wirth, Herman Felix (06.05.1885, 27.07.1932); to Wirth, *Die Meinung anderer Leute über Herman Wirth* (BA (ehem. BDC) Ahnenerbe: Wirth, Herman Felix (06.05.1885, 10.12.1933)

Rosenberg, A., *Der Mythus des 20. Jahrhunderts* [*The Myth of the 20th Century*] (Newport Beach, CA: Noontide Press, 1982); *Tagebuch* [*Diary*] (National Archives and Records Administration, 1934)

Rowley-Conwy, P., *From Genesis to Prehistory* (Oxford: OUP, 2007)

Rubio, J., *Nazi Archaeology in the Canary Islands* (London: Lulu Press, 2009)

Runciman, S., *The Medieval Manichee* (Cambridge: CUP, 1947)

Runge, F., '*Westfälische Bibliographie*' in *Westfälisch–Niederrheinisches Institut für Zeitungsforschung Stadt- und Landesbibliothek*, 1 January 1973 (Dortmund, 2010)

Ruse, M., *The Darwinian Revolution* (Cambridge: CUP, 1999)

Ryback, T., *Hitler's Private Library: The Books that Shaped His Life* (New York: Knopf, 2008)

Sabeheddin, M., 'Otto Rahn & the Quest for the Holy Grail' in *New Dawn Magazine* No. 43, July–August 1997

Salta, M., 'National Archaeological Museum' in *Archaeology in Greece* pp. 116-119 (Athens: History of Civilisations No. 2, 2002)

Salvador, A. A., *Truth and Symbolism of Holy Grail* (1999)

Sanden, van der, W., *Through Nature to Eternity* (Amsterdam: Batavian Lion International, 1996)

Sax, M., Walsh, J. M., Freestone, I. C., Rankin, A. H., and Meeks, N. D., 'The Origins of Two Purportedly Pre-Columbian Mexican Crystal Skulls' in *Journal of Archaeological Science* Issue 10, Vol. 35, pp. 2751-2760, October 2008

Schäfer, E., *Berge, Buddhas und Bären* [*Mountains, Buddhas and Bears*] (Berlin: Verlag Paul Parey, 1933); *Dach der Erde* [*Roof of the World*] (Berlin: Verlag Paul Parey, 1938); *Fest der weissen Schleier; eine Forscherfahrt durch Tibet nach Llahsa, der heiligen Stadt des Gottkönigtums* [*Festival of the White Gauze Scarves: A Research Expedition through Tibet to Lhasa, the Holy City of the God Realm*] (Braunschweig: Vieweg-Verlag, 1961); *Four New Birds from Tibet* (Philadelphia: Proceedings of the Academy of Natural Sciences, 1937); *Geheimnis Tibet, erster Bericht der deutschen Tibet–Expedition, 1938/39* (Munich: F. Bruckmann, 1943); *Unbekanntes Tibet* [*Unknown Tibet*] (Berlin: Verlag Paul Parey, 1938)

Schellenberg, W., *The Schellenberg Memoirs* (London: Andre Deutsch, 1956)

Schjellerup, I. R., *Incas and Spaniards in the Conquest of the Chachapoyas* (Göteborg: Göteborg University, 1997)

Schlosser, W., and Cierny, J., *Sterne und Steine. Eine praktische Astronomie der Vorzeit* (Darmstadt: Wissenschaftliche Buchgesellschaft, 1996)

Schmidt, H., *Externstein-Führer* (Detmold: Hermann Bösmann GmbH Verlag, 1973)

Schneider, T., *Ägyptologen im Dritten Reich* (Brill, reprinted 2013); *Egyptology Under National Socialism: Arizona Lecture 2014* (Vancouver: University of British Columbia, 2014)

Schöbel, G., and Reinerth H., '*Forscher—NS-Funktionär—Museumsleiter*' in Leube, A. and Hegewisch, M., *Prähistorie und Nationalsozialismus. Die mittel- und osteuropäische Ur- und Frühgeschichtsforschung in den Jahren 1933-1945* pp.

321-396 (Heidelberg: *Studien zur Wissenschafts- und Universitätsgeschichte* 2, 2002)

Sebottendorff von, R., *Bevor Hitler kam [Before Hitler Came]* (Munich: Deukula-Grassinger, 1933)

Shimon, G., and Jacobson, D., *Below the Temple Mount in Jerusalem* (Oxford: British Archaeological Reports, 1996)

Shirer, W. L., *The Rise and Fall of the Third Reich* (London: Simon and Schuster, 1960)

Shnirelman, V., 'From Internationalism to Nationalism' in Kohl, P. L., and Fawcett, C., *Nationalism, Politics and the Practice of Archaeology* (Cambridge: CUP, 1995)

Shnirelman, V., 'From Internationalism to Nationalism' in Kohl, P. L., and Fawcett, C., *Nationalism, Politics and the Practice of Archaeology* pp. 120-138 (Cambridge: CUP, 1995)

Sieg, U., *Deutschlands Prophet. Paul de Lagarde und die Ursprünge des modernen Antisemitismus* (München: Carl Hanser, 2007)

Sievers, W., *Abrechnung fur die Tripolis-Reise von* (BA (ehem.BDC) Ahnenerbe, Kiss: Edmund (10.12.1886, 16.02.1939); to Altheim (BA (ehem. BDC) Ahnenerbe: Altheim, Franz (06.10.1898, 13.05.1939); to Bousset (NARA, RG242, T580/203/686, 30.07.1936); *Bericht über die Forschungsfahrt 1936* (NARA, RG242, T580/203/686, 12.06.1936); to Galke (NARA, RG242, A3345 DS G113. Bose, Fritz: (28.07.1906, 31.05.1938); to Grönhagen (NARA, RG242, T580/206/716, 07.10.1937) to Himmler (BA (ehem. BDC) Ahnenerbe: Wirth, Herman Felix (06.05.1885, 07.05.1936); to Himmler (NARA, RG242, A3345 DS G119: Grönhagen, Yrjö von (03.10.1911, 17.04.1937); to Himmler (NARA, RG242, T580/124/35, 14.01.1939); to Himmler (BA, NS 21/123, 18.08.1939); to Koehler and Amelang (BA, NS 21/ 166, 09.12.1937); to Kotte (BA (ehem. BDC) Ahnenerbe: Kottenrodt, Wilhelm (11.11. 1904) 07.04.1937); to Reichsführer–SS. Personlicher Stab (NARA, RG242, T580/151/229 13.03.1941); *Tagebuch* (BA, NS 21/127, 10.12.1941); to Trautmann (BA (ehem. BDC) Ahnenerbe: Trautmann, Erika: (15.04.1897, 01.11.1937); to Wüst, including Grönhagen's report, *Arbeitsplan der Abteilung Pflegestätte für indogermanisch–finnische Kulturbeziehungen* (NARA, RG242, T580/206/716, 21.04.1937)

Silberman, N. A., *Between Past and Present* (New York: Henry Holt, 1989); 'Promised lands and chosen Peoples' in Kohl, P. L., and Fawcett, C., *Nationalism, Politics and the Practice of Archaeology* pp. 249-262 (Cambridge: CUP, 1995)

Silverstein, K., 'Ford and the Führer' in *The Nation* 270 (3), 2000, pp. 11-16

Sklar, D., *The Nazis and the Occult* (New York: Dorset Press, 1977)

Snyder, L., *Encyclopedia of the Third Reich*, 2nd Ed. (Boston, Mass: Da Capo Press, 1994); 'Houston Stewart Chamberlain and Teutonic Nordicism' in *Race, A History of Modern Ethnic Theories,* Chapter VIII (London: Longmans, Green and Co, 1939)

Soage, A. B. 'Hasan al-Banna or the Politicisation of Islam' in *Totalitarian Movements and Political Religions* 9(1), 2008, pp. 21-42

Speer, A., *Inside the Third Reich* (New York: Avon, 1971)

Spivey, N., *How Art Made the World* (London: BBC Books, 2005)

Steigmann-Gall, R., *The Holy Reich* (Cambridge: CUP, 2003)

Stelzig, C., *Felix von Luschan. Ein kunstsinniger Manager am Königlichen Museum für Völkerkunde zu Berlin* (Münster: Unrast, 2005)

Stevens, J., *Storming Heaven* (New York: Grove Press, 1987)

Stevenson, D., *The Origins of Freemasonry* (Cambridge: CUP, 1988)

Stoddart, T. L., *Racial Realities in Europe* (New York: Charles Scribner's Sons, 1924);

The Rising Tide of Color Against White World-Supremacy (New York: Charles Scribner's Sons, 1921)

Strabo, *The Geography of Strabo I.4.2.* (Cambridge: CUP, 2014)

Strange, J., *Cæsarii Heisterbacensis Dialogus Miraculorum* (Cologne: J. M. Heberle, 1851)

Strohmeyer, A., *Der gebaute Mythos. Das Haus Atlantis in der Bremer Böttcherstrasse. Ein deutsches Missverständnis* (Bremen: Donal, 1993)

Sturluson, S., *The Prose Edda* (Oakland: University of California Press, 1964)

Sünner, R., *Schwarze Sonne* (Freiburg: Herder, 1999)

Sverdlov, I. V., *Kenning Morphology* (Durham and York: 13th International Saga Conference, 2006)

Sykes, C., *Wassmuss: 'The German Lawrence'* (New York: Longmans, Green and Co., 1936)

Tacitus [transl. Birley), *Agricola and Germany* (Oxford: Oxford World's Classics, 2009)

Tauxe, L., *Paleomagnetic Principles and Practice* (Dordrech: Kluwer, 1998)

'The Swastika' in *Annual Report of the Board of Regents of the Smithsonian Institution* (Washington DC: Smithsonian Institution, n.d.)

Tolkein, C., 'The Battle of the Goths and the Huns' in *Saga-Book* (University College, London, for the Viking Society for Northern Research, 1955)

Tong, E., 'Thirty Years of Chinese Archaeology (1949-1979)' in Kohl, P. L., and Fawcett, C., *Nationalism, Politics and the Practice of Archaeology* pp. 177-197 (Cambridge: CUP, 1995)

Topinard, P., *l'Anthropologie* (Paris: C. Reinwald et cie, 1893)

Trautmann, E., *Anmerkung* (NARA, RG242, A3345 DS G112: Altheim, Franz (06.10.1898, 30.06.1938); *Deutsches Reich Reisepass* (BA, NS 21/165 and 687); to RFSS (BA (ehem. BDC) Trautmann, Erika (15.04.1897, 15.10.1937)

Tresidder, J., *Dictionary of Symbols* (San Francisco: Chronicle Books, 1998)

Trinkhaus, E., and Shipman, P., *The Neanderthals* (New York: Alfred A. Knopf, 1993)

Tuchel, J., and Schattenfroh, R., *Zentrale des Terrors* (Berlin: Siedler, 1987)

Tyldesley, J., *Nefertiti* (Harmondsworth: Penguin, 1998)

Tylor, E. B., *Anthropology an Introduction to the Study of Man and Civilization* (London: Macmillan and Co, 1881); *Primitive Culture. Volume 1* (London: John Murray, 1871); 'Professor Adolf Bastian' in *Man 5*, 1905, pp. 138-143

United States Holocaust Memorial Museum, *Homosexuals: Victims of the Nazi Era 1933–1945* (Washington D.C.: United States Holocaust Memorial Museum, 2003)

Volkischer Beobachter (NA, CDS, T580, R202, 22.8.38)

Wagner, W., *Romance and Epics of Our Northern Ancestors, Norse, Celt and Teuton* (New York: Norroena Society Publisher, New York, 1906)

Weindling, P., *Health, Race and German Politics between National Unification and Nazism, 1870-1945* (Cambridge: CUP, 1989)

Weisthor to Wolff (NARA, RG242, A3345 DS G113: Bose, Fritz (28.07.1906, 01.07.1937)

Wennerholm, E., *Sven Hedin 1865–1952* (Wiesbaden: F. A. Brockhaus Verlag, 1978)

Whitaker, I., 'The Problem of Pytheas' Thule' in *The Classical Journal* 77(2), December 1981-January 1982, pp. 148-164

Williamson, R. A., *Houston Stewart Chamberlain* (Santa Barbara: University of California, 1973)

Wirth, H., *Bericht* (BA (ehem. BDC) Ahnenerbe: Wirth, Herman Felix: (06.05.1885, 25.08.1935); *Bericht über die Hällristningar–Expedition des 'Deutschen Ahnenerbe' vom 27.08 his 03.09.1935* (BA (ehem. BDC) REM: Wirth, Herman (06.05.1885, 03.09.1935); *Bericht uber die erste Hällristningar-Expedition des*